# ARTS INTEGRATION AND SPECIAL EDUCATION

*Arts Integration and Special Education* contributes to research, policy, and practice by providing a theory of action for studying how linguistic, cognitive, and affective student engagement relates to arts integrated learning contexts and how these dimensions of engagement influence content area and literacy learning.

*Arts Integration and Special Education* connects the interdisciplinary framework in human development and linguistics, special education, and urban education with primary action research by special educators trained in arts integration, working in an inclusive urban charter school with middle-school-age students. Upper elementary to middle-grade-level student learning is relatively understudied and this work contributes across fields of special education and urban education, as well as arts education. Moreover, the classrooms in which the action research occurs are made up of students with a diverse range of abilities and needs. The book's interdisciplinary model, which draws on developmental and educational psychology, special education, and speech/language pathology research and practice, is the first to posit explanations for how and why AI contexts facilitate learning in students with language and sensory processing disorders, and those at-risk for school failure due to low socioeconomic status conditions.

**Alida Anderson** is Associate Professor of Special Education in the School of Education, Teaching, and Health in the College of Arts & Sciences at American University. She was formerly an artist and special education K-12 teacher.

# ARTS INTEGRATION AND SPECIAL EDUCATION

An Inclusive Theory of Action for Student Engagement

Edited by Alida Anderson

Routledge
Taylor & Francis Group

NEW YORK AND LONDON

First published 2015
by Routledge
711 Third Avenue, New York, NY 10017

and by Routledge
2 Park Square, Milton Park, Abingdon, Oxon OX14 4RN

*Routledge is an imprint of the Taylor & Francis Group, an informa business*

© 2015 Taylor & Francis

The right of Alida Anderson to be identified as the author of the editorial material of this work, and of the authors for their individual chapters, has been asserted by them in accordance with sections 77 and 78 of the Copyright, Designs and Patents Act 1988.

*Library of Congress Cataloguing in Publication data*
　Arts integration and special education : an inclusive theory of action for student
　engagement / edited by Alida Anderson.
　　pages　cm
　Includes bibliographical references and index.
　1. Special education–Art.　I. Anderson, Alida.
　LC3970.A78 2014
　371.9–dc23
　2014021505

ISBN: 978-0-415-74417-1 (hbk)
ISBN: 978-0-415-74418-8 (pbk)
ISBN: 978-1-315-81315-8 (ebk)

Typeset in Bembo
by Out of House Publishing

Printed and bound in the United States of America by Publishers Graphics, LLC on sustainably sourced paper.

For my husband Florencio Lennox Campello, My son Anderson Lennox Campello, My parents Jane Jaspersen Anderson and William Howard Anderson, And my sister and best friend Greta Jean Anderson.

# CONTENTS

# FIGURES

# TABLES

# CONTRIBUTORS

**Katherine A. Berry**, *the George Washington University*, is a doctoral candidate in the Department of Special Education and Disability Studies at The George Washington University, with research interests in dramatic arts integration, language acquisition, and students with specific learning disabilities. Previously, Berry served as a DC Teaching Fellow and worked as a special education teacher for grades 4–6 in DC public and charter schools. Berry holds a B.A. from the University of Virginia and an M.A. in Special Education from Trinity Washington University. Berry's dissertation research is an exploratory study investigating the influence of a dramatic arts strategy on the on-task behavior of students with language-based learning disabilities in inclusive elementary classroom settings. Her work has been featured in *Preventing School Failure*, the *American Journal of Obstetrics and Gynecology*, and The George Washington University Policy Paper Series. Recent presentations have included papers given at international and national conferences of the American Educational Research Association, Council for Exceptional Children, International Neuropsychology Society, and the National Arts Education Association.

**Christina Bosch**, *Center for Applied Special Technology (CAST), Wakefield, MA*, is an Instructional Designer/Research Associate interested in the application of cognitive science, psychology, and neuroscience research to teaching and learning practices and policies. After earning a B.A. in English at the University of Vermont, Bosch earned a Certificate of English Language Teaching to Adults in Hanoi, Viet Nam, and taught English as a Second Language while living abroad. She returned to the US and began classroom teaching at an inclusive, arts-integrated, public charter elementary school while earning an M.A. in Special Education: Learning Disabilities, from American University (AU). She was highly influenced by the progressive models of practice around learning differences at the Lab School of Washington and at the School for Arts in Learning. A subsequent Graduate Certificate in Arts Integrated Instruction from AU grounded her pedagogy in the framework of Universal Design for Learning as well as the potentials of action research. Driven by her later experience as a pull-out, push-in special education teacher, she obtained an M.Ed. in Mind, Brain, and Education from the Harvard Graduate School of Education in the pursuit of improving the experiences of both students and teachers affected by the conventional special education system. Bosch's interests include the effects of reflection and internal focus on creative thinking; fostering creativity through interdisciplinary curriculum design; writing and composition instruction, especially involving students with language and behavioral disabilities; supporting teacher socio-emotional competency; and bridging research and practice in education. She has co-authored two articles published in *JSD: The Learning Forward Journal.*

**James S. Catterall,** *University of California Los Angeles,* is Professor Emeritus and past Chair of the Faculty at the UCLA Graduate School of Education and Information Studies, and is an Affiliate Faculty member at the UCLA Center for Culture, Brain, and Development. In July 2011, Dr. Catterall became Director and Principal Investigator at the Centers for Research on Creativity. Professor Catterall's research focuses on measurement of children's cognitive and social development and motivation in the context of learning in the arts. He is the author of *Doing well and doing good by doing art* (2009), a 12-year longitudinal study of the effects of learning in the arts on the achievements and values of young adults. Dr. Catterall and colleagues published *The arts and achievement in at-risk youth: Findings from four longitudinal studies,* released in 2012 by the National Endowment for the Arts. Professor Catterall has published leading studies on learning in music and its effects on visual and spatial intelligence; and on learning in the visual arts and the development of creativity, originality, and self-efficacy beliefs. His latest research points to significant overlaps in the neural circuitry and neuroanatomy of empathetic responses and artistic expressions. Professor Catterall holds degrees in economics (with honors) from Princeton University and in public policy analysis from the University of Minnesota; he holds a Ph.D. in Education from Stanford University.

**Jean B. Crockett,** *University of Florida,* is a Professor of Special Education, and Director of the School of Special Education, School Psychology, and Early Childhood Studies in the University of Florida College of Education. Earlier in her career she served as a music educator, classroom teacher, and school administrator. Dr. Crockett holds a B.A. from Marymount Manhattan College, an M.A. in Liberal Studies from the State University of New York at Stony Brook, a professional diploma in Administration and Supervision from St. John's University, and a Ph.D. in Special Education from the University of Virginia. Her research interests

address the connections between policy initiatives, leadership development, and the instruction of students with disabilities. She has published five books in addition to multiple book chapters, and articles in peer-reviewed journals. She is a past president of the Division for Research of the Council for Exceptional Children, and serves on the editorial boards of seven professional journals. She is an associate editor for the *Journal of Special Education Leadership*, and the special education editor for the *Journal of Law and Education*. Dr. Crockett is affiliated with The CEEDAR Center (Collaboration for Effective Educator Development, Accountability, and Reform), a national technical assistance center based at the University of Florida dedicated to supporting states in developing effective teachers and leaders who can prepare students with disabilities for successful futures.

**Robyne Davis,** *Private Practice*, is a Licensed Professional Counselor and Board-Certified Dance/Movement Therapist working in private practice. She has worked with children, adolescents, and adults in hospitals, schools, and community counseling centers over the past 20 years. She earned a B.A. in Psychology from the University of North Carolina, Chapel Hill, an M.A. in Dance/Movement Therapy from Goucher College, MD, and a Graduate Certificate in Curriculum and Instruction from American University. In Davis' private practice, she provides educational consulting and counseling services for students, parents, and schools. Davis has presented at events and conferences of the American Mental Health Counselors Association, American Association of State Counseling Boards, Substance Abuse and Mental Health Services Administration Children's Mental Health Awareness Day, VSA Arts and Special Education, and American Dance Therapy Association (ADTA). She was featured in the American Counselor Association's March 2009 edition of *Counseling Today*. She is a member of the American Counselor Association and the ADTA, and has served in leadership roles in the ADTA, such as chapter president and Government Affairs Chair, and is also a member of the National Alliance of Specialized Instructional Support Personnel. Davis is an M.A. candidate in the Education and Human Development program, with an emphasis on Secondary Special Education and Transition Services, at the George Washington University.

**Sandra M. Loughlin,** *University of Maryland*, is a lecturer in the College of Education. Dr. Loughlin has a strong background in arts integration, educational psychology, and curriculum and instruction, particularly in relation to text and painting comprehension. On these topics, Dr. Loughlin has published empirical and theoretical research, taught undergraduate and graduate coursework, presented at national and international conferences, provided professional development and consultative services, and written arts-focused curriculum and assessments. Dr. Loughlin is a former teacher and staff developer in arts-integrated elementary and middle schools and was a research assistant on the Artful Thinking Project at Harvard Project Zero. She holds a B.A. in Elementary Education from

Washington Adventist University, an M.Ed. in Arts in Education from Harvard University, and a Ph.D. in Human Development from the University of Maryland, College Park, with a specialization in Educational Psychology. Her work has been featured in *Educational Psychology Review*, *Learning and Instruction*, and *Instructional Science*, and in handbooks devoted to psychology and reading. Presentations have included papers given at international conferences of the American Educational Research Association, American Psychological Association, Council for Exceptional Children, and European Association for Research on Learning and Instruction.

**Kristin Nagy,** *Bridges Public Charter School, Washington, DC*, is the Coordinator for Arts Integration, where she works with students and teachers on integrated arts learning across subject areas. Ms. Nagy began her career as a special education teacher working with elementary school students with severe emotional and behavioral disabilities. Over the past decade she has worked with students from Pre-K through high school as a language arts teacher, special education teacher, and visual art teacher. As a special educator, she developed an interest in teaching and learning through the arts and began to incorporate many of her own skills as a visual artist into her lessons. Later, Nagy developed an interest in media arts and began integrating film studies and filmmaking, as a form of both visual and dramatic art, into her language arts classes. Ms. Nagy holds a B.A. from Michigan State University, an M.A. in Special Education from Trinity Washington University, a Graduate Certificate in Curriculum and Instruction from American University, and an Ed.M. in Arts in Education from Harvard University.

# PREFACE

This volume is among the first to address arts integration (AI, hereafter) from multidisciplinary perspectives, and it was my hope that it would embody many of the themes and directions in the fields of special and general education, educational psychology, and human development. It evolved from my research and practice with students over the past 25 years, as an artist (1985–1995), as a special educator (1991–2003), and as a researcher and teacher-of-teachers (1998–present). My work with students, families, teachers, and colleagues has brought forth an inclusive theory of action for integrating language, cognition, affect, and arts learning through a discussion of contextual factors. As a special educator, I have worked in various classroom settings with preschool, elementary, adolescent, and adult students with mild, moderate, and severe communication disorders (autism spectrum disorders [ASD], specific language impairments, developmental delays, intellectual disabilities, learning disabilities [LD], pervasive developmental disorders, and cerebral palsy). Each of my students has taught me to reconceptualize learning and engagement according to their unique strengths and needs. My academic and professional interests have been greatly influenced by Professors Joanne Carlisle, Doris Johnson, C. Addison Stone, and Steven Zecker during my studies in communication sciences and disorders at Northwestern University; and by Professors Carol Kinne, John Knecht, and Lynn Schwarzer during my studies of art and art history at Colgate University. Also, I am grateful for the creative and innovative work that Sally Smith pioneered at the Lab School of Washington over 50 years ago.

In developing a plan for this book, I had an initial purpose to provide an explanatory hypothesis for how and why the arts support students with diverse learning needs based on core language development, cognition, and special education principles. The state of the current research on student learning through

AI is ripe for pioneering investigations to substantiate theoretical constructs, such as the engagement hypothesis detailed further in Part I of the book. In 2009/10, I served as the principal investigator on a project to design and implement a professional development program for educators that encompassed AI and special education principles and practices. The project's public charter school partner was dedicated to the arts and followed an inclusion model, with 60% of its population having identified disabilities. In addition, the majority of its students qualified for free or reduced meals. Three action research demonstrations of practice investigating the influence of AI on student outcomes in language, cognition, and social-emotional skills, conducted at the partner school and written collaboratively with my graduate students, are summarized in Part II. These demonstrations of practice provide evidence of the facilitative aspects of AI within content-based academic classes. Part III of the book focuses on where AI is now in understanding its contributions to student learning and engagement, and where future research opportunities and practical challenges lie.

This book takes a different approach from most in AI and education by its grounding and framework in allied fields of human development and linguistics, instructional design, special education, and arts education. Its first aim is to contribute to research, policy, and practice in providing a theory of action for studying how student engagement (linguistic, cognitive, and/or affective) relates to AI learning contexts, and how these dimensions of engagement influence content area (mathematics, language arts, social studies) and literacy (oral and written language comprehension, productivity, and specificity) learning.

Another aim of this book is connecting the interdisciplinary framework in human development and linguistics, special education, and general education with primary action research by special educators trained in AI, working in an inclusive urban charter school with middle-school-age students. Upper elementary to middle-grade-level student learning is relatively understudied and this work contributes across fields of special education and urban education, as well as arts education. Moreover, the classrooms in which the research is grounded were made up of students with a diverse range of abilities and needs. The multidisciplinary model presented in this book draws on developmental and educational psychology, special education, and speech/language pathology research and practice, and is the first to posit explanations for how and why AI contexts influence learning outcomes in students with language- and sensory-based processing disorders in inclusive classroom settings.

Most importantly, this book on AI and special education aims to contribute to better understanding *how* and *why* AI facilitates students' development of language, social, emotional, and academic skills in such learning contexts, with the hope of further specifying the relations between arts and education (e.g., Hetland & Winner, 2000; Hetland, Winner, Veenema, & Sheridan, 2008). The book contributes to the 'next wave' in research by framing AI as contextualized learning, and examining developmental (linguistic, cognitive, and affective) dimensions of this learning context to better explain students' performance in contextualized (i.e., AI) and decontextualized (i.e., conventional) classroom activities.

Given the current pedagogical model, the book quickly changed from an independent to a collaborative project. Experts from allied AI and special education fields contribute to the topics of AI and human development, including foci on students with language- and sensory-based processing disorders. Our combined efforts support the theoretical framework for student engagement first presented in Part I's Chapter 4, and then revisited in Part II of the book, through three 'voices from the field' action research chapters. Each of these chapters has sections entitled 'Voices from Higher Education' examining the linguistic, cognitive, and affective dimensions of students' learning within the inclusive engagement framework. The framework dimensions are reconsidered in Part III with a synthesis of findings in relation to the present and future directions in the field of AI and educational research and practice. I am pleased to present this collaborative and inclusive theory of action, with supporting evidence and directions for research and practice, with great thanks to my esteemed contributors.

## References

Hetland, L., & Winner, E. (2001). The arts and academic achievement: What the evidence shows. *Arts Education Policy Review,* 102(5), 3–6.

Hetland, L., Winner, E., Veenema, S., & Sheridan, K. (2007). *Studio thinking: The real benefits of visual arts education.* New York: Teachers College Press.

# ACKNOWLEDGEMENTS

The demonstrations of practice discussed in this book are based on research supported by a sub-contract from the US Department of Education and American University. A great number of colleagues and students have given invaluable help in the investigation of arts integration across classroom environments. I would like to thank especially my contributors, Sandra M. Loughlin at University of Maryland; Jean B. Crockett at University of Florida; James S. Catterall at University of California Los Angeles, Katherine A. Berry at the George Washington University; and at my own American University Vivian Vasquez, Franzi Rook, Nicole Scifo, Kathy Tenhula, and Sarah Irvine Belson.

Among the many colleagues whose friendship has been such a necessary support I want to give special thanks to Margie Linn, Lauren McGrath, Stephen Vassallo, Elizabeth Worden, and Toni Barton. And finally, thanks to my esteemed colleague Rachel Gabrielse for her support and thorough attention to detail in bringing this collaborative project to life.

# ABOUT THE EDITOR

**Alida Anderson, Ph.D.,** *American University*, is Associate Professor of special education and learning disabilities, with research interests in the contextualization of language in learning environments, language development, and literacy acquisition in diverse populations. As a post-baccalaureate, Anderson studied printmaking and photography at the School of the Art Institute of Chicago, shifting to art therapy to support exceptional students' learning through the arts. For over two decades, as a specialist/case manager, early childhood special educator, and university professor, she has developed and disseminated information to students, families, and care providers on inclusive and integrated arts approaches and has been a teacher-therapist with students having developmental and learning disabilities. Dr. Anderson holds a B.A. from Colgate University, an M.A. in Communication Sciences and Disorders from Northwestern University, and a Ph.D. in Special Education from the University of Maryland, College Park. Her work has been featured in *Dyslexia, Child Language Teaching and Therapy, Urban Education, PACEC Journal, Journal of Research in Reading, Reading and Writing: An Interdisciplinary Journal, Journal of International Teacher Education, Journal of Training and Educational Studies, Learning Disabilities: A Multidisciplinary Journal* and *Preventing School Failure.* Presentations have included papers given at international conferences of the Society for the Scientific Study of Reading, Council for Exceptional Children, American Educational Research Association, British Dyslexia Association, VSA International, and the National Council for the Teachers of Mathematics.

PART I

# Theoretical and Methodological Issues in the Study of Arts Integration in Education

## Introduction

This section provides an overview of theoretical and methodological approaches to the study of arts integration (AI) in general and special education, with particular emphasis on interdisciplinary approaches to addressing learners' individual needs within classroom contexts. Thorough examination of the background and historical context of AI is presented, as well as the interdisciplinary language, educational psychology, and special education research and practice that support its use in educational settings. Arts integration research and practice, from its foundations to its current status as a multidisciplinary learning approach, is described in relation to the book's theoretical framework on student engagement. Notably, this volume explores the question of whether arts *integration* may in fact be a response to the dis*integration* of education over two decades due to reform education movements, beginning in the late 1990s to the present, that have focused primarily on achievement outcomes rather than students' acquisition or mastery of concepts.

Part I's organization is as follows. In Chapter 1, Sandra M. Loughlin and I examine operational definitions for AI in general education and special education, and include historical and research perspectives on AI from the past or 'yesterday' and present, or 'today.' Chapter 1 reviews the status of AI research from a multidisciplinary perspective to highlight the emphasis on developing a theory of action to study learning processes that occur in general education and special education settings with its use.

Chapter 2 outlines the linguistic-cognitive theoretical contributions to the study of AI's influence on language and literacy outcomes in students with learning and sensory processing disabilities, as well as for students at-risk for school failure due to low academic achievement and/or social-emotional difficulties. This chapter draws upon theory and research from developmental and speech-language research and practice to understand how and why AI contexts support language outcomes in student populations, and provides information on the contextualized–decontextualized language continuum (Scott, 1994; Ukrainetz, 2006) in relation to AI. The principles of Universal Design in Learning (UDL) (Rose & Meyer, 2002) are presented in relation to this linguistic-cognitive orientation, highlighting the role of linguistic engagement through contextualization.

In Chapter 3, Katherine A. Berry and Sandra M. Loughlin critically examine AI research and practice focused on cognitive and affective dimensions of engagement in students with and without disabilities in a variety of educational settings. Directions for AI research and practice, with attention to cognitive and affective engagement, are presented relative to students who have learning and sensory processing disabilities, as well as for students who are at-risk for academic failure due to social-emotional challenges.

Chapter 4 presents a unifying theory of action for engagement through AI, which is expressed through linguistic, cognitive, and affective dimensions. This interdisciplinary engagement model draws on developmental and educational psychology, special education, and speech and language pathology research and practice to explain how and why AI addresses individual learning needs of students with language- and sensory-based disabilities, and those at-risk for school failure due to social-emotional and behavioral challenges. The multi-component engagement framework posits connections between linguistic, cognitive, and affective dimensions to operationalize it as an outcome across arts and non-arts (conventional academic) learning contexts. This theory of action will be applied to the AI demonstrations of practice in Part II of the book, and will be reconsidered in light of the current and future directions in the field of AI in general and special education in Part III.

## Part I Questions for the Reader

- What is AI and why do we need it?
- Why do we need arts integration (AI) in education?
- What are the characteristics of effective schools and teachers?
- How has the role of the arts in education changed over time?
- How does arts *integration* address students' educational dis*integration*?

## References

Rose, D., & Meyer, A. (2002). *Teaching every student in the digital age: Universal design for learning*. Alexandria, VA: Association for Supervision and Curriculum Development.

Scott, C. (1994). A discourse continuum for school-age students. In G. Wallach & K. Butler (Eds.), *Language learning disabilities in school-age children and adolescents: Some principles and applications* (pp. 219–252). New York: Macmillan.

Ukrainetz, T. A. (Ed.). (2006). *Contextualized language intervention*. Eau Claire, WI: Thinking Publications.

# 1

# A HISTORICAL REVIEW OF ARTS INTEGRATION RESEARCH AND PRACTICE

## Lessons Learned

*Sandra M. Loughlin and Alida Anderson*

Connections between arts and non-arts disciplines have been made in a variety of arenas for decades, even centuries, in philosophy, linguistics, psychology, and educational practice (Loughlin, 2013). These connections have translated into powerful beliefs about learning and intelligence (Gardner, 1983) and highly influential educational initiatives (Bloom, Hastings, & Madaus, 1971). More recently, the rich history connecting arts and non-arts learning has been manifested in an increasingly popular educational practice, often called arts integration. Arts integration (hereafter, AI) is colloquially described as teaching and learning in and through the arts, and is evident in instruction for students with and without disabilities. Indeed, the United States Department of Education (2010) has emphasized arts-based learning as a way to reach and teach all children and a number of states have standards specifically relating to arts integration (Burnaford, Brown, Doherty, & McLaughlin, 2007). Given AI's rising popularity and influence, the President's Committee on the Arts and Humanities (Committee on the Arts and Humanities, 2011) recently stated that "Arts integration has ... generated a lot of enthusiasm from classroom teachers, school administrators and policy researchers for its ability to produce results" (p. 19).

While AI's benefits are increasingly acknowledged, its parameters remain a point of debate. AI has been differentially termed, defined, and operationalized in the literature (Bresler, 2001; Burnaford et al., 2007; Cornett, 2007) and agreed-upon definitions and practices remain elusive. Practices falling under the umbrella term AI vary on virtually all possible dimensions: *who* does AI (e.g., teaching artists, arts teachers, classroom teachers), *what* is being integrated (e.g., content standards, thinking processes, shared fundamental concepts), *when* AI occurs (e.g., during the school day, after school), *where* AI takes place (e.g., school classrooms, museums, arts organizations), *how* AI lessons are developed (e.g., co-teaching, artists-in-residence, single teachers), and *why* do AI at all.

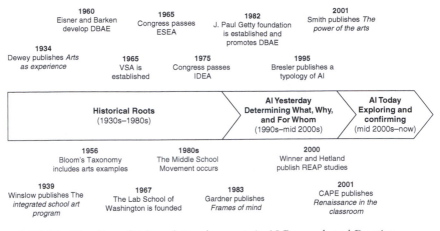

**FIGURE 1.1** Timeline of Selected Developments in AI Research and Practice.

Despite these differences in focus and scope, at their core all perspectives on AI assume that learning in and through the arts is linked to learning in non-arts domains – cognitively, linguistically, motivationally, affectively, or socially – and that harnessing those linkages enhances teaching and learning. Accordingly, the Consortium of the National Arts Education Associations (2002) defines the goal of interdisciplinary arts education as enabling students to "identify and apply authentic connections between two or more disciplines and/or understand essential concepts that transcend individual disciplines" (p. 3). Deasy (2002) defines AI as "the effort to build a set of relationships between learning in the arts and learning in the other skills and subjects of the curriculum" (p. 2). Similarly, and in an effort to better pinpoint the types of connections, conceptions, and relationships afforded by AI, this book defines AI as the linking of an arts area (e.g., drama, music, dance, visual art) with a content area (e.g., language arts, mathematics) for the purposes of reaching a deeper level of engagement, learning, and reflection than would be possible without inclusion of the art form (Anderson, 2012).

Like other educational initiatives, AI has been subjected to the buffeting winds of theories of learning, research agendas, politics, and finances (Eisner, 1998). As a consequence, justifications for AI and research efforts around it have changed dramatically over the decades (Aprill, 2010). What has remained constant, though, is the belief that AI can benefit all learners. Although most AI research and practice has occurred in general education settings, AI also has a rich history in special education contexts (Gerber & Guay, 2006; Smith, 2001). In the special education literature, there have been numerous exploratory investigations (e.g., Carrigan, 1994; Clements & Clements, 1984) and policy papers (Anderson, 1975; Andrus, 1994; Keifer-Boyd & Kraft, 2003; Kraft, 2003, 2004) on the ways in which the arts enhance inclusive learning opportunities for students 'at-risk' for school failure, including students with identified disabilities. Interestingly, none of these studies used the term 'arts integration,' despite clearly linking arts to content in an effort to reach and teach students. Only recently has 'arts integration' been applied to describe the practice of integrating art and content learning for students in inclusive classroom settings (see Abedin, 2010; Anderson, 2012).

This chapter foregrounds the research and practice outlined in this book by describing historical and current developments in AI research and practice, focusing on student learning in both general and special education. In particular, it describes the historical roots of AI (i.e., research and practice from approximately the 1930s to 1980s), AI yesterday (i.e., research and practice from approximately the 1990s to mid-2000s), and AI today (i.e., research and practice from approximately the mid-2000s to today). Selected developments in these periods are presented in Figure 1.1.

Based on this analysis, the current chapter argues that the field has moved from defining, describing, and legitimizing AI, to identifying theoretically grounded relations between art and non-arts learning through exploration and confirmation. The chapter concludes by deriving lessons from the history of AI that may inform AI research tomorrow, and outlining how the volume's theory of action and demonstrations of practice address those research aims.

## Historical Roots of Arts Integration

John Dewey may have been the first formal advocate for curricular integration in general (Beane, 1993), and AI in particular (Burnaford et al., 2007). In his writings, including the classic 1934 work, *Art as experience*, Dewey argued that learning is a holistic experience, requiring individuals to bring to bear knowledge from multiple disciplines to deeply and meaningfully understand the world. Thus, he suggested that experience is the proper unit of analysis for understanding and fostering learning, rather than the narrower and somewhat arbitrary confines of traditional academic disciplines. From this perspective, Dewey called for educational approaches that emphasized the interrelation of subjects with one another, in an effort to build true understanding, and argued that the arts and aesthetics comprised an essential aspect of the learning experience.

Building on Dewey's theories, several general and arts-specific integration practices soon followed. Shortly after publication of *Art as experience*, the National Council of Teachers of English published *The correlated curriculum* (Weeks, 1936), which argued for both subject-specific and interdisciplinary learning opportunities, and described a number of 'correlations' between English and other subject areas. Curricular efforts particular to the arts were also developed at this time. For instance, Leon Winslow published *The integrated school art program* in 1939, proposing that the arts and all subject areas be connected in order to provide a richer educational experience for learners. According to Bresler (2001), the Music Educators National Conference Yearbooks of 1934 and 1935 included titles that infused the arts into academic disciplines.

These and other Dewey-inspired beliefs and practices were challenged, how-ever, by the dominant educational paradigm of the age: behaviorism. As noted by Loughlin and Alexander (2012), because of behaviorism's emphasis on the stimu-lation of learning, rather than the process of learning itself, assessments and object-ives of learning were imprecise, vaguely worded goals, making reliable assessments difficult and cumbersome (Snowman & Biehler, 2000). As a result, by the 1950s, the field of education was in the midst of an instructional objectives movement spawned by industrial and military psychology, wherein complex, whole tasks were broken down into discrete behaviors that were observable and measurable and often ordered in hierarchical frames (Saettler, 1990).

This pendulum swing away from Dewey's notion of holistic experiences spawned a number of efforts to improve learning objectives. Of these, perhaps most notable are Bloom and colleagues' seminal works (Bloom, Engelhart, Furst, Hill, & Krathwohl, 1956; Bloom et al., 1971; Krathwohl, Bloom, & Masia, 1964), which broke apart and outlined distinct hierarchical taxonomies for cognitive, affective, and psychomotor learning – an antithesis to Dewey's integrative, experi-ential argument. Interestingly, however, a close examination of the cognitive framework (Bloom et al., 1956, 1971), also known as Bloom's Taxonomy, reveals a critical rationale for current AI efforts. To demonstrate the viability of their taxonomy for education, Bloom and colleagues (1971) set out to show its broad applicability by providing examples of the six levels of cognitive objectives (i.e., knowledge, comprehension, application, analysis, synthesis, and evaluation) across the curriculum in art, mathematics, social studies, language arts, and science. By showing that art, for example, is as legitimate a vehicle as science for teaching the six types of cognitive objectives, Loughlin (2011) suggests that Bloom's Taxonomy stands as an example of one relation that can be drawn between the arts and non-arts disciplines: cognitive processes.

Despite the efforts of Dewey, Bloom, and a host of others to emphasize the importance of arts education and the interrelation of arts and non-arts disciplines, the ensuing several decades were marked by a perceived divide between the 'hard' sciences on the one hand, and the 'soft' arts on the other (Kliebard, 1987). This distinction is often attributed to the launch of Sputnik in 1957, which shocked the United States and led to a massive 'back to basics' effort that emphasized math and science, while de-emphasizing the social sciences and the arts. This effort was reinforced in 1983, with the publication of *A nation at risk* (National Commission on Excellence in Education, 1983), which argued that the failure of American schools was undermining the nation's ability to compete in an increasingly glo-bal economy (Burnaford et al., 2007). As a result, with the exception of pockets of progressive education touting a child-centered approach emphasizing creative self-expression (Duke, 1988) and a brief rekindling of interest in the wake of President Johnson's 'Great Society' effort (Burnaford et al., 2007), the arts were largely marginalized in mainstream education for several decades (Duke, 1988) and larger curricular integration efforts were stalled (Beane, 1993).

Despite being a low point for arts learning, this period is notable for significant improvements in the education of students from environmentally disadvantaged backgrounds and those with disabilities. In 1965, Congress passed the Elementary and Secondary Education Act (ESEA), with the intent to enable access, participation, and progress of students in public education through early intervention (e.g., Head Start) and additional programs and supports (e.g., Title I). The civil rights of individuals with disabilities also took center stage during this period. Historically, individuals with disabilities were segregated from mainstream school environments. If students with disabilities were receiving education, it was occurring in nonpublic day schools, institutions, or homes (Hardman, Drew, & Egan, 2011). This changed in 1975, with the passage of the Education for All Handicapped Children Act (EHA), a public and federally funded mandate for students ages six through 21 to receive free and appropriate special education services. This landmark legislation, now entitled the Individuals with Disabilities Education Improvement Act (i.e., IDEA, 2004), has been amended several times (e.g. 1992, 1997) over the past three decades to reflect the current climate of the US education system towards inclusion.

Also noteworthy in the roots of arts integration and special education was the emergence of Very Special Arts (VSA) in 1974. Originally known as the National Committee – Arts for the Handicapped, VSA was founded to provide arts and education opportunities to individuals with disabilities. Very Special Arts operated under the premise that individuals with disabilities deserve access to high-quality arts learning opportunities. This premise translated into the creation of local, national, and international arts programs and program development that supports academic learning through and with the arts for children, youth, and adults with disabilities.

During the 1980s, several critical developments took hold and set the stage for the rise of inclusive AI efforts for students with and without disabilities. These were the curricular integration movement, the establishment of the Getty Center for Education in the Arts, and publication of Gardner's influential *Frames of mind* (1983).

Arts integration is a specialized form of curricular integration, the latter of which was the focus of a significant effort during this time to tailor education for early adolescents (Alexander, 2001). The Middle School Movement, as it is known, sought to establish developmentally appropriate learning environments for adolescents and to serve as an intermediary between the skill-building focus of elementary school and the discipline-knowledge focus of high school. Included in this middle school curriculum effort were exploratory programs, the block schedule to allow for deep engagement, and interdisciplinary teams of teachers that would identify and communicate overarching themes and concepts linking together content areas (Beane, 1993). Thus, integrated learning was cast as a major driver and rationale for middle schools, and received significant attention both in middle school contexts and in the larger educational community.

Also, the value of curricular integration was identified for students with disabilities. Sally Smith, a special education pioneer, founded The Lab School of Washington, DC initially to meet the needs of her son with dyslexia. Her method was to focus the curriculum around academic 'clubs.' This approach, which was largely inspired by Bruner (1975), Dewey (1934), and Montessori (1917), focused on the use of the environment to create the context for learning. Smith's club method integrated the academic content learning within particular themes, such as 'cave club,' or 'the Renaissance club,' in which students were actively engaged in art- and project-based learning to support their simultaneous content learning in social studies, language arts, history, and science.

In parallel with the push toward curricular integration in general and special education, there was a shift in the field of arts education. According to Duke (1988), the J. Paul Getty Trust established the influential Getty Center for Education in the Arts (the Center) in 1982 to improve the quality and status of the arts in America under the assumption that human beings are truly educated when their learning includes a comprehensive curriculum in the arts. In an effort to improve the perception of the arts among the public and in schools, the Center suggested that a more comprehensive approach – one that moved beyond art-making – would need to be adopted. Duke (1988) quotes Harold Williams, then president of the J. Paul Getty Trust, who summed up the problem: "the arts have been assigned a marginal position in today's curriculum, and art education is valued most exclusively as a means of enhancing self-expression and creativity, rather than as an organized body of knowledge requiring the same kind of substance and intellectual rigor we expect in the sciences and humanities" (p. 8).

The more comprehensive approach adopted by the Center – with the goal to ensure a serious place for the arts alongside reading, writing, and arithmetic – was Discipline-Based Art Education (DBAE). Discipline-Based Arts Education is a comprehensive curricular approach to the study of art that includes four interrelated disciplines: art production, art history, art criticism, and aesthetics (Eisner, 1988). Developed in the 1960s by Manuel Barkan and Elliot Eisner, DBAE represented a different paradigm from the one that had dominated art education in the previous several decades. As described by Duke (1988), art education in the 1940s and 1950s romanticized child art, focused on the product of art-making rather than the process the led to it, and characterized art primarily from the inside out. In contrast, DBAE valued the artistic product, used models of adult art accomplishment as a means of setting standards for child art development and education, and viewed art as an outside–inside process in which the art-maker utilizes learned knowledge and strategies – including knowledge of art history and aesthetic standards – to create increasingly sophisticated artwork.

Partly due to the influence of the Center, support for the tenets of DBAE quickly followed from the four national arts organizations (i.e., National Art Educators Association, National Dance Education Organization, Music Educators

National Conference, and American Alliance for Theater and Education), as well as the College Board, the National Endowment for the Arts, and the United States Department of Education. Eventually, DBAE provided the framework for the development of numerous state standards of the arts, and its impact is still being felt in very recent articulations of arts-learning standards.

From the perspective of AI, the wide acceptance of DBAE indicated that learning different art forms had several significant parallels. For instance, learning music entailed critique, as did visual art. Likewise, knowledge of history was essential for both dance and drama learning. Thus, DBAE provided four meaningful connections between the four arts disciplines and set the stage for considering the degree to which meaningful connections could and should be made between the arts and non-arts disciplines.

The curricular integration efforts of Beane (1993) and Smith (2001) might not have intersected with implications drawn from DBAE, however, were it not for the publication of one tremendously influential book: *Frames of mind* (Gardner, 1983). In this, Gardner articulated what is widely known and described as Multiple Intelligences (MI) theory, arguing that human intelligence is better understood as multiple intelligences: bodily-kinesthetic, interpersonal, intrapersonal, linguistic, logical-mathematical, musical, naturalistic, and spatial. Moreover, Gardner suggested that only a few of these intelligences (i.e., logical-mathematical and linguistic) are valued in schools and on traditional intelligence tests, but that all are essential components of humanness and success beyond education settings. By distinguishing different types of intelligence and arguing that no intelligence is superior to another, MI theory provided a compelling argument for the increased role of the arts in schools.

Gardner's works proved highly influential in AI efforts at the broadest level. Gardner's argument that arts and non-arts disciplines entail distinct and worthwhile intelligences fueled larger efforts to integrate curricula around the arts for students with and without disabilities. Thus, although the early 1980s were a notable low point in the status of arts in general education curricula and practice, the combined efforts to integrate curriculum, the wide acceptance of DBAE, and the influence of Gardner's MI theory set the stage for AI research and practice in the 1990s and early 2000s.

## Arts Integration Yesterday: Determining What, Why, and for Whom

During the 1990s, the educational community was in the midst of the Standards movement, focused on clear sequences of instruction and on accountability measures, as well as experiencing decreased funding at the federal and state levels. Nevertheless, during this period, there were some important developments with regard to arts in education. The passage of the Goals 2000: Educate America Act in 1994 established, for the first time, the arts as fundamental academic subjects.

The 1990s also saw a surge in AI efforts for students with and without disabilities (Bresler, 1995). Partnership and program initiatives proliferated, such as the Chicago Arts Partnerships in Education (Burnaford, Aprill, Weiss, & CAPE, 2001) and Very Special Arts, which since 2010 has been known as VSA. Additionally, a number of practitioner-focused resources were published to help teachers teach general and special education students in and through the arts (Cornett, 1998; Gerber & Guay, 2006; Smith, 2001).

The increased profile of the arts was not without its drawbacks, though. As described by Winner and Cooper (2000), several high-profile studies published during this period (e.g., Leng, Shaw, & Wright, 1990) were misinterpreted by the general public and policy officials to suggest that arts learning caused improvements in cognitive function and unbounded enthusiasm for learning. Thus, despite the apparent boon to the arts educational community with the description of the arts in the Goals 2000: Educate America Act (1994), the combination of standardization efforts, public misperception of scientific research, and the competition for scarce funds translated into research and intervention focused on how the arts could aid in academic achievement, often under the assumption that the arts transfer to non-arts areas. As a result, artists, researchers, and practitioners in the arts community expressed concerns that the arts were burdened with justifying their existence as facilitators of 'academic competencies.'

Two types of efforts are discernible during this period: efforts to define and describe high-quality AI practices for students with and without disabilities, and studies linking arts learning to non-arts academic outcomes. Although research of these types has continued more recently (e.g., Aprill, 2010; Catterall, Dumais, & Hampden-Thompson, 2012; DeMoss, 2005; Mishook & Kornhaber, 2006), in an effort to identify patterns in research, these lines of inquiry are discussed in relation to the time period under examination here due to their predominance.

## Defining and Describing Arts Integration

Efforts to define and describe high-quality AI in general and special education occurred largely in tandem, but on parallel tracks. Thus the following section describes definitions and descriptions of AI first within the field of general education, and then focuses on parallel developments in special education.

### General education

The proliferation of AI efforts during this period resulted in a wide variety of practices, representing an equally wide variability in artistic quality (Catterall & Waldorf, 1999; Day, Eisner, Stake, Wilson, & Wilson, 1984; Stake, Bresler, & Mabry, 1991). For instance, the Chicago Arts Partnerships in Education developed AI programming that focused on identifying meaningful connections between arts and non-arts learning and lessons in which arts standards were as important as the non-arts content standards (Catterall & Waldorf, 1999). In contrast, a large-scale study of schools promoting AI conducted by Stake, Bresler, and Mabry (1991) found that AI instruction involved the arts as "topic enhancements" and "motivators for learning basic skills objectives" (p. 304). According to the authors, typical AI efforts included singing the names of the presidents, concluding that the AI lessons had little or no connection to authentic arts learning goals. The variety of AI efforts identified in these studies, particularly those efforts that appeared to 'use' the arts only to enhance non-arts learning, reignited the debate in the arts community regarding the intrinsic versus instrumental role of the arts in education.

In light of this debate, a primary concern in the early 1990s was making a clear and consistent argument that any efforts to pursue AI must not supplant traditional, discipline-based arts education opportunities for students. For instance, in 1992, a publication issued by a consortium of the national arts education associations (Consortium of National Arts Education Associates, 2002) highlighted the continued necessity for all students to experience educational opportunities in which they received sequential, comprehensive arts instruction by qualified art, music, theater, and dance educators. In this position paper, the consortium noted that AI efforts were welcome additions to comprehensive arts education, given that AI instruction was valid, useful, well designed, and well taught.

As noted by Stake et al. (1991), though, high-quality AI instruction was not commonly observed, and several attempts were made to discriminate between integration efforts in which arts were used merely as instruments in service of non-arts learning, and quality AI, in which the intrinsic value of the arts was maintained and even enhanced in concert with non-arts content (Bresler, 1995; Catterall, 1998; Consortium of National Arts Education Associates, 2002). For instance, Bresler (1995) forwarded a typology of four potential interactions between arts and non-arts learning: the subservient approach; the affective style; the social integration style; and the co-equal, cognitive integration style. In the subservient approach, the arts were used to "spice" non-arts content, serving as a "handmaiden" to non-arts instruction and learning. As suggested by the work of Stake et al. (1991), Bresler (1995) found that the subservient approach was most prevalent in practice. The affective and social integration styles, although focused on teaching non-arts content standards, were equally lacking in meaningful arts learning. The affective style was characterized by using the arts to create a calming environment, as aesthetic pleasure apart from meaningful learning, and as a means of self-expression. The social integration style, in contrast, highlighted the role of arts activities as community-developers (e.g., a school Christmas concert), again without efforts to develop in students deeper knowledge of or engagement with the arts.

Only the fourth type of arts integration identified by Bresler (1995) involved real and valuable arts learning. This co-equal, cognitive integration was characterized by learning in both arts and non-arts disciplines and by the engagement of "higher-order cognitive skills" (p. 34). By way of example, Bresler described the work of a social studies teacher who incorporated into her lessons information about and discussion around the cultural, particularly musical, contexts of particular time periods. To this point, the teacher guided students to engage with musical compositions and meaningfully consider how the music of the day represented the trends and values of the time period.

Using this and other definitions of AI, a number of researchers attempted to identify and describe qualities of authentic AI learning contexts (AEP, 1999, 2002; Bresler, 1997; Burnaford et al., 2001; Collins & Chandler, 1993; Seidel, 1999; Smith, 2001; Smith & Herring, 1996). For instance, Bresler (1997) conducted a naturalistic case study of five arts-integrated high schools that promised the "best conditions for integration." She found that AI was generally afforded by the identification of common issues, themes, or broad questions, and that students were introduced to artistic ways of seeing, analyzing, and creating compositions. Additionally, the study indicated that the AI curricula emphasized connection-making, focusing on personal and social relevance and finding relations between contemporary American culture and cultures in the past or around the world.

## Special education

Historically in special education, and in conjunction with experience-based approaches to education, the arts have been used as an alternative to conventional general education approaches, which have failed to meet the developmental (e.g., cognitive, linguistic, social-emotional, motor) needs of diverse learners. What most effective special educators have understood, yesterday and today, is that recognizing where individual students are in terms of their language, cognitive, social-emotional, and physical-motor development is key to providing them with appropriate and individualized educational programming. The best educators have noted that the arts are a valuable tool for this purpose. This position is reflected in Smith's (1991, 2000, 2001) writings, in which she argued that one of the benefits of the arts in special education programs was that they empowered exceptional students to take ownership of their disabilities and helped teachers find the methods that best accommodated students' learning.

To better illuminate the nature of arts-based special education, examinations of high-quality arts-integrated and arts-based learning efforts also were undertaken and described for students with disabilities (Smith, 1991, 2000, 2001; VSA, 2014b). In her pioneering book, *The power of the arts* (2001), Smith documents how arts-based curricula support students with learning- and sensory-based disorders to meet their individualized language-learning, cognitive, social, and emotional goals. Although Smith never explicitly describes her approach as 'arts integrated,' her descriptions meet the standard set out by Bresler (1995) by promoting learning in the arts and higher-order cognition. As such, it is recognized here as AI.

According to Smith, students with disabilities often have difficulty with – and are rarely challenged to engage in – higher-order thinking. However, through the arts, these challenges are more readily met. Thus, a hallmark of successful AI curricula for students with disabilities lies in the effort to help them discover relationships, nuances, and concepts; and to bridge the gulf between literal meanings and abstractions. According to Smith (2000), "young children use the arts – pretending, constructing, dancing, and doing – to make sense of their environment" (p. 32). In AI contexts, the arts become instruments through which students understand their conditions and develop skills for working around and celebrating their differences.

Another key to successful AI curricula for students with disabilities lies in the creation of art objects. According to Smith (2000), students with moderate to severe learning difficulties are passive, often waiting for adults to take the initiative and "pour knowledge into their brains" (p. 7). In contrast, art-making requires students to take a more active role in their learning by generating idiosyncratic solutions to problems and taking ownership of their work. Additionally, the process of creating requires students to pay attention to space and time. These are critical competencies in the development of every child, but students with disabilities have greater need for activities that cultivate these skills because they do not develop them as readily.

Smith also describes development of students' social and emotional selves as an essential component of AI learning. She terms this the fourth R: in addition to learning reading, writing, and arithmetic, students need to learn to form relationships at school. In particular, Smith argues that involvement in the arts offers students an outlet to cultivate their passions, to uncover hidden talents, and to discover their self-worth. Smith also claims that exceptional learners often have issues with working as members of a team, and that arts contexts help them to develop this capacity and inclination.

## Linking Arts Learning to 'Academic' Outcomes

The 1990s and early 2000s also saw the undertaking of a number of empirical studies that sought to link arts learning to non-arts outcomes (for reviews of many of these studies, see Eisner, 1998; Winner & Hetland, 2000). In addition to the descriptive-type research discussed previously, there was a rise in studies using correlational or experimental/quasi-experimental methodologies.

Correlational studies measure the strength and directionality of two variables. In the case of AI research, the two variables were arts experiences or learning and non-arts outcomes, such as SAT scores, GPAs, or academic awards. For instance, Catterall, Chapleau, and Iwanaga (1999) conducted a widely cited and influential study which examined the relation between arts and achievement outcomes using a large-scale database. They found that students who were highly engaged in arts experiences had higher achievement scores than did students with low arts

engagement. The researchers also identified a correspondence between instrumental music training and math achievement and a similar association between theater involvement and reading proficiency, motivation, and empathy.

Another group of studies used an experimental or quasi-experimental design, which included a treatment (i.e., arts experiential) group and a control (i.e., non-arts) condition. For example, Gardiner, Fox, Knowledge, and Jeffrey (1996) conducted a study in eight first-grade classrooms, four of which incorporated music and art instruction that emphasized sequential skill-development (i.e., treatment) while the remaining four classrooms received the standard art and music curriculum (i.e., control). After seven months, the students took standardized math and reading assessments and their scores were compared. The results of the study indicated that, although the treatment and control groups did not differ with respect to reading scores, the math achievement scores of students in the treatment condition were significantly higher.

As noted by Winner and Hetland (2000), a critical concern related to the growing number of studies, both qualitative and quantitative in nature, was the frequent and erroneous description of their findings as indicating causality or transfer of learning; claims often made by arts advocates and, occasionally, by the authors themselves. For instance, Catterall (2002) described the studies included in the frequently cited Champions of Change synthesis of arts research (Deasy, 2002) as having been selected for inclusion in the document due to "their ability to make causal suggestions" (p. 154) regarding the transfer of arts experiences to non-arts outcomes. However, as noted by Winner and Hetland (2003), the threshold for causality was often not met in the included studies.

This example captures well the significant problem of the search for, or assumption of, transfer in arts research during this period, which, according to some (Eisner, 1998; Smith, 1995), risked attaching an unattainable and misguided burden to the arts. Pogrebin (2007) quotes Winner's explanation of this potentially dangerous research orientation:

> We feel we need to change the conversation about the arts in this country. These instrumental arguments are going to doom the arts to failure, because any superintendent is going to say, "If the only reason I'm having art is to improve math, let's just have more math." Do we want to therefore say, "No singing," because singing didn't lead to spatial improvement? You get yourself in a bind there. The arts need to be valued for their own intrinsic reasons. Let's figure out what the arts really do teach.

As well as being controversial, the attempts to demonstrate transfer or causality from arts experiences to non-arts outcomes was largely unsuccessful from a methodological perspective. This point was made very clearly in the influential Reviewing Education and the Arts Project (REAP; Winner & Hetland, 2000). This monumental undertaking involved collecting over 1,000 studies examining arts experiences and non-arts outcomes, both published and unpublished; retaining all studies whose methodologies could substantiate a transfer or causality claim (i.e., correlational or experimental/quasi-experimental); and then subjecting the roughly 200 remaining studies to a series of statistical meta-analyses, in an effort to determine the degree to which, as a collective, the studies indicated transfer from arts experiences to non-arts outcomes.

The results of the meta-analyses concluded that there was sufficient support for three causal relations: listening to music and spatial-temporal reasoning, learning to play music and spatial reasoning, and classroom drama and verbal skills. However, the studies did not find support for additional instrumental claims: that arts-rich education impacts verbal or math achievement; that the arts promote creativity; and that visual art, dance, or music impacts reading outcomes.

Although hotly contested and widely debated (for a summary of the debate, see Winner & Hetland, 2001), the REAP studies signaled a sea-change in arts-related research. After 'muting' the unsubstantiated causal claims made about how the arts benefit non-arts outcomes, the researchers challenged the field to deeply examine the affective, social, and cognitive aspects afforded by arts learning, to both better understand the benefits of quality arts education in its own right, and to develop grounded rationales for how and why arts learning might relate to learning in other areas.

The challenge inherent in the REAP studies resonated with other critiques of the state of arts research (Eisner, 1998, 2002; Melnick, Witmer, & Strickland, 2011; Mishook & Kornhaber, 2006; Parsons, 2004). For instance, Eisner's (1998) review noted the dearth of theoretical rationales linking experience in the arts with academic achievement. He called for research that moved beyond correlations or examinations of outcomes – particularly standardized testing data – to examine the processes underlying quality arts experiences and the degree to which those processes overlapped with processes essential to non-arts learning. Parsons (2004) suggested that one valuable avenue to examining the how and why of arts research may lie in a deeper understanding of the psychology of learning. This point was also articulated by noted cognitive scientist Robert Sylwester:

> The problem in evaluating arts is our inability of codifying particulars. Most have looked at the results of skills rather than the thinking processes which underpin them … If one only looks at specifics of art that may be transferred, rather than focusing on the process, few skills may be demonstrated or applied elsewhere. However, the thinking processes are probably used throughout.
>
> *(quoted in Melnick et al., 2011, p. 156)*

This quotation captures current trends in arts and AI-related research for students with and without disabilities. Indeed, many of today's research efforts are oriented toward unearthing the mechanisms or affordances that gave rise to the descriptions of learning in high-quality AI for all students and the positive findings of the empirical research. Specifically, today's AI research endeavors to address the theoretical rationale gap noted by Eisner (1998) and the thinking processes suggested by Sylwester (Melnick et al., 2011). In short, if the AI research of yesterday was focused on the *what* of learning in AI settings, the research of today emphasizes the *how* and *why*.

## Arts Integration Today: Exploring and Confirming

The educational climate of today has not reduced its relentless focus on standardization and high-stakes accountability, particularly in light of the increasing achievement gap that separates students from diverse backgrounds (i.e., diversity in ability, ethnicity, culture, and socioeconomic status). Indeed, due to the continued perception that US students lag behind much of the world in academic competence and are ill-prepared for success in the workplace, there is a concerted effort, once again, to raise the stakes for education (Gewertz, 2011). This effort is manifest in the creation and wide-spread adoption of the Common Core State Standards (CCSS) Initiative. The CCSS have been developed through an unprecedented collaboration between state governors and consists of agreed-upon standards of learning across the curriculum. To date, 45 states, the District of Columbia, and four US territories have adopted the CCSS and high-stakes tests are being developed to assess students on these standards (Common Core State Standards Initiative, 2014). This near-universal collaboration and adoption of the CCSS is notable, particularly given the fact that education efforts have been greatly impacted by a global economic downturn, which has resulted in the scarcity of funds at every level. Concurrently, across the educational landscape, evidence-based practice in virtually all aspects of schooling, from reading programs to social work, has become a reality (Odom, Buysse, & Soukakou, 2011; Odom, Collet-Klingenberg, Rogers, & Hatton, 2010). In special education research, the combination of evidence-based practice and practice-based evidence has come to be regarded as the most feasible and sustainable model of intervention and service provision (Cook & Cook, 2013; Rumrill, Cook, & Wiley, 2011).

For these reasons, federal, state, and local education policymakers are critically examining the role of arts in academic programming and budgeting, and are seeking rigorous qualitative and quantitative data detailing the contribution of arts to student outcomes, particularly for those considered 'at-risk' (see Novosel, Deshler, Pollitt, & Mitchell, 2011) for academic failure, including students with and without disabilities (Clark, Evans, Loughlin, Staret, & Taytslin, 2012; National Art Education Association, 2009; National Endowment for the Arts, 2010; Robinson, 2013). In 2010, the National Endowment for the Arts (NEA) expanded its strategic plan to cultivate and communicate evidence of the value and impact of the arts through an arts-research agenda (NEA, 2010). The NEA's approach reflects the calls put forth by the REAP studies and others (Bresler,

2001; Eisner, 2002), focusing on better understanding what happens in high-quality arts-learning experiences and how and why those learning experiences might relate to learning in non-arts contexts.

An examination of recent research on arts and AI learning (i.e., over approximately the past decade) reveals two general approaches with the goal of identifying theoretically grounded relations between art and non-arts learning: what this chapter terms Exploratory and Confirmatory. Although following a different course, both approaches aim to identify meaningful connections between arts and non-arts learning and have the potential to impact arts integration research, policy, and practice. This section describes the Exploratory and Confirmatory approaches, provides examples of lines of inquiry reflective of each with regard to students with and without disabilities, and discusses implications for AI research and practice.

## The Exploratory Approach

The first, and likely better-known, approach to today's AI research explores arts learning contexts, including high-quality AI settings, to determine their salient social, affective, and cognitive aspects. This research approach is termed Exploratory because it emphasizes unrestricted and close examination to determine patterns and practices, rather than imposing hypotheses or predictive frameworks on the arts learning context. Indeed, one goal of this research is to identify the patterns or practices inherent in arts learning, in an effort to *generate* hypotheses or predictive frameworks for the future.

Although several examples of the Exploratory approach are evident in the literature (DeMoss, 2005; Henley, 1992; Winner, 1996; Zhbanova, Rule, Montgomery, & Nielsen, 2010), perhaps the most influential instance of this research type is reflected in the Studio Thinking line of inquiry (Hetland, Winner, Veenema, & Sheridan, 2007). This study consisted of an in-depth analysis of two excellent arts high schools in the Boston area, and comprised analysis of videotaped visual art lessons, field observations, and teacher interviews. The research focused on identifying and describing the habits of mind cultivated by serious study of visual art. The results of this study were eight dispositions, or 'studio habits of mind': develop craft, engage and persist, envision, express, observe, reflect, stretch and explore, and understand the art world. These findings served two valuable purposes: better understanding of what is learned in high-quality arts contexts, and the identification of potential relations to learning in non-arts areas. Indeed, the researchers concluded that the identification of the studio habits of mind was the first in a series of steps, culminating in testing the hypotheses that particular habits of mind learned in the arts transfer to non-arts learning, possibly in an AI context. Sheridan's (2011) application of the Studio Thinking framework is evidence that this research trajectory is yielding results.

Similarly, McCurrach and Darnley (1999) used an Exploratory approach to closely examine the patterns and processes evidenced when individuals with a range of learning and sensory difficulties created drama. Specifically, the authors framed students' cognitive and social skills learning objectives around the production of the play *Macbeth*. The results showed that students' participation and experience supported their understanding and use of language, the formation of relationships, as well as demonstration of affective engagement through excitement, enjoyment, joint attention, and eye contact, among other individualized outcomes for students.

The Exploratory research approach has significant potential to influence AI efforts in both general and special education. As noted by many (e.g., Perkins, 2001), curricula and research linking arts learning to non-arts outcomes has little hope of yielding consistent, significant, and positive relations unless there is better understanding of what should be taught and what should be measured. A first step, as illustrated by this Exploratory approach, is to identify what is salient about arts learning. Only once this goal is achieved can the field develop meaningful AI curricula that deliberately tap into those salient attributes and study the degree to which those attributes are evident in the non-arts learning context as well.

Significant progress has been made in the past decade to develop an understanding of how people learn in high-quality arts contexts; however, much more research in this area is needed. For instance, although the Studio Thinking research (Hetland et al., 2007) illuminated some critical aspects of learning in visual arts contexts, a similar approach should be taken to better understand learning in other high-quality arts and AI contexts, including traditional and emergent art forms. Also, following the example of Sheridan (2011), future research should test the relations between the habits of mind developed in arts contexts and those essential for learning in non-arts disciplines.

The Exploratory approach is extraordinarily valuable to the arts education and AI fields, and has the potential to be equally valuable to education policy and practice globally. However, there is a communication burden. Because studies of this nature are focused closely on arts learning, they are likely to be primarily published in arts-related outlets and therefore read by, and influential to, those already steeped in the arts. As such, communicating these findings to a non-arts audience and making clear the implications for AI practice for students with and without disabilities must be a concerted and deliberative effort.

## The Confirmatory Approach

In contrast to the Exploratory research, the Confirmatory approach begins with predictions drawn from theory and constructs in arts-allied fields, and then examines the degree to which those predictions are confirmed in arts contexts. In other words, the Confirmatory approach brings to bear what is known about the learning process in non-arts disciplines in an effort to better understand what might occur for students with and without disabilities learning in AI contexts.

An example of the Confirmatory research lens is the recent work of Rinne, Gregory, Yarmolinskaya, and Hardiman (2011). Rinne and colleagues applied several well-known theories in cognitive psychology to AI learning. Specifically, the authors argue that AI learning promotes rehearsal, elaboration, generation, enactment, oral production, pictorial representation, effort after meaning, and emotional arousal – all of which have been shown to significantly improve long-term memory. The authors suggested that these constructs be used to frame AI research under the rationale that AI may improve long-term retention of content and, as a consequence, improve overall learning.

Anderson (Anderson, 2012; Anderson, Berry, & Loughlin, 2014; Anderson, Loughlin, & Berry, 2013) also used the Confirmatory approach in studies of language use in drama-integrated settings. To better understand how classroom drama facilitates students' language use – a well-established relation without a clear explanatory mechanism – Anderson applied a theory from the language-learning literature. Under examination was the degree to which classroom drama primed students to use specific literate language, or to 'talk like books,' when communicating with other students and with the teacher. For instance, Anderson (2012) found that students performing significantly below grade level in reading, both with and without disabilities, produced significantly more literate language during those lessons integrating classroom drama than in lessons without. Anderson concluded that classroom drama placed a higher burden on all students to communicate their ideas and understanding of texts and, in so doing, to understand and use language that was more specific and precise. Moreover, this work indicated that the dramatic AI context facilitated linguistically specific discourse among students with and without language-based disabilities.

These studies and others reflecting the Confirmatory approach (Loughlin & Alexander, 2012; Loughlin, Anderson, & Berry, 2013; Millis & Larson, 2008; Solso, 1999; Tishman & Palmer, 2006; VSA, 2008) have harnessed theories and constructs in arts–allied fields to inform understanding of how students learn in AI settings. However, much more Confirmatory-type research remains to be done, particularly with respect to illuminating why AI might be related to deeper and more meaningful learning. For instance, linkages between AI and learning may be better understood by examining how AI affects students' executive function skills (Welsh, Pennington, & Groisser, 1991), self-theory (Dweck, 1999), engagement (Corno & Mandinach, 1983), achievement motivation (Wigfield & Eccles, 2000), self-efficacy (Bandura, 1977), self-regulation (Zimmerman & Schunk, 2001), and individual and situational interest (Hidi, 1990), amongst others.

As a field, the arts may look to special education research as a model in this respect. Today, special education is a diverse field, which encompasses multidisciplinary perspectives on development and learning from psychology, linguistics, sociology, medicine, and education. Special education perspectives are informed by developmental linguistics and psychology, as well as by practical work with students who have diverse learning needs and their families.

As with Exploratory research, there are difficulties to overcome with Confirmatory-style research if it is to be influential. Primarily, in order to bring to bear theories and constructs from other disciplines, those interested in AI must be aware of and proficient in an arts-adjacent discipline. Research using a Confirmatory framework is often published in books or in discipline-specific journals and may not include explicit references to the arts or to students with disabilities. As such, those interested in developing AI-related research or pedagogy must begin to read widely, often beyond the arts fields, in order to identify concepts or theories with the potential to improve the current understanding of how AI impacts learners.

There is significant upside to this effort, however. Many relevant constructs in arts-adjacent fields have deep research bases and wide acceptance in the larger educational community. Thus, framing AI research with these constructs could propel arts research into the larger conversation. For example, Anderson's work (Anderson, 2012; Anderson et al., 2013, 2014) is focused on oral and written language use, which are significant predictors of academic success (Westby, 2006, 2010) and are, therefore, the target of significant policy and research efforts (RAND Reading Study Group, 2002). Similarly, the approach promoted by Rinne et al. (2011) suggests that AI learning is facilitative because it incorporates multiple representations of an idea (e.g., text and visuals). Not only is this suggestion based on significant research in cognitive psychology (Mayer, 2002; Paivio, 1971; Schnotz & Bannert, 2003), it is the foundation of several current federally funded research initiatives in science (e.g., Cromley et al., 2013).

Another benefit of undertaking studies with a Confirmatory framework is the tie to research funding and policy implementation. In a recent address to the national forum of the Arts Education Partnership, John Easton of the Institute for Education Sciences urged the arts community to develop and present studies with a clearly articulated 'theory of action' – what this chapter terms Confirmatory – describing how and why a given arts experience was shown to impact students or school (Clark et al., 2012). Easton went on to say that connecting the arts to evidence-based funding (e.g., grants awarded by the Institute for Education Sciences) would help solidify the link between arts education and academic achievement and bolster support for the arts.

Easton's call for compelling theories of action with regard to arts and AI learning requires the research community to consider alternative frameworks to the status quo. For example, MI theory has often been used to frame AI efforts because it supports the notion that arts are as essential in the curriculum as other content areas. However, MI theory does not itself provide a viable explanation for how or why AI learning occurs. In fact, as argued by Parsons (2004), MI theory emphasizes the differences among content areas (i.e., each represents a unique intelligence), and so does not explain how or why two content areas can or should be integrated. It is essential that, as a field, AI researchers consider theories and constructs that will present a better rationale for AI.

Several other theories of action might prove more viable for Confirmatory research efforts. For example, social semiotics theory and the related work of the New London Group (1996) have been used to frame how and why the creation of artworks may relate to the creation of other, non-arts compositions (e.g., Kress & van Leeuwen, 1996). These theories can be used to frame AI studies in which the integration occurs in the overlapping of creative efforts (e.g., writing and drama). On the other side of the creation-comprehension continuum are the Trans-Symbolic Comprehension (Loughlin, 2013; Loughlin & Alexander, 2012) and Artful Thinking (Tishman & Palmer, 2006) frameworks, which examine the degree to which arts and non-arts compositions require similar approaches to thinking and understanding. These frameworks can be used to examine how students understand arts and non-arts compositions in AI contexts.

The call for more Confirmatory research was recently made by Rinne and colleagues (2011). In discussing the significance of their study, the authors called attention to the considerable potential that arts-adjacent fields have for furthering AI research efforts.

> In addition, the work undertaken here is at a minimum suggestive of the possibility that there is a wealth of scientific knowledge already in existence that can inform [AI] policy and practice. This underscores the importance of ensuring that researchers and educators alike are constantly making an effort to seek out such knowledge and apply it in sensible, meaningful, and measured ways for the benefit of all students.
>
> *(p. 94)*

## Arts Integration Research: Lessons Learned

The foregoing discussion of the history of AI suggests several lessons for AI researchers: develop a theory of action, focus on high-quality AI instruction, examine the role of AI in the learning of students with and without disabilities, and consider research findings in light of future trends in educational policy and practice. These lessons were considered in the development of this volume.

This book posits a theory of action and then provides action research to confirm it. Specifically, it takes a Confirmatory approach to examining the degree to which AI is related to increases in cognitive, affective, and linguistic engagement in students with disabilities and, by extension, their oral and written language. In so doing, it draws on literature in educational psychology and speech and language pathology to develop a theory of action to explain how and why AI might be associated with greater increases in these students' oral and written language use than are evidenced using a conventional approach to instruction. This theory of action uses engagement as an umbrella and postulates contributions from language, cognition, and affective/social-cognitive domains of learning to better understand the influence of AI contexts on student learning. For example, it considers the degree to which linguistic, cognitive, and affective dimensions of engagement – individually and collectively – relate to learning outcomes for students.

This volume also focuses heavily on the role of AI learning for students with disabilities. Recently, Catterall et al. (2012) examined several large-scale datasets to determine the relation between arts learning and students at-risk for academic failure. The extensive analysis concluded that (1) students from at-risk backgrounds with high levels of arts engagement performed better than did their low-engagement peers on a host of academic and behavioral measures and (2) that most of the positive associations between arts involvement and academic achievement were more significant for students from at-risk backgrounds than for their lower-risk peers. Most recently, Robinson's (2013) evaluation of AI research published between 1995 and 2011 conducted with disadvantaged student populations – including economically disadvantaged students, English language learners, and students with disabilities – also found positive effects of AI on student learning.

Despite the impressive conclusions drawn by Catterall et al. (2012) and Robinson (2013), others (e.g., O'Thearling & Bickley-Green, 1996; Parsad, Spiegelman, & Coopersmith, 2012) have found disproportionally fewer arts opportunities in schools serving students from at-risk backgrounds. The juxtaposition generated by these studies suggests a significant area for future AI research: namely, investigating how and why the arts and AI might impact students from at-risk backgrounds. Thus, there is a felt need for AI researchers and practitioners to examine high-quality AI learning in schools or programs that serve students from urban, minority, special education, and/or English language-learning backgrounds. This book takes on the challenge of crafting research that examines how and why AI might benefit a group of students among those at-risk for academic disenfranchisement and failure: those with disabilities.

The final lesson to be learned from this study of the history of AI research and practice is that it is essential to look ahead. In this effort, Part III of this volume considers the future of AI research and highlights possible directions for the field. These ideas are offered as a conclusion to this chapter's lessons learned for the research and practice of tomorrow, as well as for the reader's further consideration while reading the demonstrations of AI in inclusive classrooms from Part II of the book.

## References

Abedin, G. (2010). *Exploring the potential benefits of arts-based education for adolescents with learning disabilities: A case study of engagement in learning through the arts.* Retrieved from ProQuest Dissertations & Theses (3409864).

Alexander, W. M. (2001). *Making the transition to curriculum integration: A curriculum design in middle level schools* (Unpublished doctoral dissertation). University of Maine, Orono, ME. Retrieved from http://www.library.umaine.edu/theses/pdf/AlexanderWM2001.pdf

Anderson, A. (2012). The influence of process drama on elementary students' written language. *Urban Education*, 47(5), 959–982.

Anderson, A., Berry, K., & Loughlin, S. M. (2014, April). *The influence of drama on elementary students' narrative written language and on-task behavior*. Presentation at the 2014 AERA Annual Meeting, Philadelphia, PA.

Anderson, A., Loughlin, S. M., & Berry, K. (2013, April). *The influence of dramatic arts integration on teacher and student language in language arts contexts*. Presentation at the 2013 AERA Annual Meeting, San Francisco, CA.

Anderson, F. E. (1975). Mainstreaming art as well as children. *Art Education*, 28(8), 26–27.

Andrus, L. (1994). Art education: An equalizing force in the inclusion setting. In *Inclusion: Buzzword or hope for the future* [Monograph]. Albany, NY: New York State Council of Educational Assessment.

Aprill, A. (2010). Direct instruction vs. arts integration: A false dichotomy. *Teaching Artist Journal*, 8(1), 6–15.

Arts Education Partnership. (1999). *Gaining the arts advantage: Lessons from school districts that value arts education*. Washington, DC: Author.

Arts Education Partnership. (2002). *Critical links: Learning in the arts and student academic and social development*. Washington, DC: Author.

Bandura, A. (1977). Self-efficacy: Toward a unifying theory of behavioral change. *Psychological Review*, 84, 191–215.

Beane, J. (1993). *A middle school curriculum: From rhetoric to reality*. Columbus, OH: National Middle School Association.

Bloom, B. S., Engelhart, M. D., Furst, E. J., Hill, W. H., & Krathwohl, D. R. (Eds.). (1956). *Taxonomy of educational objectives: Handbook I: The cognitive domain*. New York: David McKay.

Bloom, B. S., Hastings, J. T., & Madaus, G. F. (1971). *Handbook on formative and summative evaluation of student learning*. New York: McGraw-Hill.

Bresler, L. (1995). The subservient, co-equal, affective, and social integration styles and their implications for the arts. *Arts Education Policy Review*, 96(5), 31–37.

Bresler, L. (1997). *General issues across sites: The role of the arts in unifying high school curriculum*. A report for the College Board/Getty Center for the Arts.

Bresler, L. (2001). Agenda for arts education research: Emerging issues and directions. In M. McCarthy (Ed.), *Enlightened advocacy: Implications for research for arts education policy and practice* (pp. 43–71). College Park, MD: University of Maryland.

Bruner, J. S. (1975). The ontogenesis of speech acts. *Journal of Child Language*, 2, 1–19.

Burnaford, G., Aprill, A., Weiss, C., & Chicago Arts Partnerships in Education (CAPE) (Eds.). (2001). *Renaissance in the classroom: Arts integration and meaningful learning*. Mahwah, NJ: Lawrence Erlbaum Associates.

Burnaford, G., Brown, S., Doherty, J., & McLaughlin, H. J. (2007). *Arts integration frameworks, research, and practice: A literature review*. Washington, DC: Arts Education Partnership.

Carrigan, J. (1994). Paint talk: An adaptive art experience promoting communication and understanding among students in an integrated classroom. *Preventing School Failure: Alternative Education for Children and Youth*, 38(2), 34–37.

Catterall, J. S. (1998). Does experience in the arts boost academic achievement? A response to Eisner. *Art Education*, 51(4), 6–11.

Catterall, J. S. (2002). The arts and the transfer of learning. In R. J. Deasy (Ed.), *Critical links: Learning in the arts and student academic and social development* (pp. 151–157). Washington, DC: Arts Education Partnership.

Catterall, J. S., Chapleau, R., & Iwanaga, J. (1999). Involvement in the arts and human development: General involvement and intensive involvement in music and theater arts. In E. B. Fiske (Ed.), *Champions of change: The impact of the arts on learning* (pp. 1–18). Washington, DC: Arts Education Partnership.

Catterall, J. S., Dumais, S. A., & Hampden-Thompson, G. (2012). *The arts and achievement in at-risk youth: Findings from four longitudinal studies.* Washington, DC: National Endowment for the Arts.

Catterall, J. S., & Waldorf, L. (1999). Chicago Arts Partnerships in Education: Summary evaluation. In E. B. Fiske (Ed.), *Champions of change: The impact of the arts on learning* (pp. 47–62). Washington, DC: Arts Education Partnership.

Clark, E., Evans, J., Loughlin, S., Staret, C., & Taytslin, H. (2012). *Are we there yet? Arts evidence and the road to student success. AEP 2012 national forum report.* Washington, DC: Arts Education Partnership.

Clements, C. B., & Clements, R. D. (1984). *Art and mainstreaming: Art instruction for exceptional children in regular classes.* Springfield, IL: Charles C Thomas.

Collins, E. C., & Chandler, S. (1993). Beyond art as product: Using an artistic perspective to understand classroom life. *Theory into Practice, 32*(4), 199–203.

Committee on the Arts and Humanities. (2011). *Reinvesting in arts education: Winning America's future through creative schools.* Washington, DC: Author.

Common Core State Standards Initiative. (2014). *In the states.* Retrieved February 10, 2014 from http://www.corestandards.org/in-the-states

Consortium of National Arts Education Associations. (2002). *Authentic connections: Interdisciplinary work in the arts.* Reston, VA: National Art Education Association.

Cook, B. G., & Cook, S. C. (2013). Unraveling evidence-based practices in special education. *Journal of Special Education, 47*(2), 71–82.

Cornett, C. E. (1998). *The arts as meaning makers: Integrating literature and the arts throughout the curriculum.* Upper Saddle River, NJ: Merrill.

Cornett, C. E. (2007). *Creating meaning through literature and the arts: An integration resource for classroom teachers* (3rd ed.). Upper Saddle River, NJ: Pearson Education.

Corno, L., & Mandinach, E. (1983). The role of cognitive engagement in classroom learning and motivation. *Educational Psychologist, 18,* 88–108.

Cromley, J. C., Bergey, B. W., Fitzhugh, S., Newcombe, N., Wills, T. W., Shipley, T. F., & Tanaka, J. C. (2013). Effects of three diagram instruction methods on transfer of diagram comprehension skills: The critical role of inference while learning. *Learning and Instruction, 26,* 45–58.

Day, M., Eisner, E., Stake, R., Wilson, B., & Wilson, M. (1984). *Art history, art criticism, and art production: An examination of art education in selected school districts.* Santa Monica, CA: RAND.

Deasy, R. J. (Ed.). (2002). *Critical links: Learning in the arts and student academic and social development.* Washington, DC: Arts Education Partnership.

DeMoss, K. (2005). How arts integration supports student learning: Evidence from students in Chicago's CAPE Partnership schools. *Arts and Learning Research Journal, 21*(1), 91–118.

Dewey, J. (1934). *Art as experience.* New York: Minton, Balch & Company.

Duke, L. L. (1988). The Getty Center for Education in the Arts and Discipline-Based Art Education. *Art Education, 41*(2), 7–12.

Dweck, C. (1999). *Self-theories: Their role in motivation, personality, and development.* Philadelphia, PA: Psychology Press.

Education for All Handicapped Children Act of 1975, Public Law 94–142, 20 U.S.C. §
1400 et seq. (1975).

Eisner, E. W. (1998). Does experience in the arts boost academic achievement? *Art Education*,
51(1), 7–15.

Eisner, E. W. (2002). *The arts and the creation of mind*. New Haven, CT: Yale University
Press.

Eisner, E. W., & Getty Center for Education in the Arts. (1988). *The role of Discipline-Based
Art Education in America's schools*. Los Angeles: Getty Center for Education in the Arts.

Elementary and Secondary Education Act of 1965, Public Law 89–10, 20 U.S.C. § 6301
et seq. (1965).

Gardiner, M. F., Fox, A., Knowledge, F., & Jeffrey, D. (1996). Learning improved by arts
training. *Nature*, 381(6580), 284.

Gardner, H. (1983). *Frames of mind: The theory of multiple intelligences*. New York: Basic
Books.

Gerber, B. L., & Guay, D. P. (2006). *Reaching and teaching students with special needs through art*.
National Art Education Association.

Gewertz, C. (2011). Higher education is goal of GED overhaul. *Education Week*, 31(12).
Retrieved February 12, 2014 from http://www.edweek.org/ew/articles/2011/11/16/
12ged.h31.html?qs=GED

Goals 2000: Educate America Act of 1994, Public Law 103–227, 20 U.S.C. § 5801 et seq.
(1994).

Hardman, M. L., Drew, C. J., & Egan, M. W. (2011). *Human exceptionality: School, community,
and family* (10th ed.). Boston: Cengage Learning.

Henley, D. R. (1992). *Exceptional children, exceptional art: Teaching art to special needs*. Worcester,
MA: Davis.

Hetland, L., Winner, E., Veenema, S., & Sheridan, K. (2007). *Studio Thinking: The real benefits
of visual arts education*. New York: Teachers College Press.

Hidi, S. (1990). Interest and its contribution as a mental resource for learning. *Review of
Educational Research*, 60(4), 549–571.

Individuals with Disabilities Education Improvement Act of 2004, Public Law 108–446, 20
U.S.C. § 1401 et seq. (2004).

Keifer-Boyd, K., & Kraft, L. M. (2003). Inclusion policy in practice. *Art Education*, 56(6),
46–53.

Kliebard, H. (1987). *The struggle for the American curriculum: 1893–1958*. New York:
Routledge & Kegan Paul.

Kraft, M. (2003). Equality and inclusion: Creating a communitarian environment. *Journal of
Cultural Research in Art Education*, 21, 68–75.

Kraft, M. (2004). Least restrictive environment: Policy analysis and case study of a high
school art class. *Visual Arts Research*, 30(1), 22–34.

Krathwohl, D. R., Bloom, B. S., & Masia, B. B. (1964). *Taxonomy of educational objectives: The
classification of educational goals. Handbook II: Affective domain*. New York: David McKay
Co., Inc.

Kress, G. R., & van Leeuwen, T. (1996). *Reading images: A grammar of visual design*. London:
Routledge.

Leng, X., Shaw, G. L., & Wright, E. L. (1990). Coding of musical structure and the trion
model of cortex. *Musical Perception*, 8(1), 49–62.

Loughlin, S. M. (2011, April). Trans-symbolic comprehension and higher-order thinking. In
K. Muis (Chair), *Thinking critically about higher-order thinking: New perspectives on a familiar*

*construct*. Symposium conducted at the annual meeting of the American Educational Research Association, New Orleans, LA.

Loughlin, S. M. (2013). *Examining trans-symbolic and symbol-specific processes in poetry and painting* (Unpublished doctoral dissertation). University of Maryland, College Park.

Loughlin, S. M., & Alexander, P. A. (2012). Explicating and exemplifying empiricist and cognitivist paradigms in the study of human learning. In L. L'Abate (Ed.), *The role of paradigms in model construction*. London: Springer-Verlag.

Loughlin, S. M., Anderson, A., & Berry, K. (2013, April). *Reading between the lines: Classroom discourse and academic rigor in traditional and drama-integrated language arts*. Presentation at the 2013 AERA Annual Meeting, San Francisco, CA.

Mayer, R. E. (2002). Multimedia learning. *Psychology of Learning and Motivation*, 41, 85–139.

McCurrach, I., & Darnley, B. (1999). *Special talents, special needs: Drama for people with learning disabilities*. Philadelphia, PA: Jessica Kingsley Publishers.

Melnick, S., Witmer, J., & Strickland, M. (2011). Cognition and student learning through the arts. *Arts Education Policy Review*, 112(3), 154–162.

Millis, K., & Larson, M. (2008). Applying the construction-integration framework to aesthetic responses to representational artworks. *Discourse Processes*, 45(3), 263–287.

Mishook, J. J., & Kornhaber, M. L. (2006). Arts integration in an era of accountability. *Arts Education Policy Review*, 107(4), 3–11.

Montessori, M. (1917). *The Montessori elementary material* (A. Livingston, Trans.) (Vol. 2). New York: Frederick A. Stokes.

National Art Education Association. (2009). *NAEA research agenda: Creating a visual arts research agenda for the 21st century*. Washington, DC: Author.

National Commission on Excellence in Education. (1983). *A nation at risk: The imperative for educational reform*. Washington, DC: National Commission on Excellence in Education.

National Endowment for the Arts (2010). *Art works for America: Strategic Plan, FY 2012–2016*. Retrieved November 6, 2011 from http://www.nea.gov/about/Budget/NEAStrategicPlan2012-2016.pdf

New London Group. (1996). A pedagogy of multiliteracies: Designing social futures. *Harvard Educational Review*, 66(1), 60–92.

Novosel, L., Deshler, D., Pollitt, D., Mark, C., & Mitchell, B. (2011). At-risk learners (characteristics). In N. Seel (Ed.), *Encyclopedia of the science of learning* (pp. 1–5). New York: Springer.

Odom, S. L., Buysse, V., & Soukakou, E. (2011). Inclusion for young children with disabilities: A quarter century of research perspectives. *Journal of Early Intervention*, 33(4), 344–356.

Odom, S. L., Collet-Klingenberg, L., Rogers, S. J., & Hatton, D. D. (2010). Evidence-based practices in interventions for children and youth with autism spectrum disorders. *Preventing School Failure: Alternative Education for Children and Youth*, 54(4), 275–282.

O'Thearling, S., & Bickley-Green, C. A. (1996). Art education and at-risk youth: Enabling factors of visual expression. *Visual Arts Research*, 22(1), 20–25.

Paivio, A. (1971). *Imagery and verbal processes*. New York: Holt, Rinehart, and Winston.

Parsad, B., Spiegelman, M., & Coopersmith, J. (2012). *Arts education in public elementary and secondary schools: 1999–2000 and 2009–2010*. Washington, DC: United States Department of Education.

Parsons, M. (2004). Art and integrated curriculum. In E. W. Eisner & M. D. Day (Eds.), *Handbook of research and policy in art education* (pp. 775–794). Mahwah, NJ: Lawrence Erlbaum.

Perkins, D. (2001). Embracing Babel: The prospects of instrumental uses of the arts for education. In E. Winner & L. Hetland (Eds.), *Beyond the soundbite: What the research actually shows about arts education and academic outcomes* (pp. 117–124). Los Angeles: J. Paul Getty Trust.

Pogrebin, R. (2007, August 4). Book tackles old debate: Role of art in schools. *The New York Times.* Retrieved January 31, 2014 from http://www.nytimes.com/2007/08/04/arts/design/04stud.html?_r=0

RAND Reading Study Group (RRSG). (2002). *Reading for understanding: Toward an R&D program in reading comprehension.* Santa Monica, CA: Author.

Rinne, L., Gregory, E., Yarmolinskaya, J., & Hardiman, M. (2011). Why arts integration improves long-term retention of content. *Mind, Brain, and Education,* 5(2), 89–96.

Robinson, A. H. (2013). Arts integration and the success of disadvantaged students: A research evaluation. *Arts Education Policy Review,* 114(4), 191–204.

Rumrill Jr, P. D., Cook, B. G., & Wiley, A. L. (2011). *Research in special education: Designs, methods, and applications.* Springfield, IL: Charles C. Thomas.

Saettler, P. (1990). *The evolution of American educational technology.* Englewood, CO: Libraries Unlimited, Inc.

Schnotz, W., & Bannert, M. (2003). Construction and interference in learning from multiple representation. *Learning and Instruction,* 13(2), 141–156.

Seidel, S. (1999). "Stand and unfold yourself": A monograph on the Shakespeare & Company Research Study. In E. B. Fiske (Ed.), *Champions of change: The impact of the arts on learning* (pp. 79–90). Washington, DC: Arts Education Partnership.

Sheridan, K. M. (2011). Envision and observe: Using the Studio Thinking Framework for learning and teaching in digital arts. *Mind, Brain, and Education,* 5(1), 19–26.

Smith, J., & Herring, J. (1996). Literature alive: Connecting to story through arts. *Reading Horizons, 37*(2), 102–115.

Smith, R. (1995). The limits and costs of integration in arts education. *Arts Education Policy Review,* 96, 21–25.

Smith, S. L. (1991). *Succeeding against the odds: How the learning disabled can realize their promise.* New York: Jeremy P. Tarcher/Perigee.

Smith, S. L. (2000). *The power of the arts: Teaching academic skills to the non-traditional learner through the arts.* Baltimore: Paul H. Brookes.

Smith, S. L. (2001). *Power of the arts: Creative strategies for teaching exceptional learners.* Baltimore: Paul H. Brookes.

Snowman, J., & Biehler, R. (2000). *Psychology applied to teaching* (9th ed.). Boston: Houghton-Mifflin.

Solso, R. L. (1999). *Cognition and the visual arts.* Cambridge, MA: MIT.

Stake, R., Bresler, L., & Mabry, L. (1991). *Custom and cherishing: Arts education in the US.* Urbana, IL: Council for Research in Music Education, University of Illinois.

Tishman, S., & Palmer, P. (2006). *Artful thinking: Stronger thinking and learning through the power of art. Final report to Traverse City Public Schools.* Cambridge, MA: Project Zero, Harvard Graduate School of Education.

United States Department of Education. (2010). *Issue brief: Arts education through the US Department of Education.* Washington, DC: Author. Retrieved May 12, 2013 from http://www.artsusa.org/get_involved/advocacy/aad/issue_briefs/2007/advocacy_issue-brief_004.asp#

VSA. (2008). *The contours of inclusion: Frameworks and tools for evaluating arts in education.* Washington, DC: The Kennedy Center. Retrieved March 19, 2014 from http://www.kennedy-center.org/education/vsa/resources/vsa_research.cfm

VSA. (2014a). *The international organization on arts and disability: About VSA*. Washington, DC: The Kennedy Center. Retrieved March 19, 2014 from http://www.kennedy-center.org/education/vsa/

VSA. (2014b). *The international organization on arts and disability: VSA research*. Washington, DC: The Kennedy Center. Retrieved March 19, 2014 from http://www.kennedy-center.org/education/vsa/resources/vsa_research.cfm

Weeks, R. M. (1936). *A correlated curriculum: A report of the Committee on Correlation of the National Council of Teachers of English*. New York: Appleton-Century.

Welsh, M., Pennington, B., & Groisser, D. (1991). A normative-developmental study of executive function: A window on prefrontal function in children. *Developmental Neuropsychology*, 7(2), 131–149.

Westby, C. E. (2006). There's more to passing than knowing the answers: Learning to do school. In T. A. Ukrainetz (Ed.), *Contextualized language intervention* (pp. 319–387). Eau Claire, WI: Thinking Publications.

Westby, C.E. (2010). Word of mouth: A newsletter dedicated to speech and language in school-age children. *Word of Mouth*, 21(5), 1–6.

Wigfield, A., & Eccles, J. S. (2000). Expectancy-value theory of achievement motivation. *Contemporary Educational Psychology*, 25(1), 68–81.

Winner, E. (1996). Commentary: What drawings by atypical populations can tell us. *Visual Arts Research*, 22(2), 90–95.

Winner, E., & Cooper, M. (2000). Mute those claims: No evidence (yet) for a causal link between arts study and academic achievement. *Journal of Aesthetic Education*, 34(3/4), 11–75.

Winner, E., & Hetland, L. (2000). The arts in education: Evaluating the evidence for a causal link. *Journal of Aesthetic Education*, 34(3/4), 3–10.

Winner, E., & Hetland, L. (2001). Research in arts education: Directions for the future. In E. Winner & L. Hetland (Eds.), *Beyond the soundbite: What the research actually shows about arts education and academic outcomes* (pp. 143–148). Los Angeles: J. Paul Getty Trust.

Winner, E., & Hetland, L. (2003). Beyond the evidence given: A critical commentary on *Critical Links*. *Arts Education Policy Review*, 104(3), 13–15.

Winslow, L. L. (1939). *The integrated school art program*. New York: McGraw-Hill Book Co.

Zhbanova, K., Rule, A., Montgomery, S., & Nielsen, L. (2010). Defining the difference: Comparing integrated and traditional single-subject lessons. *Early Childhood Education Journal*, 38(4), 251–258.

Zimmerman, B. J., & Schunk, D. H. (2001). *Self-regulated learning and academic achievement: Theoretical perspectives* (2nd ed.). Mahwah, NJ: Erlbaum.

# 2

# ARTS INTEGRATION AS A CONTEXTUALIZED LANGUAGE-LEARNING ENVIRONMENT

*Alida Anderson*

## Introduction

As detailed in Chapter 1, arts integration (AI) research studies from the past two and a half decades have described the characteristics and effects of AI in a variety of learning contexts. In this spirit, Chapter 2 provides the first dimension of a three-part theoretical framework for the next 'wave' of AI research to focus on *how* and *why* AI works in order to validate its use in education from a language-learning perspective.

This chapter presents the first dimension of the book's framework in describing how and why AI operates as a contextualized language-learning environment (e.g., Kavanaugh, 1991; Scott, 1994; Ukrainetz, 2006). This linguistic dimension of the book's engagement framework draws on developmental and educational psychology, special education, and speech and language pathology research and practice to explain how and why AI facilitates language learning for students with language- and sensory-based challenges; e.g., those students with learning disabilities (LD), attention deficit hyperactivity disorder (ADHD), developmental delay (DD), autism spectrum disorder (ASD), and language impairments.

First, Universal Design for Learning (UDL; CAST, 2011; Rose & Meyer, 2002) and differentiated instruction principles (Tomlinson, 2001), which have been identified as particularly effective in increasing student engagement, are overviewed to better understand how the instructional environment of AI interacts with these principles. Next, AI as a language-learning context is considered within the contextualized–decontextualized language continuum (Scott, 1994; Ukrainetz, 2006) and support for AI as a contextualized learning environment is presented. The chapter closes with the posited influence of linguistic engagement on affect and cognition, both of which are considered within the dimensions of the book's framework and presented in Chapter 3.

## What We Know about Why AI Works in Inclusive Classrooms: Intersections among UDL, Differentiated Instruction, and AI

Universal Design for Learning is among the most important sets of principles for addressing the needs of every student; these principles (CAST, 2011) support the first part of the book's theoretical framework, in which AI is framed as a contextualized language-learning environment. The primary goal of UDL is to promote student access, participation, and progress in academic settings through increased engagement, an objective supported by AI through experiential learning. Also, this section highlights the opportunity for differentiated instruction (Tomlinson, 2001) to occur within an AI learning context, facilitating learning in inclusive environments for students with and without disabilities.

Universal Design for Learning (UDL) is a learning approach involving the design of curricular materials and activities that offer flexibility to match students' strengths and needs to ultimately support their individual goals. The UDL framework considers students' different abilities "to see, hear, speak, move, read, write, comprehend English, attend, organize, engage, and remember" (Orkwis, 2003, p. 2). Three essential elements of UDL provide the foundation for responsive AI lesson planning to meet the needs of students with diverse learning needs in inclusive classrooms. They are: (1) multiple means of representation, (2) multiple means of action and engagement, and (3) multiple means of expression (CAST, 2011). These three UDL principles provide the foundation for the arts integrated action research projects described in Part II. [Notably, the principles of representation, engagement, and expression are supported by social-cognitive learning theory (see Sideridis, Morgan, Botsas, Padeliadu, & Fuchs, 2006; Stone & Reid, 1994; Wang, 1997 for applications to students with learning difficulties) and Multiple Intelligences theory (Gardner, 1983).]

1. *Multiple means of representation* (*recognition networks*) refers to students having a variety of ways to receive, understand, and interpret information. This is also known as the 'what' of teaching and learning.
2. *Multiple means of engagement* (*affective systems*) focuses on students' backgrounds, interests, preferences, strengths, and needs to motivate and sustain their engagement. Engagement is connected with social interaction and self-efficacy (relationships with others and beliefs about one's ability to succeed).
3. *Multiple means of action and expression* (*strategic systems*) refers to how students respond to a particular learning activity. This can be organized by modality-specific forms of output (auditory, visual, tactile-kinesthetic, oral, written), as well as contextual forms (affective-social, technology-based).

**TABLE 2.1** Comparing UDL, Differentiated Instruction, and Dramatic Arts Integration

| UDL (multiple means of …) | Differentiated Instruction | Dramatic Arts Integration |
|---|---|---|
| *Representation* Content is presented to students in several ways, utilizing more than conventional text reading. | *Content* Content is evaluated and presented in light of students' readiness, interests, and learning profiles. | Drama arts and content area standards are addressed with and through the experience of dramatic arts. |
| *Engagement* Students are provided with a variety of activities or means of interacting with content to sustain participation. | *Process* Activities, methods, and strategies are selected based on students' readiness, interests, and learning profiles. | Drama activities provide students access to and interaction with content through activities such as See Think Wonder routines, in-role, mantle of the expert, and tableaux. |
| *Expression* Students' understandings of content and concepts are demonstrated through a variety of processes, products, and presentations. | *Product* Outcomes reflect students' readiness, interests, and learning profiles. | Dramatic presentations, as well as more conventional outcomes, are used to assess students' understanding through visual, auditory, tactile-kinesthetic, choral/group/ individual modalities. |

## How Does AI Support UDL and Differentiated Instruction?

Based on the current educational climate supporting inclusion, differentiated instruction is seen as the leading instructional process for providing flexible ways to teach students from diverse backgrounds in general education classrooms (Mastropieri & Scruggs, 2014). Differentiated instruction focuses on dimensions of *content* (what will be taught), *process* (how students process the information), and *product* (flexible ways for students to demonstrate their learning) (Tomlinson, 2001) for facilitating individual student engagement. It is well documented that UDL supports differentiated instruction (Hall, Strangman, & Meyer, 2003) by encouraging diversification of instructional strategies. Just as differentiated instruction considers students' unique interests and abilities, UDL considers individual strengths and needs to tailor instruction within the context of the group learning environment. Table 2.1 shows how UDL principles align with definitions of differentiated instruction and components of dramatic AI. For example, *multiple means of representation* (UDL) aligns with the differentiated instructional principle of *content*, and can be addressed through the *integration of arts and academic content*.

Likewise, the UDL principle of *engagement* aligns with the differentiated instructional principle of *process*, and can be operationalized through dramatic AI routines such as See Think Wonder (Harvard Project Zero, n.d.), in-role (Baldwin, 2008; Morgan & Saxton, 1989), mantle of the expert (Heathcote & Herbert, 1985), and tableau (Neelands, 1998). The UDL component of multiple means of *expression* aligns with the differentiated instructional principle of *product* and can be operationalized in AI through multisensory as well as interactive and individual learning activities.

By addressing students' strengths, needs, readiness, skills, and interests, all three learning approaches create increased opportunities for students with and without exceptionalities to engage more fully with academic content, vocabulary, and concepts.

## Arts in Education

Another useful way of thinking about AI's unique contribution to education is to place it on a continuum from the most commonly known and conventional form of *arts in education* (e.g., art, music classes within the school day) to the less typically occurring *arts as therapy*, which is far less conventional as an educational context. As shown in Figure 2.1, AI bridges these two approaches.

Figure 2.2 shows how AI approaches feature both process and product outcomes, and take place across general and special education settings. Moreover, AI is typically implemented by both general and special educators, and encompasses content standards from both arts and academic content domains.

**FIGURE 2.1** Continuum of the Arts in General and Special Education.

|  | Arts in Education | Arts Integration | Arts Therapy |
| --- | --- | --- | --- |
| **Art form:** | Product-oriented | Process and product-oriented | Process-oriented |
| **Setting:** | General education | General and special education | Special education |
| **Teacher:** | General educator | General and special educator | Special educator/therapist |
| **Content:** | Arts standards | Arts and academic standards | Arts and academic standards |

**FIGURE 2.2** The Role of Art Form, Setting, Teacher, and Content across Arts Educational Settings.

## Contextualized–Decontextualized Language Continuum and Linguistic Specificity and Productivity

Language learning through contextualization (Scott, 1994; Ukrainetz, 2006), or placement within students' immediate environment, is supported by research that relates development of linguistic specificity and productivity to the strategy of scaffolding from contextualized to decontextualized language use and to cognitive-social learning theories. As children engage in symbolic representation, assimilation and accommodation (Piaget, 1926, 1963), and social interaction (Vygotsky, 1978), they use increasingly complex and specific language features such as adverbs, conjunctions (causal, temporal, and sequential), noun phrases, and mental/linguistic verbs (Anderson, 2011; Curenton & Justice, 2004; Paul, 2002; Pellegrini, 1985). Social interaction theory has been used to interpret children's increased understanding and use of specific language features such as noun phrases, conjunctive clauses, adverbs, and mental and linguistic verbs in dramatic-symbolic play contexts with peers (Kempe, 2003; Pellegrini, 1985; Peter, 2003).

The degree to which language is tied to the immediate environment, or degree of contextualization, is a critical consideration in the development of specific and precise language (Curenton & Justice, 2004; Paul, 2002; Scott, 1994). A number of language researchers distinguish between two types of language use: *contextualized* and *decontextualized* (see Table 2.2; Paul, 2002; Scott, 1994). Westby (1991, 1994) depicts a continuum representing differences in the function and structure of language, the extremes of which are described as contextualized and decontextualized. Contextualized oral language is related to 'everyday' language activities such as face-to-face conversations, in which shared knowledge and vocabulary, the use of gestures, interactive negation of meaning, and listener feedback facilitate the apprehension of meaning (Snow, 1991a). Contextualized language is generally marked by topic familiarity (e.g., participant-shared knowledge or context), extralinguistic contextual clues (e.g., prosody or gesture), simple syntax, and repetitive or high-frequency vocabulary. According to Westby (1991), contextualized language is used to immediately present and share information about concrete and practical matters with a dialogic partner.

In contrast, decontextualized language, often in the form of written text from which the author is absent, is associated with unfamiliar topics, more complex syntax, and semantic diversity. This type of language is used primarily to communicate ideas about the past or future, and share information about abstract objects, events, or situations that are not available in the immediate environment. Decontextualized language is usually associated with classroom academic language tasks, particularly reading and writing text, in which the speaker is removed from the context. Decontextualized language tasks such as text reading are grounded in time and space, do not assume shared knowledge and vocabulary, and are often linguistically complex (De Temple, Wu, & Snow, 2009). Thus, decontextualized language is "comprehensible to an unknown audience without support from

**TABLE 2.2** Continuum of Contextualized to Decontextualized Discourse Features

| Contextualized | Decontextualized |
|---|---|
| Informal | Formal |
| Familiar | Unfamiliar |
| Oral | Written |
| Dialogue | Monologue |
| Concrete | Abstract |
| (refers to immediate environment) | (diverse vocabulary, complex syntax) |
| Conversational | Literate |
| – repetitive | – specific/precise use of adverbs, |
| – high frequency vocabulary |   conjunctions, noun phrases, and verbs |
| – simple syntax | – complex syntax |

**Contextualized**                                                             **Decontextualized**

Pretend play--------------------------------Narration--------------------------------Scientific report

Conversation--------------------------------Narrative/storytelling--------------------Book reading

**FIGURE 2.3** Continuum of Contextualized–Decontextualized Language Activities.

others" (Westby, 1994, p. 56). Table 2.2 shows how the features of contextualized and decontextualized discourse function on a continuum.

Another way to think of this contextualized–decontextualized language continuum is in the spectrum of activities in which contextualization is associated. Figure 2.3 provides examples of activities ranging from contextualized to decontextualized with respect to the way that participants use language.

Notably, both contextualized and decontextualized language involves literate language. Literate language development rests on the premise that children are exposed to linguistically specific or 'literate language' in events such as contextualized story sharing and symbolic play activities, with an increasing shift to less familiar contexts such as school-based tasks (Pellegrini & Galda, 1998), in which they use increasingly decontextualized language. Thus, children's language production in literacy contexts such as storybook sharing and narration is typically characterized as their first experience with explicit (Snow, 1991a) and decontextualized (Snow, 1991b) language. Literacy researchers identify literate language use in these contexts as the bridge between oral and written discourse, since literate language use develops across contextualized, oral language activities such as conversations, and also is required in decontextualized, written language activities (Dickinson & McCabe, 1991; Kavanaugh, 1991; Paul, 2002). Currently, adolescent language intervention approaches aimed at the Common Core State Standards (CCSS, 2012) proficiencies target literate language use as an intervention outcome (Montgomery, 2013) in recognition of the important role that these discourse features play in conveying information and ideas (e.g., causal, sequential, and temporal ideas through conjunction use; elaboration and description of thoughts and ideas through the use of adverbs, elaborated noun phrases, and mental and linguistic verbs).

The contextualized–decontextualized language continuum has been used to explain children's attainment of school-based literacy skills, particularly in relation to linguistic specificity, or literate language use. For instance, Westby (1994), in her work with school-age populations, used this continuum to describe students' attainment of school-based literacy skills across a variety of academic contexts (e.g., language arts, science, and mathematics), finding increased literate language use differentiated high-performing from low-performing students (see Pellegrini & Galda, 1998, pp. 120–155 for a review). Also, Wallach and Butler (1994) indicated associations between elementary age students' academic performance and linguistic specificity, in that students who effectively used literate language early on in their academic careers were more likely to meet teachers' expectations and to be rewarded, encouraged, and motivated in school than students who did not.

The contextualized–decontextualized continuum has also been used to characterize development of specific language registers in African American English, in which children use language features such as noun phrases, conjunctions, and adverbs (i.e., literate language) in less familiar or unknown contexts (i.e., school), as compared to familiar (i.e., home) (Charity, Scarborough, & Griffin, 2004; Curenton & Justice, 2004; Heath, 1983). In this application, researchers have described how children transition from familiar or contextualized oral language communication of events, to unfamiliar or decontextualized forms of classroom-based oral and written discourse.

Only a few studies, however, have investigated the influence of context on written language (Anderson, 2012; Anderson, Loughlin, & Berry, 2013; Craig, 2006; Jones & Pellegrini, 1996). Jones and Pellegrini (1996) found that contextualized writing, as defined by interaction between first-grade students and their friends as well as their teachers, had a facilitating effect on the quality of students' written narratives, in comparison to solitary writing activities. Craig (2006) also examined the effect of a contextualized interactive approach on kindergarten-age children's early literacy skills. Features of this contextualized instruction included teachers' use of supportive, interactive discourse to mediate children's participation and maximize children's involvement (Mariage, 2001; Pinnell & McCarrier, 1994). Children participating in contextualized activities made greater gains in word reading and comprehension achievement than children participating in solitary reading activities. Ukrainetz et al. (2005) found that an interactive, oral-narrative, storytelling activity using picture sequences influenced early elementary-age students' academic (i.e., decontextualized language such as literate language) and artistic (e.g., quality of ideas, content, interest, individuality, and engagement) oral expression. More recently, Anderson (2012) found that fourth- and fifth-grade students with and without language-based disabilities used literate language more evidently and measurably in their writing in dramatic arts contexts than in conventional language arts activities. This research shows that contextualization positively influences linguistic specificity and productivity in oral and written discourse. Notably, speech-language researchers have identified literate language features as oral and written language intervention targets for adolescents with language disorders (see Joffe & Nippold, 2012; Montgomery, 2013). The growing emphasis on decontextualized language competence through literate language use beginning in early childhood and extending to upper elementary and adolescent student populations is detailed next.

## Contextualized–Decontextualized Language and Students with Literacy Challenges

Oral and written language mutually influence students' development of linguistic specificity and productivity, since the structure and function of the language features is shared in expressing relationships among ideas (e.g., coordinating and subordinating conjunctions), open class-content words, noun phrases with attributive adjectives, relative clauses, and prepositional phrases (Paul, 2002). Thus, students with problems in linguistic specificity in oral language evident first in early childhood also have ongoing difficulties with understanding and expressing literate oral and written language (Scott, 2004). In particular, students with language-based exceptionalities (e.g., learning disabilities [LD], developmental disabilities [DD]) have documented struggles with linguistic specificity and productivity stemming from early deficits in semantic diversity and syntactic knowledge (Scott, 1994, 1995). Students with language-based LD have been reported to use less literate language across both contextualized and decontextualized activities than their peers, particularly in oral narrative storytelling, despite similar exposure (Gillam & Johnston, 1992; Kaderavek & Sulzby, 2000; Ukrainetz & Gillam, 2009). However, only a few studies have compared literate language use in children with and without language-based exceptionalities across contextualized and decontextualized language-learning activities (Anderson, 2011; McKeough, 1984; Ukrainetz & Gillam, 2009). McKeough (1984) showed a strong relationship between literate language use and dramatic play in oral narrative retellings by 8 to 12 year-old students with and without LD. Ukrainetz and Gilliam (2009) found both elementary-age children with and without LD to show increased oral language productivity and specificity using contextualized support (pictures and interactive practice) in narrative storytelling. Anderson (2011) found that preschool-age children with and without language impairments had significantly greater linguistic specificity and productivity (as measured through literate language use) in contextualized play, as compared to storybook reading, children's presumed earliest decontextualized language experience (Snow, 1991a). More recently, Anderson (2012) and Anderson, Loughlin, and Berry (2013) found that third- and fourth-grade students with language- and sensory-based disorders in inclusive drama-integrated language arts classroom settings produced significantly greater amounts of oral and written language, as compared to conventional language arts instructional contexts.

Likewise, students from low socioeconomic status (SES) backgrounds enter school with less semantic diversity and syntactic knowledge than their age-matched peers from middle-to-high SES backgrounds (Hart & Risley, 1995). Similarly, students with emotional-behavioral disabilities (EBD) struggle with linguistic productivity and specificity in academic settings due to emotional and/or behavioral issues affecting motivation and engagement (Brown, 2007; Foley, 2001; Nelson, Benner, Neill, & Stage, 2006). Employing instructional strategies that bridge the gap between contextual or informal language and decontextualized, formal language provides all students, but especially those with individual language-learning needs, with necessary scaffolds to access, participate, and progress in academic tasks.

## AI as a Mechanism of Linguistic Engagement and Its Posited Influence on Affect and Cognition

Frequent and varied opportunities to engage in activities that bridge contextualized and decontextualized language use in classroom settings, particularly in the form of narrative and play activities, are critical to the development of language skill. For instance, Pellegrini (1985) examined literate behavior in the context of interactive, scripted, social-symbolic play in a preschool sample and found that students in the dramatic-play condition with concrete props used more literate language than their peers in the solitary play or construction play conditions. He interpreted children's increased literate language use in dramatic play as evidence of mental representation of concrete/contextual events and objects. Activities bridging contextualized and decontextualized language activities enhance students' understanding and use of specific and precise discourse features, also known as literate language, in the form of noun phrases, conjunctive clauses, and adverbs. This relation likely arises through the 'facilitating mechanisms' of social interaction (Luciarello & Nelson, 1987) and setting (Dickinson & McCabe, 1991; 2001; Snow, 1991a, 1991b; Wells, 1985), which are the hallmarks of contextualized AI settings. Specifically, as children acquire and integrate information to form increasingly sophisticated mental representations in AI contexts, they gain experience with, and come to rely on, specific and complex language features to express their ideas in increasingly decontextualized contexts such as academic settings.

Since AI contexts are ones in which students invent and represent ideas, concepts, or situations for themselves, in these contexts students are working 'with' and 'through' the art form to reach academic, social, and personal goals (Anderson, 2012; Cornett, 2007, p. 13). As mentioned previously, AI is commonly identified as a process-oriented approach, which activates "learners' imaginations by using arts forms and structures associated with a larger field to explore content area curriculum, texts, relationships readers have with texts, issues connected to texts, and other aspects of literacy learning in diverse educational settings" (Schneider, Crumpler, & Rogers, 2006, p. xiv).

The relation between AI activities and student achievement has been shown to be powerful for elementary and secondary students from diverse socio-economic, linguistic, and cultural backgrounds (Ingram & Seashore, 2003; Kempe, 2003; see review by Robinson, 2013). In particular, researchers have reported reliable causal relationships between AI activities and gains in students' reading, writing, and verbal skills (Anderson, 2012; Brouillette & Jennings, 2010; Brouillette, Walker, Burge, & Fitzgerald, 2008; de la Cruz, 1995; Hui & Lau, 2006; Moore & Caldwell, 1993; Rose, Parks, Andoes, & McMahon, 2010). For instance, a study by Hui and Lau (2006) found that first- and fourth-grade students from Hong Kong who participated in an afterschool drama program were more expressive and elaborate in storytelling activities and had greater improvement in their communicative-expressive language than did their peers in a control condition. Anderson (2012) found that urban students in the US with and without language-based LD were more linguistically specific and productive in contextualized dramatic arts writing activities than in conventional language arts instructional contexts.

Anderson and colleagues (2013) found that AI positively influenced oral and written language skills of students with and without language and sensory processing disabilities such that students' language use was more productive and specific during AI activities involving written language as compared to conventional language arts writing tasks. This initial evidence suggests that AI was a scaffold for students' linguistic representations of causal, temporal, sequential, and relational events and concepts.

Also, AI has been shown to influence students' written language productivity and specificity in their transfer of gains in contextualized writing to decontextualized writing tasks (Anderson et al., 2013). These authors suggest that this transfer was likely due to students' exposure, experience, and initial success with contextualized AI literacy activities. These findings showed that students' language use was influenced by their direct experience with the learning context (i.e., their emotional engagement with the subject matter and their success in contextualized written language activities). The findings indicated that the contextualized AI writing activities scaffolded students' increased productivity in decontextualized written language tasks.

Additionally, this research (Anderson et al., 2013) showed that AI positively influenced students' behavioral engagement during literacy activities, in which 100% of the students showed active participation, as compared to 47% of students in conventional literacy activities. These findings are consistent with those focused on the role of contextualization (i.e., the use of concrete and/or representational activities) to support concept development and expression of ideas for students with language, sensory processing, and emotional-behavioral disorders (Mastropieri, Scruggs, & Fulk, 1990; Miller & Hudson, 2006).

To date, however, the majority of studies examining the role of AI in students' reading, writing, and language achievement in schools have focused primarily on the outcomes – that is, a comparison of outcome data (i.e., reading comprehension scores or the quality of written text) between AI and non-AI conditions – rather than on the reasons for the evidenced differences, or in the likely influential relationships between language learning and other aspects of engagement (affective and/or cognitive). The next chapter presents the dimensions of affective and cognitive engagement in relation to AI as an influential learning context for students with language- and sensory-based challenges in a variety of classroom settings.

## References

Anderson, A. (2011). Linguistic specificity through literate language use in preschool age children with specific language impairment and typical language. *Child Language Teaching and Therapy*, 27(1), 1–15.

Anderson, A. (2012). The influence of process drama on elementary students' written language. *Urban Education*, 39(4), 1–24.

Anderson, A., Loughlin, S., & Berry, K. (2013, April). *The influence of dramatic arts integration on teacher and student language in language arts contexts.* Presentation at the 2013 AERA Annual Meeting, San Francisco, CA.

Baldwin, P. (2008). *The practical primary drama handbook.* London: Sage.

Brouillette, L., & Jennings, L. (2010). Helping children cross cultural boundaries in the borderlands: Arts program at Freese Elementary creates cultural bridges. *Journal for Learning through the Arts: A Research Journal on Arts Integration in Schools and Communities*, 6(1). Retrieved from http://escholarship.org/uc/item/1kf6p9th#page-1

Brouillette, L. R., Walker, P., Burge, K., & Fitzgerald, W. (2008). Teaching writing through the arts in urban secondary schools: A case study. *Journal for Learning through the Arts: A Research Journal on Arts Integration in Schools and Communities*, 4(1). Retrieved from http://escholarship.org/uc/item/6fg4n7gv

Brown, T. M. (2007). Lost and turned out: Academic, social, and emotional experiences of students excluded from school. *Urban Education*, 42(1), 432–455.

CAST. (2011). *Universal Design for Learning Guidelines version 2.0.* Wakefield, MA: CAST. Retrieved from http://www.udlcenter.org/aboutudl/udlguidelines

Charity, A., Scarborough, H., & Griffin, D. (2004). Familiarity with school English in African-American children and its relation to early reading achievement. *Child Development*, 75, 1340–1356.

Common Core State Standards. (2012). *Implementing the Common Core Standards.* Retrieved February 13, 2014 from http://www.corestandards.org/

Cornett, C. (2007). *Creating meaning through literature and the arts.* Saddle River, NJ: Pearson.

Craig, S. A. (2006). The effects of an adapted interactive writing intervention on kindergarten children's phonological awareness, spelling, and early reading development: A contextualized approach to instruction. *Journal of Educational Psychology*, 98(4), 714–731.

Curenton, S., & Justice, L. (2004). Low-income preschoolers' use of decontextualized discourse: Literate language features in oral narratives. *Language, Speech, and Hearing Services in Schools*, 35, 240–253.

de la Cruz, R. E. (1995). *The effects of creative drama on the social and oral language skills of children with learning disabilities* (Doctoral dissertation). Illinois State University, Bloomington, IL.

De Temple, J. M., Wu, H., & Snow, C. E. (2009). Papa Pig just left for Pigtown: Children's oral and written picture descriptions under varying instructions. *Discourse Processes*, 14(4), 469–495.

Dickinson, D., & McCabe, A. (1991). The acquisition and development of language: A social-interactionist account of language and literacy development. In J. Kavanaugh (Ed.). *The language continuum: From infancy to literacy* (pp. 1–40). Parkton, MD: York Press.

Dickinson, D., & McCabe, A. (2001). Bringing it all together: The multiple origins, skills, and environmental supports of early literacy. *Learning Disabilities Research and Practice*, 16, 186–202.

Foley, R. M. (2001). Academic characteristics of incarcerated youth and correctional educational programs: A literature review. *Journal of Emotional and Behavioral Disorders*, 9(4), 248–259.

Gardner, J. (1983). *Frames of mind: The theory of multiple intelligences*. New York: Basic Books.

Gillam, R. B., & Johnston, J. (1992). Spoken and written language relationships in language/learning-impaired and normally achieving school-age children. *Journal of Speech and Hearing Research*, 35, 1303–1315.

Hall, T., Strangman, N., & Meyer, A. (2003). *Differentiated instruction and implications for UDL implementation*. Wakefield, MA: National Center on Accessing the General Curriculum. Retrieved January 24, 2014 from http://aim.cast.org/learn/historyarchive/backgroundpapers/differentiated_instruction_udl#.VBnk5BZibKd

Hart, B., & Risley, R. T. (1995). *Meaningful differences in the everyday experience of young American children*. Baltimore: Paul H. Brookes.

Harvard Project Zero. (n.d.). *Artful thinking*. Retrieved March 27, 2014 from http://www.pzartfulthinking.org/see_think_wonder.php

Heath, S. (1983). *Ways with words: Language, life and work in communities and classrooms*. Cambridge: Cambridge University Press.

Heathcote, D., & Herbert, P. (1985). A drama of learning: Mantle of the expert. *Theory into Practice*, 24(3), 173–180.

Hui, A., & Lau, S. (2006). Drama education: A touch of the creative mind and communicative-expressive ability of elementary school children in Hong Kong. *Thinking Skills and Creativity*, 1(1), 34–40.

Ingram, D., & Seashore, K. S. (2003). *Arts for academic achievement: Summative evaluation report*. Minneapolis, MN: Center for Applied Research and Educational Improvement. Retrieved from http://hdl.handle.net/11299/143655

Joffe, V., & Nippold, M. A. (2012). Progress in understanding adolescent language disorders. *Language, Speech, and Hearing Services in Schools*, 43(4), 438–444.

Jones, I., & Pellegrini, A. D. (1996). The effects of social relationships, writing media, and microgenetic development on first-grade students' written narratives. *American Educational Research Journal*, 33(3), 691–718.

Kaderavek, J., & Sulzby, E. (2000). Narrative production by children with and without specific language impairment: Oral narratives and emergent readings. *Journal of Speech, Language, and Hearing Research*, 43, 34–50.

Kavanaugh, J. (Ed.). (1991). *The language continuum: From infancy to literacy* (pp. v–viii). Parkton, MD: York Press.

Kempe, A. (2003). The role of drama in the teaching of speaking and listening as the basis for social capital. *Research in Drama Education: The Journal of Applied Theatre and Performance*, 8(1), 65–78.

Luciarello, J., & Nelson, J. (1987). Remembering and planning: Talk between mothers and children. *Discourse Processes*, 10, 219–235. (EJ360623)

Mariage, T. V. (2001). Features of an interactive writing discourse: Conversational involvement, conventional knowledge, and internalization in morning message. *Journal of Learning Disabilities*, 34, 172–206.

Mastropieri, M. A., & Scruggs, T. E. (2014). *The inclusive classroom: Strategies for effective instruction* (5th ed.). Upper Saddle River, NJ: Prentice Hall.

Mastropieri, M. A., Scruggs, T. E., & Fulk, B. J. M. (1990). Teaching abstract vocabulary with the keyword method: Effects on recall and comprehension. *Journal of Learning Disabilities*, 23(2), 92–96.

McKeough, A. (1984, April). *Developmental stages in children's narrative composition*. Paper presented at the 68th Annual Meeting of the American Educational Research Association, New Orleans, LA. (ED249461)

Miller, S. P., & Hudson, P. J. (2006). Helping students with disabilities understand what mathematics means. *Teaching Exceptional Children*, 39(1), 28–35.

Montgomery, J. K. (2013). Teaching words to adolescents with language disabilities. *SIG 1 Perspectives on Language Learning and Education*, 20, 67–74.

Moore, B. H., & Caldwell, H. (1993). Drama and drawing for narrative writing in primary grades. *Journal of Educational Research*, 87(2), 100–110.

Morgan, N., & Saxton, J. (1989). *Teaching drama: A mind of many wonders*. Cheltenham, UK: Nelson Thornes.

Neelands, J. (1998). *Beginning drama 11–14*. London: David Fulton Publications.

Nelson, J. R., Benner, G. J., Neill, S., & Stage, S. A. (2006). Interrelationships among language skills, externalizing behavior, and academic fluency and their impact on the academic skills of students with EBD. *Journal of Emotional and Behavioral Disorders*, 14(4), 209–216.

Orkwis, R. (2003). Universally Designed Instruction. ERIC/OSEP Digest. Retrieved from http://eric.ed.gov/?id=ED475386

Paul, R. (2002). *Language disorders from infancy through adolescence: Assessment and intervention*. St. Louis, MO: Mosby.

Pellegrini, A. (1985). Relations between preschool children's symbolic play and literate behaviors. In L. Galda & A. Pellegrini (Eds.), *Play, language and stories: The development of children's literate behavior* (pp. 79–97). Norwood, NJ: Ablex.

Pellegrini, A., & Galda, L. (1998). Peer interaction, play, and literate language: naturalistic and experimental evidence from preschool and primary classrooms. In A. Pellegrini & L. Galda (Eds.), *The development of school-based literacy: A social-ecological perspective* (pp. 60–88). New York: Routledge.

Peter, M. (2003). Drama, narrative and early learning. *British Journal of Special Education*, 30(1), 21–28.

Piaget, J. (1926). *The language and thought of the child*. New York: Harcourt Brace.

Piaget, J. (1963). *The origins of intelligence in children* (2nd ed.). New York: Norton.

Pinnell, G. S., & McCarrier, A. (1994). Interactive writing: A transition tool for assisting children in learning to read and write. In E. Hiebert & B. Taylor (Eds.), *Getting reading right from the start: Effective early literacy interventions* (pp. 149–170). Needham, MA: Allyn & Bacon.

Robinson, A. H. (2013). Arts integration and the success of disadvantaged students: A research evaluation. *Arts Education Policy Review*, 114(4), 191–204.

Rose, D., & Meyer, A. (2002). *Teaching every student in the digital age: Universal design for learning*. Alexandria, VA: Association for Supervision and Curriculum Development.

Rose, D. S., Parks, M., Androes, K., & McMahon, S. D. (2010). Imagery-based learning: Improving elementary students' reading comprehension with drama techniques. *Journal of Educational Research*, 94(1), 55–63.

Schneider, J., Crumpler, T., & Rogers, T. (2006). *Process drama and multiple literacies: Addressing social, cultural, and ethical issues*. Portsmouth, NH: Heinemann.

Scott, C. (1994). A discourse continuum for school-age students. In G. Wallach & K. Butler (Eds.), *Language learning disabilities in school-age children and adolescents: Some principles and applications* (pp. 219–252). New York: Macmillan.

Scott, C. (1995). Syntax for school age children: A discourse perspective. In M. Fey, J. Windsor, & S. Warren (Eds.), *Language intervention: Preschool through the elementary years* (pp. 107–143). Baltimore: Paul H. Brookes.

Scott, C. (2004). Syntactic contributions to literacy learning. In C. Stone, E. Silliman, B. Ehren, & K. Apel (Eds.), *Handbook of language and literacy: Development and disorders* (pp. 340–362). New York: Guilford Press.

Sideridis, G. D., Morgan, P. L., Botsas, G., Padeliadu, S., & Fuchs, D. (2006). Predicting LD on the basis of motivation, metacognition, and psychopathology: An ROC analysis. *Journal of Learning Disabilities*, 39(3), 215–229.

Snow, C. (1991a). The theoretical basis for relationships between language and literacy development. *Journal of Research in Childhood Education*, 6, 5–10.

Snow, C. (1991b). Diverse conversational contexts for the acquisition of various language skills. In J. Miller (Ed.), *Research on child language disorders: A decade of progress* (pp. 105–124). Austin, TX: Pro-Ed.

Stone, C. A., & Reid, D. K. (1994). Social and individual forces in learning: Implications for instruction of children with learning difficulties. *Learning Disabilities Quarterly*, 17(1), 72–86.

Tomlinson, C. A. (2001). *How to differentiate instruction in mixed-ability classrooms* (2nd ed.). Alexandria, VA: Association for Supervision and Curriculum Development.

Ukrainetz, T. A. (Ed.). (2006). *Contextualized language intervention*. Eau Claire, WI: Thinking Publications.

Ukrainetz, T. A., & Gillam, R. B. (2009). The expressive elaboration of imaginative narratives by children with specific language impairment. *Journal of Speech, Language, and Hearing Research*, 52, 883–898.

Ukrainetz, T. A., Justice, L. M., Kaderavek, J. N., Eisenberg, S. L., Gillam, R. B., & Harm, H. M. (2005). The development of expressive elaboration in fictional narratives. *Journal of Speech, Language, and Hearing Research*, 48, 1363–1377.

Vygotsky, L. (1978). *Mind in society: The development of higher psychological processes* (M. Cole, V. John-Steiner, S. Scribner, & E. Souberman [Eds.]). Cambridge, MA: Harvard University Press.

Wallach, G., & Butler, K. (1994). Creating communication, literacy, and academic success. In G. Wallach & K. Butler (Eds.), *Language learning disabilities in school-age children and adolescents* (pp. 2–26). New York: Macmillan.

Wang, M. C. (1997). *Serving students with special needs through inclusive education approaches*. Philadelphia, PA: National Research Center on Education in the Inner Cities. (ED419076)

Wells, G. (1985). Preschool literacy-related activities and success in school. In D. Olson, N. Torrance, & A. Hildyard (Eds.), *Literacy, language, and learning: The nature and consequences of reading and writing* (pp. 229–253). Cambridge: Cambridge University Press.

Westby, C. (1991). Learning to talk, talking to learn: Oral and literate language differences. In C. S. Simon (Ed.), *Communication skills and classroom success* (pp. 334–357). Eau Claire, WI: Thinking Publications.

Westby, C. (1994). The effects of culture on genre, structure, and style of oral and written texts. In G. Wallach & K. Butler (Eds.), *Language learning disabilities in school-age children and adolescents* (pp. 180–218). New York: Macmillan.

# 3

# COGNITIVE AND AFFECTIVE ENGAGEMENT, ARTS INTEGRATION, AND STUDENTS WITH DISABILITIES

*Katherine A. Berry and Sandra M. Loughlin*

To those invested in student learning – students, families, educators, and researchers – the importance of engaging students in their school communities and classwork has long been clear. Engaged students are interested, motivated, and involved, and, as a result, they are more likely to enjoy and succeed in school (Klem & Connell, 2004; Newman & Davies, 2005). By contrast, disengaged students are bored, unmotivated, and uninvolved. They frequently struggle and often drop out of school (Christenson, Reschly, Appleton, Berman-Young, Spangers, & Varro, 2008). As a result, the study of student engagement has grown in both depth and prominence, under the assumption that engagement-related strategies may promote students' desire to learn and persist in school.

Unfortunately, recent evidence suggests that both typically developing students (Appleton, Christenson, & Furlong, 2008; Fredricks & Eccles, 2002; National Research Council, 2004) and those with disabilities (Bridgeland, Dilulio, & Morison, 2006; Kastner & Gottlieb, 1995; Vaughn, Elbaum, & Boardman, 2011) are increasingly disengaged from traditional school. With respect to students with language- and sensory-based challenges (e.g., those students with learning disabilities [LD], attention deficit/hyperactivity disorder [ADHD], autism spectrum disorders [ASD], and language impairments), the lack of access to the general education curriculum is a posited deterrent to engagement in learning. Theoretical and applied studies suggest a relation among students' deficits, their engagement, and classroom performance (Sideridis, Morgan, Botsas, Padeliadu, & Fuchs, 2006). According to this view, students' deficits lead them to struggle with acquiring key academic skills, which leads to decreased engagement and more task-avoidant behavior, and eventually, a more generalized set of deficits impacting classroom performance (Sideridis et al., 2006). Therefore, interventions or programs that accommodate students' deficits and promote students' psychological and emotional investment in learning may improve their educational outcomes.

Arts integration has been promoted as one such avenue for increasing engagement for students with (Abedin, 2010; Durham, 2010; Whittaker, 2005) and without disabilities (Baum, Owen, & Oreck, 1997; Catterall, 2002; Ingram & Seashore, 2003). The use of arts in educational contexts provides a medium for the engagement of students who struggle in academic areas such as mathematics, reading, and writing by providing alternative ways to learn that may be more compatible with their interests and preferences. Further, arts education in the school curriculum provides students who struggle with academic learning additional opportunities for participation and success (Abedin, 2010; Robinson, 2013). In particular, research and theory suggest that learning in and through the arts is related to students' persistence in school and in learning tasks, positive behavior, self-concept, and self-efficacy.

Given the theoretical and emerging empirical relations between arts integration and student engagement, this volume examines the degree to which arts integration facilitates engagement and improved student outcomes. In particular, the research in this book examines indicators of cognitive, affective, and linguistic engagement in arts-integrated settings for students with and without disabilities.

The purpose of this chapter is to present two aspects of engagement – cognitive and affective – and to offer a foundation for the discussion of the theoretical model in Chapter 4 and the demonstrations of practice in Part II of the volume. In this effort, attempts to define, conceptualize, measure, and parse engagement are discussed. Next, the cognitive and affective components of engagement are reviewed. For each, findings from empirical studies of engagement for students with and without disabilities in conventional and arts-integrated settings are briefly reviewed. Finally, this chapter is positioned relative to what is known and unknown about cognitive and affective engagement in inclusive and arts integrated settings.

## Components of Student Engagement

Despite its demonstrated impacts on academic achievement, prosocial behavior, and academic persistence (Janosz, Archambault, Morizot, & Pagani, 2008), definitions and conceptions of student engagement are highly variable (Appleton et al., 2008; Lawson & Lawson, 2013). Also, ways in which student engagement is measured are inconsistent (Appleton et al., 2008). Indeed, in their commentary in the comprehensive *Handbook of research on student engagement* (Christenson, Reschly, & Wylie, 2012), Eccles and Wang (2012) entitled their contribution "So what is engagement, anyway?" Most of the conceptual, definitional, and methodological challenges surrounding engagement can be attributed to the scope of the construct. By many accounts (Christenson et al., 2012; Guthrie & Wigfield, 2000), engagement is a "meta-construct," encompassing several distinct but related components. Although the number and nature of components ranges from two to four, most scholars consider engagement to have three basic components: cognitive, behavioral, and affective (Appleton et al., 2008). This chapter uses the definitions of these components offered by Fredricks, Blumenfeld, and Paris (2004).

Cognitive engagement refers to students' psychological investment in academic tasks (Fredricks et al., 2004), and encompasses both students' thoughts about school (i.e., their disposition toward school work) and participation in learning tasks (i.e., in-the-moment engagement). As a result, there are a variety of elements associated with cognitive engagement: investment in learning, willingness to work hard, self-regulation, goal setting, perceived relevance of school to future, use of cognitive and metacognitive skills and strategies, effort, and flexibility.

Behavioral engagement targets students' participation in school and academic tasks, with the perspective that student conduct is indicative of students' desires to achieve academically and reflects the norms and expectations of school (Fredricks et al., 2004). Behavioral engagement includes such measures as time spent on homework, time on task during class activities, compliance with school rules, absenteeism, suspensions, extracurricular participation, and truancy. Behavioral engagement is perceived to be a necessary precursor to positive academic outcomes and is crucial to preventing school dropout.

Researchers describe affective engagement as students' perceived social, emotional, and psychological attachment to school (Fredricks et al., 2004). Affective engagement has two dimensions. The first describes students' engagement with their academic tasks, and includes students' perceptions of their interest, anxiety, boredom, and enjoyment relative to school work. The second dimension relates to students' engagement with the institution and culture of school. This dimension includes engagement with teachers, administrators, and peers, and relates to students' feelings of belonging, relatedness, and identification. Collectively, the two dimensions of affective engagement suggest that students who feel a sense of attachment to their academic tasks and the people at their school are more academically motivated and are less likely to experience behavioral challenges than those students who do not.

## Cognitive and Affective Engagement, Arts Integration, and Students with Disabilities

Having considered the nature of cognitive and affective engagement, this section examines how these components of engagement are manifest in and between two areas of interest to this volume: arts integration and students with disabilities. In this effort, findings from a review of the literature relative to each component are presented. Specifically, these studies address cognitive engagement in arts-integrated classrooms, cognitive engagement among students with disabilities, and cognitive engagement among students with disabilities in arts-integrated classrooms. The same approach is taken in a discussion of affective engagement, by presenting studies of affective engagement in arts-integrated classrooms first, then affective engagement and students with disabilities, and finally affective engagement and students with disabilities in arts–integrated classrooms.

In examining these literatures, a rigorous methodology was employed. First, six databases likely to yield relevant studies were identified: Academic Search Complete, ArtsEdSearch, Education Source, ERIC (EBSCO), ProQuest Dissertations and Theses Online, and PsychINFO. Then, search terms were created to target the four areas of interest to the review: cognitive engagement, affective engagement, arts integration, and students with disabilities. The search terms used for each construct are presented in Figure 3.1.

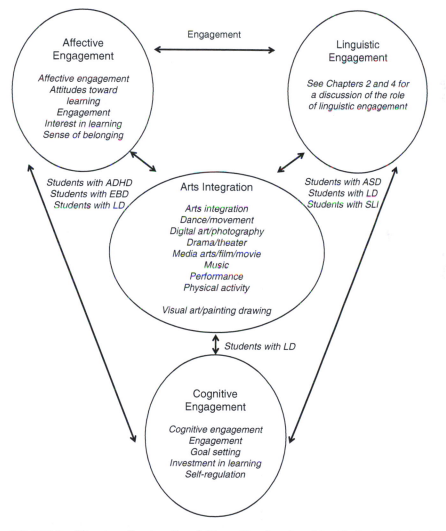

**FIGURE 3.1**   Literature Review Search Terms Employed to Identify Studies Related to Cognitive Engagement, Affective Engagement, Arts Integration, and Students with Disabilities. (Search Terms in Italic within Figure.)

To narrow the scope of the search, three delimitations were employed. First, only empirical studies published in English-language peer-reviewed journals were included. Second, to reflect this volume's focus on elementary and middle school, studies and articles were limited to K-8 academic classroom settings. As such, the review excluded articles with high school participants as well as studies that were conducted after school, as part of summer programs, in residential facilities, in home environments, and exclusively in arts, music, dance, physical education, or drama classes. Third, studies explicitly focused on students with low-incidence disabilities such as significant intellectual disabilities, serious physical impairment, multiple disabilities, and deaf/blindness were excluded from this review.

Given these delimitations, varied combinations of search terms were applied to the six target databases. The results of this methodology yielded several studies in each of the categories under consideration. Five studies described cognitive engagement and arts integration, five focused on cognitive engagement and students with disabilities, and four emphasized cognitive engagement, arts integration, and students with disabilities. With regard to affective engagement, nine studies describing affective engagement and arts integration, two focused on affective engagement and students with disabilities, and four considering the intersection of affective engagement, arts integration, and students with disabilities were identified. The 29 identified studies are discussed here by type of engagement.

## Cognitive Engagement

This section presents the literature on cognitive engagement (i.e., students' psychological investment in academic tasks) and its relation to arts integration, cognitive engagement and students with disabilities, and cognitive engagement and arts integration for students with disabilities.

### Cognitive engagement and arts integration

The review yielded five studies in the area of cognitive engagement and arts integration. Two large-scale studies (DeMoss & Morris, 2002; Ingram & Meath, 2007) examined K-8th-grade students' cognitive engagement after they participated in classes taught by Chicago Arts Education Partnership (CAPE) teaching artists (DeMoss & Morris, 2002) and after they were exposed to the Arts for Academic Achievement program (AAA; Ingram & Meath, 2007). Findings from student and teacher interviews, classroom observations, and teacher surveys suggested that students improved their ability to assess their own learning, developed greater intrinsic motivation (DeMoss & Morris, 2002), and increased their engagement in instruction and learning (Ingram & Meath, 2007) as a result of the arts-integrated lessons and AAA program. Also, a comparative case study (Stevenson & Deasy, 2005) of 10 schools with integrated arts curricula revealed that the arts-integrated curriculum enhanced students' metacognitive skills by fostering their adaptability and flexibility as they developed solutions to academic problems (Stevenson & Deasy, 2005). In his study of second graders, McFadden (2010) showed that integrating theater into literacy lessons proved beneficial for improving elements of cognitive engagement. Results from qualitative teacher interviews and focus groups indicated that the students improved their higher-level thinking and problem-solving skills after participating in 10 drama-integrated literacy lessons. Lastly, Baum and Owen (1997) determined that fourth-, fifth-, and sixth-grade students used more self-regulative capacities, such as problem-solving, self-initiating, asking questions, and paying attention during instructional time, when they were in arts-integrated classes than in more conventional classes.

## Cognitive engagement and students with disabilities

A search of studies in the area of cognitive engagement and students with disabilities generated similarly few results. To date, only five studies have reported findings that describe elements of cognitive engagement and students with ADHD, emotional/behavioral disorders (EBD), and LD; no studies included students with ASD or speech and language impairments (SLI). According to self-rating scales, seventh-grade students with LD demonstrated lower levels of predicted effort and investment in learning compared to their typically developing peers (Lackaye & Margalit, 2006). Data from the National Education Longitudinal Study of 1988 revealed that eighth-grade students with LD and EBD self-reported as less engaged (i.e., bored and useless) than their classmates without disabilities (Reschly & Christenson, 2006). Similarly, Anderson (2004) determined that cognitive engagement variables, specifically the importance of one's education to the future (i.e., utility) and boredom, were significant predictors of dropout and completion rates for eighth-grade students with LD and EBD after accounting for achievement test scores, grade retention, and socioeconomic status (SES; Anderson, 2004). Two studies (Hutchison, 2007; Palincsar, Collins, Marano, & Magnusson, 2000) highlighted the use of a Guided Inquiry supporting Multiple Literacies (GIsML) approach and an engagement intervention for improving the cognitive engagement of students with LD. Results from individual case studies revealed that guided inquiry (i.e., GIsML) fostered feelings of personal success and investment in literacy learning for fourth graders with LD (Palincsar et al., 2000) and the engagement intervention improved levels of persistence and effort for two adolescents with LD (Hutchison, 2007).

## Cognitive engagement, arts integration, and students with disabilities

The examination of studies conducted at the intersection of cognitive engagement, arts integration, and students with disabilities yielded only four related studies to date. Two dissertation studies (Abedin, 2010; Durham, 2010) examined the benefits of arts integration for students with adolescents with LD and/or ADHD (Abedin, 2010) and for first through sixth graders with LD (Durham, 2010). Qualitative analysis of classroom observations, parent, student, and teacher interviews, and student artifacts (i.e., arts-related products) revealed that the arts increased students' ability and willingness to engage in learning, enhanced their self-regulatory skills (Abedin, 2010), and improved their metacognitive skills, cognitive processing, and perseverance (Durham, 2010). An additional dissertation (Jacobs, 2005) evaluated the effects of a drama program called Drama Discovery on the self-efficacy of students with EBD. Used in conjunction with bibliotherapy (i.e., utilizing literary sources to support student understanding of a topic), Drama Discovery positively improved students' feelings of self-efficacy, as measured by qualitative observations, audiotapes, student journals, and interviews (Jacobs, 2005). A final study (Wilhelm, 1995) found that integrating visual art activities such as creating cutouts or illustrating objects into literacy lessons helped two seventh graders with EBD to take a more active role in reading and to develop their metacognitive skills by allowing them to visualize what they were reading.

## Affective Engagement

This section presents findings on affective engagement (i.e., students' positive and negative reactions to teachers, classmates, academics, learning tasks, and school) and its relation to arts integration, affective engagement and students with disabilities, and affective engagement and arts integration and students with disabilities.

### Affective engagement and arts integration

Nine relevant studies emerged from the literature search related to affective engagement and arts integration. Results from two large-scale studies (Barry, 2010; Ffolkes-Bryant, 2008) showed that elementary-aged students who attended arts-integrated schools demonstrated positive attitudes towards learning, as measured by teacher and student surveys. Several studies (Duatepe-Paksu & Ubuz, 2009; Forseth, 1980; Healy, 2004; James, 2011) investigated the effects of using dramatic or visual arts integration for improving students' attitudes towards mathematics. Results suggested that visual arts integration improved third, fourth, and fifth graders' attitudes toward learning, math, and art, as measured by pre- and post-attitudinal tests and Likert scale surveys (Forseth, 1980; James, 2011). Similarly, middle school students who participated in drama-based geometry lessons (Duatepe-Paksu & Ubuz, 2009) and visual-arts-integrated math lessons (Healy, 2004) demonstrated improved attitudes towards mathematics, as measured by student surveys. Results from surveys, teacher interviews, classroom observations, and focus groups showed that music integration influenced middle school students' situational and personal interest in science (e.g., learning science vocabulary words, singing science-content songs, analyzing science song lyrics, etc.; Governor, Hall, & Jackson, 2013) and fifth-grade students' attitudes towards reading and music (Andrews, 1997). Lastly, the use of Reader's Theatre promoted fourth grade students' interest in literacy and reading, as measured by student surveys and performance recordings (Ward, 2007).

## Affective engagement and students with disabilities

Only two articles related to affective engagement and students with disabilities emerged from the literature review. One study (Hutchison, 2007) examined the changes in the self-perceptions and interest in writing of two students with LD after the implementation of an intervention designed to increase engagement and self-efficacy. Results from the case studies suggested that both students demonstrated increased interest in writing after the intervention (Hutchison, 2007). The second study (Haskins, 2012) investigated the influence of providing choice on the motivation to write for a student with ASD. Visual analysis from the single subject design study revealed that offering choices to the student fostered greater interest and willingness to begin writing tasks (Haskins, 2012).

## Affective engagement, arts integration, and students with disabilities

A search of studies in the area of affective engagement, arts integration, and students with disabilities generated similarly few results. Three studies (Anderson, 2012; Corcoran & Davis, 2005; Whittaker, 2005) emphasized the value of dramatic arts integration for improving the affective engagement of students with LD. The use of process drama positively influenced the attitudes and willingness of fourth graders with LD and behavior challenges to participate in written language activities (Anderson, 2012). The introduction of Reader's Theatre into language arts lessons fostered increased confidence and interest in reading for second, third, and fourth graders with LD (Corcoran & Davis, 2005; Whittaker, 2005). Positive affective engagement outcomes were found in a case study of fourth graders with EBD. Listening to music enhanced the students' attitudes towards writing, improved their focus, and increased their excitement about completing their work (Kariuki & Honeycutt, 1998).

## Discussion

The review of literature at the intersections of cognitive engagement, affective engagement, arts integration, and students with disabilities yielded several areas for discussion. First was the relative paucity of research. The search for studies within each category (i.e., arts integration, students with disabilities, and arts integration for students with disabilities) yielded five or fewer results in all but one category (i.e., affective engagement and arts integration). Given the depth of literature on engagement with traditional students in conventional settings, there is a distinct gap in research investigating engagement among students with disabilities. This finding is both surprising and concerning in light of the widespread and reasonable belief that engagement is a central benefit of participating in the arts in school (Robinson, 2013).

Likewise, given the increased prevalence of students with disabilities in inclusive elementary and middle school settings (Cortiella, 2011; McLeskey, Landers, Hoppey, & Williamson, 2011), it was concerning to find that only two studies described interventions that may foster affective engagement for students with LD and ASD and no studies considered how arts integration may influence cognitive engagement. To date, researchers have yet to investigate the affective engagement of students with other disabilities, including ADHD, EBD, and SLI. Clearly, more research on cognitive and affective engagement, in and out of arts-integrated settings, is necessary to better understand these vulnerable populations.

The review identified another area of concern related to the general lack of clarity and precision in defining and measuring constructs. The majority of studies merely referenced the term 'engagement' without explaining the specific type of engagement (i.e., cognitive or affective) and without describing how engagement was measured. Inconsistencies and difficulties in operationally defining engagement may explain the limited number of studies that were related to cognitive and affective engagement. The use of specific search terms may have inadvertently excluded relevant studies. For example, confounding terms like motivation, strategy use, and critical thinking may have yielded more numerous results, especially for students with LD. However, because studies related to these terms did not use 'engagement' to describe these constructs, they were excluded from the review. The challenge in determining which studies to include further substantiates the need for researchers to clearly define engagement and its dimensions, and to develop and use definition- and theory-driven measurements.

An additional limitation reflects the numerous studies that examined academic outcomes and presented engagement findings merely as secondary, dependent variables. Rarely were elements of cognitive or affective engagement investigated in isolation. As such, the relationship between cognitive engagement, affective engagement, arts integration, and students with disabilities is likely underspecified and underreported.

Finally, many of the studies included engagement as a variable, but did not provide an adequate theoretical or empirical rationale for how and why engagement was related to the identified academic outcomes. What, for instance, is the relationship between arts integration, engagement, and student outcomes? From a statistical standpoint, does affective engagement mediate or moderate the relation between arts integration and student outcomes? Do cognitively engaged LD students respond differently to arts integration than their less-engaged LD peers? In short, many studies in the limited pool did not adequately provide a theory of action linking variables together.

Given the limitations of the research, more robust and numerous studies related to cognitive and affective engagement, arts integration, and students with disabilities are needed. The demand for these studies is particularly timely considering the recent implementation of the Common Core State Standards (CCSS), which focus on mastery of rigorous content and the application of knowledge through higher-ordered thinking skills (National Governors Association Center for Best Practices, 2013). Future studies should investigate how best to engage (i.e., cognitively and affectively) students with disabilities to access higher-order critical thinking skills (e.g., analysis, evaluation, synthesis, etc.) reflective of the CCSS. Such examinations will determine the extent to which educational context (e.g., arts-integrated instruction) scaffolds understanding of complex academic concepts for students with disabilities.

Future studies should include one or more components of engagement as primary dependent variables, or use appropriate methodologies to link engagement to academic outcomes. Additionally, future research should operationally define engagement and the component(s) of engagement under consideration for improved and more consistent measurement. Such studies may benefit from stratification to determine which arts integration approaches (i.e., drama integration, music integration, dance integration, visual arts integration, etc.) hold the most potential for increasing cognitive or affective engagement. Similarly, future studies should isolate specific features of engagement to determine which elements, if any, are most influenced by arts integrated instruction. Finally, research could include students with ASD, ADHD, and/or SLI in addition to LD and EBD in order to further substantiate how the arts support comorbid learning needs of individual students through cognitive and affective engagement.

## Summary and Conclusion

Given the current priority on educational inclusion that promotes the placement, service delivery, and assessment of students with disabilities in general education settings, researchers and practitioners must generate inclusive learning opportunities that address diverse learning dimensions (e.g., the cognitive and affective) to maximize student engagement. The next chapter draws from the cognitive and affective dimensions of engagement to present a unified theory of action incorporating linguistic, cognitive, and affective dimensions of engagement to address how and why arts integration supports students with and without exceptionalities.

## References

*Abedin, G. (2010). *Exploring the potential of art-based education for adolescents with learning disabilities: A case study of engagement in learning through the arts.* Retrieved from ProQuest Dissertations & Theses (3409864).

★Anderson, A. (2012). The influence of process drama on elementary students' written language. *Urban Education*, 47(5), 959–982.

★Anderson, A. R. (2004). *Student engagement and dropout: An investigation with students who have mild disabilities.* Retrieved from ProQuest Dissertations & Theses (305157963).

★Andrews, L. J. (1997). *Effects of an integrated reading and music instructional approach on fifth-grade students' reading achievement, reading attitude, music achievement, and music attitude.* (Unpublished doctoral dissertation). University of North Carolina, Greensboro, NC.

Appleton, J. J., Christenson, S. L., & Furlong, M. J. (2008). Student engagement with school: Critical conceptual and methodological issues of the construct. *Psychology in the Schools*, 45(5), 369–386.

★Barry, N. H. (2010). *Oklahoma A+ Schools: What the research tells us 2002–2007.* Vol. 3, *Quantitative measures.* Edmond: Oklahoma A+ Schools/University of Central Oklahoma.

★Baum, S. M., & Owen, S. V. (1997). Using art processes to enhance academic self-regulation. In R. J. Deasy (Ed.), *Critical links: Learning in the arts and student academic and social development* (pp. 64–66). Washington, DC: Arts Education Partnership.

Baum, S. M., Owen, S. V., & Oreck, B. (1997). Transferring individual self-regulation processes from arts to academics. *Arts Education Policy Review*, 98(3), 32–39.

Bridgeland, J. M., Dilulio, J. J., & Morison K. B. (2006). *The silent epidemic: Perspectives of high school dropouts.* Washington, DC: Civic Enterprises in association with Peter D. Hart Research Associates for the Bill & Melinda Gates Foundation. Retrieved from http://www.civicenterprises.net/pdfs/thesilentepidemic3-06.pdf

Catterall, J. S. (2002). Essay: Research on drama and theatre education. In R. Deasy (Ed.), *Critical links: Learning in the arts and student academic and social development* (pp. 57–58). Washington, DC: Arts Education Partnership.

Christenson, S. L., Reschly, A. L., Appleton, J. J., Berman-Young, S., Spanjers, D. M., & Varro, P. (2008). Best practices in fostering student engagement. In A. Thomas and J. Grimes (Eds.), *Best practices in school psychology V* (pp. 1099–1119). Washington, DC: National Association of School Psychologists.

Christenson, S. L., Reschly, A. L., & Wylie, C. (Eds.). (2012). *Handbook of research on student engagement.* New York: Springer Sciences.

★Corcoran, C. A., & Davis, A. (2005). A study of the effects of Readers' Theater on second and third grade special education students' fluency growth. *Reading Improvement*, 42(2), 105–111.

Cortiella, C. (2011). *The state of learning disabilities.* New York: National Center for Learning Disabilities.

★DeMoss, K., & Morris, T. (2002). *How arts integration supports student learning: Students shed light on the connections.* Chicago: Chicago Arts Partnerships in Education (CAPE).

★Duatepe-Paksu, A., & Ubuz, B. (2009). Effects of drama-based geometry instruction on student achievement, attitudes, and thinking levels. *Journal of Educational Research*, 102(4), 272–286.

★Durham, J. (2010). *The effects of an arts-based and integrated curricular approach on the cognitive processes and personal learning characteristics of students with learning disabilities.* Retrieved from ProQuest Dissertations & Theses (193944440).

Eccles, J. S., & Wang, M. (2012). Part I commentary: So what is student engagement anyway? In S. L. Christenson, A. L. Reschly & C. Wylie (Eds.), *Handbook of research on student engagement* (pp. 133–145). New York: Springer Sciences.

★Ffolkes-Bryant, B. (2008). *Investigating the effect on student attitudes, motivation and self-esteem in performing arts elementary schools incorporating arts integration.* Retrieved from ProQuest Dissertations & Theses (304817308).

*Forseth, S. (1980). Art activities, attitudes, and achievement in elementary mathematics. *Studies in Art Education*, 21(2), 22–27.

Fredricks, J. A., Blumenfeld, P. C., & Paris, A. H. (2004). School engagement: Potential of the concept, state of evidence. *Review of Educational Research*, 74(1), 59–109.

Fredricks, J. A., & Eccles, J. S. (2002). Children's competence and value beliefs from childhood through adolescence: Growth trajectories in two male-sex-typed domains. *Developmental Psychology*, 38, 519–533.

*Governor, D., Hall, J., & Jackson, D. (2013). Teaching and learning science through song: Exploring the experiences of students and teachers. *International Journal of Science Education*, 35(18), 3117–3140.

Guthrie, J. T., & Wigfield, A. (2000). Engagement and motivation in reading. In M. L. Kamil, P. B. Mosenthal, P. D. Pearson, & R. Barr (Eds.), *Handbook of reading research* (pp. 403–422). Mahwah, NJ: Erlbaum.

*Haskins, T. M. (2012). *Influence of choice on motivation to learn for students with autism: Effect on student interest, writing achievement, latency, and behavior.* Retrieved from ProQuest Dissertations & Theses (1288420092).

*Healy, K. G. (2004). *The effects of integrating visual art on middle school students' attitude toward mathematics.* Retrieved from ProQuest Dissertations & Theses (305051220).

*Hutchison, L. A. (2007). *A pilot study of students' self-perceptions of efficacy and engagement in the writing process.* Retrieved from ProQuest Dissertations & Theses (304831471).

*Ingram, D., & Meath, M. (2007). *Arts for academic achievement: A compilation of evaluation findings from 2004–2006.* St Paul: Center for Applied Research and Educational Improvement, University of Minnesota.

Ingram, D., & Seashore, K. R. (2003). *Arts for academic achievement: Summative evaluation report.* St Paul: Center for Applied Research and Educational Improvement, College of Education and Human Development, University of Minnesota.

*Jacobs, M. N. (2005). *Drama discovery: The effect of dramatic arts in combination with bibliotherapy on the self-efficacy of students with emotional and/or behavioral disabilities regarding their understanding of their own exceptionalities.* Retrieved from ProQuest Dissertations & Theses (304994634).

*James, C.Y. (2011). *Does arts infused instruction make a difference? An exploratory study of the effects of an arts infused instructional approach on engagement and achievement of third, fourth, and fifth grade students in mathematics.* Retrieved from ProQuest Dissertations & Theses (865355330).

Janosz, M., Archambault, I., Morizot, J., & Pagani, L. S. (2008). School engagement trajectories and their differential predictive relations to dropout. *Journal of Social Issues*, 64(1), 21–40.

*Kariuki, P., & Honeycutt, C. (1998, April). *An investigation of the effects of music on two emotionally disturbed students' writing motivations and writing skills.* Paper presented at the Annual Conference of the Mid-South Research Association, New Orleans, LA.

Kastner, J., & Gottlieb, B. W. (1995). Use of incentive structure in mainstream classes. *Journal of Educational Research*, 89(1), 52–57.

Klem, A. D., & Connell, J. P. (2004). Relationships matter: Linking teacher support to student engagement and achievement. *Journal of School Health*, 74, 262–273.

*Lackaye, T. D., & Margalit, M. (2006). Comparisons of achievement, effort, and self-perceptions among students with learning disabilities and their peers from different achievement groups. *Journal of Learning Disabilities*, 39(5), 432–446.

Lawson, M. A., & Lawson, H. A. (2013). New conceptual frameworks for student engagement research, policy, and practice. *Review of Educational Research*, 83, 432–479.

*McFadden, P. J. (2010). *Using theatre arts to enhance literacy skills at the second grade level.* Retrieved from ProQuest Dissertations & Theses (3428328).

McLeskey, J., Landers, E., Hoppey, D., & Williamson, P. (2011). Learning disabilities and the LRE mandate: An examination of national and state trends. *Learning Disabilities: Research and Practice*, 26, 60–66.

National Governors Association Center for Best Practices. (2013). *Common core state standards for English/language arts*. Washington, DC: Council of Chief State School Officers.

National Research Council. (2004). *Engaging schools: Fostering high school students' motivation to learn*. Washington, DC: The National Academies Press.

Newman, L., & Davies, E. (2005). The school engagement of elementary and middle school students with disabilities. In *Engagement, academics, social adjustment, and independence: The achievements of elementary and middle school students with disabilities* (pp. 3.1–3.18) (DOE Contract No. ED-00-CO-0017). Washington, DC: US Department of Education, Office of Special Education Programs.

*Palincsar, A., Collins, K. M., & Marano, N. L. (2000). Investigating the engagement and learning of students with learning disabilities in guided inquiry science teaching. *Language, Speech, and Hearing Services in Schools*, 31(3), 240–251.

*Reschly, A. L., & Christenson, S. L. (2006). Prediction of dropout among students with mild disabilities: A case for the inclusion of student engagement variables. *Remedial and Special Education*, 27(5), 276–292.

Robinson, A. H. (2013). Arts integration and the success of disadvantaged students: A research evaluation. *Arts Education Policy Review*, 114(4), 191–204.

Sideridis, G. D., Morgan, P. L., Botsas, G., Padeliadu, S., & Fuchs, D. (2006). Predicting LD on the basis of motivation, metacognition, and psychopathology: An ROC analysis. *Journal of Learning Disabilities*, 39(3), 215–229.

*Stevenson, L., & Deasy, R. J. (2005). *Third space: When learning matters*. Washington, DC: Arts Education Partnership.

Vaughn, S., Elbaum, E., & Boardman, A. G. (2011). The social functioning of students with learning disabilities: Implications for inclusion. *Exceptionality*, 9(1–2), 47–65.

*Ward, L. (2007). *Tales of a fourth grade something: Using Readers' Theatre to promote reading comprehension*. Retrieved from ProQuest Dissertations & Theses (304851981).

*Whittaker, J. K. (2005). *Readers' Theatre: Effects on reading performance, attention and perspectives of students with reading disabilities*. Retrieved from ProQuest Dissertations & Theses (3200190).

*Wilhelm, J. D. (1995). Reading is seeing: Using visual response to improve the literary reading of reluctant readers. *Journal of Reading Behavior*, 27(4), 467–503.

# 4

# UNDERSTANDING *HOW* AND *WHY* ARTS INTEGRATION ENGAGES LEARNERS

*Alida Anderson*

## Introduction

This chapter describes the conceptual framework and research supporting *how* and *why* arts integration (AI) functions in learning engagement. An interdisciplinary model for engagement draws from allied fields of special and general education, psychology, and speech-language pathology, and is defined through linguistic, cognitive, and affective dimensions, previously detailed in Chapters 2 and 3. The current chapter proposes a theory of action to contribute to the next 'wave' of AI research focused on *how* and *why* AI facilitates student engagement for the express purpose of validating its use in education. This focus has the potential to advance allied AI fields in support of a diverse array of learners who historically have struggled with conventional teaching and learning methods and have been shown to thrive in AI learning contexts (see Chapters 1 and 8 for reviews). This chapter also sets the learning context for AI approaches in the demonstrations of practice offered in Part II.

Also, while AI may provide a 'better' learning environment for students with and without exceptionalities or other learning challenges, this chapter provides further background context for the inclusive AI classroom settings that are the focus of Part II (Chapters 5, 6, and 7). This is an important consideration in relation to the students from 'at-risk' backgrounds (see Novosel, Deshler, Pollitt, Mark, & Mitchell, 2011, for a discussion), who, until the point of their learning through AI, had experienced school failure through conventional approaches. Arguably, all students may prefer AI to conventional methods; however, the following theory of action and the demonstrations of practice in Part II do not investigate students' learning styles or preferences. Instead, the perspective is taken that AI is critical especially for students who have experienced disenfranchisement in education.

As described next in the book's theory of action, contextualization of learning through AI provides a variety of scaffolds to students' academic content learning through linguistic, cognitive, and affective dimensions of engagement.

## Background of Engagement

Teachers' journeys are often marked by attempts at using every available avenue to reach and teach their students. In particular, teachers' facilitation of students' creativity through art making, whether through mural painting, sidewalk chalk drawing, or the construction of dream houses, is not 'less than' academic. In fact, these opportunities are the opposite – they require more from both students and teachers than conventional academic tasks. Landmark educators and philosophers such as Dewey (1934), Bruner (1966), and Smith (2000) have emphasized the importance of creativity and exploration as central to authentic living and learning. The premise of this book and of AI as a valid instructional practice is the notion that all students are entitled to learn through creativity and exploration. Historically, the arts have enabled human beings to express and convey complex and critical thoughts, feelings, and ideas that transcend conventional channels; that is, the conventional literacy channels of the printed and spoken word. In this view, conventional literacy, or the command over spoken and printed words, is essentially 'tool' or technology use. Unfortunately, much of what traditional schooling focuses on is conventional literacy skill achievement, to the extent that educational outcomes are disintegrated from students' creativity, exploration, and authentic learning.

The contents of this book attempt to challenge literacy expectations held for students by facilitating their conventional oral and written language tool use through the less conventional approach of AI. Arts-integrated education has been concerned with how and why students might be engaged in using a variety of tools to achieve understandings not necessarily measured by conventional literacy metrics (Winner & Hetland, 2001). Students' interconnected communicative/linguistic, cognitive, and affective intentions are considered in this volume to be dimensions of *engagement*.

The premise of engagement (Merriam-Webster, 2013) includes the following definitions:

1. a pledge of marriage
2. an appointment or arrangement (social or business)
4. a promise, obligation, or other condition that binds
5. a period of employment
6. an action; battle.

Notably, engagement has implications of *choice*, in terms of a union or obligation. Also, it involves *voice*, such that one's engagement may be dependent on another's actions (e.g., battle, obligation, or appointment). Most significantly, the definition of engagement entails *access* in order to participate. In other words, there are necessary linguistic, cognitive, and/or affective skills for engagement.

Much has been written and studied on the ways that human development of cognition, language, and affect is rooted in sensory experiences (e.g., taste, touch, sight, hearing, movement and/or kinesthesis). For example, music has been shown to create expectations in the human brain through rhythm, tempo, and repetition (Nordoff & Robbins, 1971). Dance movement has been described as the first language of human beings, since sensory motor behavior is the primary means of understanding and expressing one's relationship with the environment (Laban, 1956). Visual art has been identified as an individual's first communication of his or her mental representations (Piaget, 1967). While the arts showcase multisensory perspectives on engagement, other disciplinary perspectives on engagement are more varied.

## Research on Engagement

There is consensus that engagement is important for success in school and in life; however, the construct of engagement has been difficult to define and even more difficult to operationalize (Fredricks, Blumenfeld, & Paris, 2004; Jimerson, Campos, & Greif, 2003; Zyngier, 2008). Zyngier (2008) suggests that educational discourse produces distinct understandings and definitions of student engagement, with a focus on dual goals of achieving social justice and academic achievement. Over a decade ago, Fredrickson and colleagues (2004) outlined the limitations of the extant research on school engagement, explaining that:

> Despite these problems, we argue that engagement has considerable potential as a multidimensional construct that unites the three components [cognitive, behavioral, emotional] in a meaningful way. In this sense, engagement can be thought of as a 'meta' construct. In fact, some scholars suggest that the term engagement should be reserved specifically for work where multiple components are present (Guthrie & Anderson, 1990; Guthrie & Wigfield, 2000).
>
> *(pp. 60–61)*

The nature of engagement as a meta-construct is a key tenet of the extant research on the topic of student engagement, and the unique contribution of the engagement framework offered in this chapter is in unifying the dimensions of language, cognition, and affect as contributing factors of a multifactorial construct of engagement (multiple pathways and influences, depending on the learner's characteristics, strengths, and needs).

Contributing to the challenges facing the study of student engagement is confusion over the unit of analysis; or exactly who or what is the focus of the engagement (Furlong, Whipple, St. Jean, Simental, Soliz, & Punthuna, 2003). Furlong and colleagues (2003) developed a common terminology to better understand research and practice focused on school-based student engagement. The 'units of measure' for understanding engagement included the school and classroom (environmental dimensions), the individual (within-student), and the peer/social (between-student) dimensions.

## Environmental dimensions

There has been clear support for the significance of environmental dimensions (school and classroom) of engagement (Katz, 2013; Klem & Connell, 2004). For instance, Klem and Connell (2004) found evidence of the relationships among teacher support, student engagement, and academic achievement in a large urban sample of secondary-age students examined longitudinally across affective and cognitive dimensions. In particular, these findings point to the nature of the relationship between teachers and students as facilitators of social and cognitive engagement. Similarly, Katz (2013) implemented a school-wide intervention based on Universal Design for Learning (UDL) principles to provide inclusive education for students with mild to moderate disabilities (including students with LD, ADHD, and EBD) across grades 1 through 12 in urban school settings. Students' affective engagement was measured by within-student behavior (e.g., active participation) and social/peer interaction (e.g., social participation). The UDL intervention context significantly increased students' affective engagement through prosocial behavior and peer interactions, as well as through students' increased autonomy and inclusion.

## Student dimensions

Within- and between-student dimensions of engagement have been examined by researchers (Park, Holloway, Arendtsz, Bempechat, & Li, 2012) aiming to establish a predictive relationship between cognitive and affective engagement among high-school-age students from low-income status backgrounds. The researchers found that specific learning contexts influenced both individual student and peer-group engagement with respect to affective engagement (e.g., autonomy, competence, and relatedness); and that students' affective engagement was predictive of their cognitive engagement (as measured by academic performance) in the same learning contexts. Similar findings were reported by Skinner, Kindermann, and Furrer (2009), who conceptualized engagement as motivational and affective, providing empirical support through emotional-behavioral skills as contrasted with behavioral (unrest) and emotional disaffection (discontent, frustration, and alienation). The authors found that the combination of affective dimensions of engagement was more valid than previous models that focused only on single dimensions of emotional or behavioral engagement (e.g., either emotional or behavioral engagement, or emotional or behavioral disaffection).

## Engagement and Special Education

For the purposes of this volume and its focus on demonstrations of AI practice with students having learning disabilities (LD), emotional-behavioral disabilities (EBD), and attention deficit hyperactivity disorder (ADHD), the engagement model presented in the following section of this chapter and throughout the volume refers to within-student and between-student measures of linguistic, cognitive, and affective engagement, with supporting evidence from special education and general education to follow.

## Engagement and students with ASD

Probably the best-known conception of engagement in special education comes from several decades of research and practice focused on individuals with autism spectrum disorder (ASD), in which seminal developmental studies have identified early deficits in engagement (see review by Kasari & Patterson, 2012). This research provides a developmental perspective on skills such as joint attention, non-verbal communication, social attention, and shared affect, to reveal that these early social-cognitive skills are precursors of later language. In this way, ASD research frames engagement as primarily cognitive and affective, with linguistic engagement following from social-cognitive dimensions. This information has been useful in developing targeted interventions for individuals with ASD.

In particular, 'engagement' is the intervention target in working with students with ASD, aimed at increasing joint attention (i.e., engagement), as well as the amount and quality of social interaction with peers (e.g., Greenspan & Wieder, 1997, 1999; Greenspan, Wieder, & Simons, 1998). For instance, Greenspan's Floortime approach (1998) engages children through interest and attraction to address communication and social interaction goals. Greenspan and colleagues (1998) explain the use of "emotions, desires, and intentions [to] guide behavior and thought, defining behavioral intent as "[coming] from affect or emotion" (pp. 13–14). In this approach, affect provides meaning for social communication and routines and is an important aspect of Greenspan's conception of engagement for students with language and sensory-based processing disorders, since "a word or activity has no meaning if there is no purpose or goal to it, no emotion invested in it" (Greenspan et al., 1998, p. 339).

Concepts of engagement vary with learners' profiles and with how engagement is measured. For students with social-communication challenges such as those with ASD, engagement is measured through shared attention and affect, joint attention skills (e.g., pointing, showing, and looking between people), social play with others, and conversation (Greenspan & Wieder, 1999; Kasari & Patterson, 2012). In this conception of engagement, cognitive and affective dimensions of engagement drive linguistic engagement.

## Engagement and students with EBD and ADHD

By contrast, students with emotional and behavioral disabilities (EBD) and ADHD are often monitored for behavioral engagement through observations of sustained attention during a particular task, through skills such as eye-contact and time-on-task (see Chapter 8 for a review; Anderson & Berry, in press). Such on-task measures assess the extent to which students are behaviorally engaged. Students' behavioral engagement is interpreted as evidence of their cognitive and affective engagement. This literature presupposes that without cognitive and affective engagement, students are unavailable to linguistically engage in academic tasks.

## Engagement and students with LD

For students with language-based disorders such as LD, engagement can be operationalized as linguistic in measuring the extent to which students use literacy 'tools' (e.g., how much students say or write, i.e., productivity; and the quality of their speaking or writing, i.e., semantic diversity, syntactic complexity, or specificity) (Anderson, 2012). Also, students with LD may experience linguistic disengagement that may impact their cognitive and affective engagement in academic tasks (Anderson & Berry, in press; Anderson, Loughlin, & Berry, 2013a, 2013b). Initial evidence of AI's influence on students' linguistic engagement (Anderson et al., 2013a, 2013b) revealed that AI positively influenced oral and written language for students with and without language and sensory processing disabilities by enhancing students' linguistic specificity and productivity. The authors argued that AI was a scaffold for conceptual and linguistic representations of causal, temporal, sequential, relational, and abstract ideas. Also, Anderson and colleagues (2013a, 2013b) reported that AI language arts approaches positively influenced behavioral engagement among students with and without disabilities in inclusive classrooms as compared to conventional language arts approaches, in which 63% of students were not engaged in conventional language arts tasks. This research indicated that students were likely to transfer their gains in contextualized writing to decontextualized writing activities with continued exposure to, and successful experience with, contextualized AI activities.

In this research, students appeared to be influenced by their direct experience with the learning context, as well as their emotional engagement with the subject matter and success with contextualized written language activities. These findings on literacy skill acquisition through meaningful and authentic experiences that build capacities for decontextualized written language through contextualized language use are consistent with research on context influences for students with

LD (see Anderson, 2012; Anderson et al., 2013a, 2013b; Durham, 2010; Joffe & Nippold, 2012; Montgomery, 2013; Ukrainetz, 1998, 2001). This body of research further indicates that experience (time/exposure) with linguistically specific discourse (oral/written) in contextualized activities influences linguistic productivity and specificity in decontextualized discourse. Moreover, concrete and representational aspects of the AI context seem to support linguistically specific discourse, which is consistent with findings on the role of context (concrete and/or representational activities) in supporting concept development and expression of ideas for students with language, sensory, and emotional-behavioral disorders (Mastropieri, Scruggs, & Fulk, 1990).

## Inclusive Engagement Frameworks

An inclusive engagement framework must consider the contributions of language, cognition, and affect within a classroom constellation of learners. Given the increased prevalence of students with disabilities in inclusive elementary and middle school settings, and the limited amount of intervention research aimed at cognitive and/or affective engagement for students with LD, ASD, ADHD, and/or EBD (see Chapter 3 for a review), there is a clear need for research aimed at the constellation of linguistic, cognitive, and affective dimensions of engagement, in and out of AI settings, to better address individual learners' needs within a classroom environment. Broadly, in general education and educational psychology, student engagement has been measured through evidence of HOT skills (e.g., Bloom's Taxonomy [1956]). There is likely a relationship between thinking skills (e.g., reasoning, analysis, opinion, interpretation) and cognitive engagement. In other words, students are more likely to be cognitively engaged in higher-order thinking (HOT) and critical thinking (CT) skills than in lower-order skills due to affective characteristics (e.g., how interested they are, how they attribute their success/failure, how much they value the task; see Eccles, Wigfield, & Schiefele, 1998; Wigfield & Eccles, 2000).

The application of cognitive and affective engagement to the study of students with disabilities is informed by Abedin's (2010) model. This dissertation study examined the relationship between engagement and inclusive AI learning opportunities for middle-school-age students with LD. Abedin conducted a qualitative analysis of classroom observations, parent, student, and teacher interviews, and student artifacts (i.e., arts-related products), and concluded that AI instruction increased students' ability and willingness to engage in learning and enhanced their self-regulatory skills. Abedin's (2010) model considered the work of Deshler (1998), who emphasizes the importance of engaging students with disabilities through inclusive educational opportunities, and Torgesen's (1989) analysis of the complex challenge of engaging these students. According to Torgesen (1989), disengagement is a secondary trait and consequence of a student's LD. However, "these secondary traits are no less important for understanding their instructional requirements than primary or specific characteristics, because once acquired, they can act causally in further limiting the child's ability to acquire new information and skills" (Torgesen, 1989, p. 167). Abedin's (2010) model also referenced Wang's (1997) identification of ways in which inclusive education can influence student learning. Wang's work suggests that innovative approaches to instruction can have a significant impact on student learning.

Preliminary research conducted with students with LD and their typical peers in inclusive elementary classrooms revealed that students' demonstration of HOT skills was indicative of their cognitive and affective engagement, both of which influenced students' increased linguistic engagement through oral and written expression (see Loughlin, Anderson, & Berry, 2013; Chapter 3 for a review). Similarly, in the field of critical literacy, engagement is a necessary connection between critical thinking or HOT skills and conventional literacy 'tool use.' Critical literacy is defined as arising from social and political conditions of our community (Mulcahy, 2011; Stevens & Bean, 2007; Vasquez, 2014). It is marked by the use of language (tools) to exercise power, enhance life, and/or question sources of privilege and injustice (Comber, 2001). It is similar to 'critical thinking' in terms of textual analysis (e.g., how does the text work; what are the effects of the text; who produced the text, under what circumstances, and for what type of audience?). However, critical literacy has the potential to increase students' affective engagement by asking, "How does this affect me?" or "Where do I see evidence of this issue or problem in my community?" In critical literacy, affective dimensions of engagement may drive students' cognitive and linguistic engagement.

Preliminary AI research findings on student engagement that yield prosocial outcomes may indicate increased affective engagement. Prosocial outcomes include social interaction skills such as teamwork, collaboration, active listening, and responding appropriately; they are outcomes that benefit other people (e.g., being nice, sharing, taking turns, and helping). Although many of these prosocial outcomes are indicative of behavioral engagement (i.e., participating in academic tasks), they entail cognitive, linguistic, and affective components. To date, the link from prosocial outcomes to cognitive and affective engagement has not been established empirically, but is most related to the affective component of engagement. In essence, prosocial academic environments with supportive teachers and peers likely help students feel a sense of belonging to school which, in turn, influences their affective engagement. Seemingly, prosocial outcomes are precursors to students' affective engagement.

Another potential direction for student engagement may occur through motivation. There is likely a relation between student engagement and literacy motivation, as defined by collaboration, choice, and challenge (Gambrell & Morrow, 1996; Morrow, Gambrell, & Duke, 2011). Although the relationship between engagement, motivation, and HOT/CT is more theoretical than empirical, interventions or programs that enhance students' cognitive engagement in learning and create positive experiences in school are likely to improve their educational opportunities by promoting increased motivation and positive affect in relation to learning. For the purposes of the discussion of linguistic, cognitive, and affective dimensions of engagement, motivation is defined as persistence and interest in literacy-related tasks, with choice, collaboration, and challenge as the central aspects of literacy motivation (Gambrell & Morrow, 1996; Morrow et al., 2011; Oldfather & Wigfield, 1996). It should be noted that motivation is not synonymous with engagement. Moreover, there are conflicting ideas about the relation between motivation and engagement; however, recent literature seems to agree (as do those who study motivation and engagement) that motivation and engagement are distinct constructs (see Reschly & Christenson, 2012).

Within this array of engagement conceptions, one shared aspect is that engagement is defined and operationalized (i.e., measured) in terms of a desirable skill set, or one that may be lacking for some students. Instead of operating from a deficit model, the following model proposes that engagement has multiple pathways and distinct dimensions: cognitive, affective, and linguistic; and that there may be particular as well as multiple pathways to engagement depending on a student's strengths and needs, similar to the way that Universal Design (CAST, 2011) and differentiated instruction (Tomlinson, 2001) principles address individual student needs (see Chapter 2 for discussion).

## How Does AI Facilitate Engagement?

In considering AI's definition from the previous chapters, and in considering the continuum of the role of the arts in education, as well as the ways in which engagement frameworks have been utilized in understanding the role of AI, we can better understand how critical literacy as well as conventional literacy skills are tapped. The past decade of AI research reflects its youthful standing in the broader field of education. In this book's application of AI to student engagement, we focus on classroom AI, as defined previously (see Chapters 1 and 2); that is, the synthesis of arts and academic content standards to support improved outcomes in both domains instead of teaching either of these content standards in isolation. The model's definition of engagement includes dimensions of **language** (oral and written discourse skills), **affect** (social, emotional, and behavioral skills), and **cognition** (evaluation, reasoning, analysis, and synthesis skills).

### AI's Influence on Linguistic Engagement

As described in Chapter 2, if AI is a contextualized learning activity, then it necessarily supports students' increased linguistic engagement because it offers a range of supports in the immediate environment that conventional decontextualized activities do not offer (e.g., book reading or lecture). In comparing the influence of AI on teacher and student discourse across AI and conventional language arts (LA) contexts, AI activities supported higher-order questioning and responding from students with and without language- and sensory-based processing disabilities in inclusive elementary classrooms, while discourse in the conventional/decontextualized LA activities remained 'lower level' and the students became quickly disengaged (Anderson et al., 2013a, 2013b). Also, comparing AI and LA contexts, AI activities support teachers to use more elaborative and inquisitive discourse with students. By contrast, teacher discourse in conventional LA is more regulative and corrective of students' behavior (not surprisingly) (Anderson et al., 2013b; Anderson & Berry, in press; Berry & Anderson, 2013; Ye, Varelas, & Guajardo, 2011).

## AI's Influence on Affective Engagement

While only a few studies (Anderson & Berry, in press; Berry & Anderson, 2014) have investigated the influence of AI on behavioral engagement (on-task behavior) of students with language- and sensory-based processing disorders, these preliminary investigations revealed that students with LD and ADHD show higher rates of on-task behavior in AI activities, to match behavioral engagement of typical peers, as compared to conventional LA contexts.

## AI's Influence on Cognitive Engagement

As mentioned previously with reference to cognitive engagement and HOT skills through abstraction levels (e.g., Bloom's Taxonomy and critical literacy), all students are entitled to have experiences interpreting, evaluating, and synthesizing information – we might agree that these activities are more cognitively and affectively engaging than lower-order experiences of recall and recognition. However, the challenge to students who have not mastered conventional literacy skills (i.e., two to four years below grade level in reading and writing skills) has two additional hurdles: accessing the academic content initially and subsequently producing a written expression of their thoughts as evidence of content learning. While higher-order concepts may be difficult to understand and express linguistically, instruction requiring a lower cognitive level of recall and recognition will likely result in students who are disengaged cognitively and affectively. Lessons utilizing AI can provide students with experiential and contextualized avenues for accessing content as well as alternative means of expressing their understanding. One student explained this idea succinctly as "When I draw, I can think. Art helps me show that I'm not stupid." The proposed model of engagement through AI simultaneously addresses students' needs on both ends of the abstraction continuum.

Also, it is plausible that, depending on the particular student, cognitive engagement is primary, with affective and linguistic engagement being secondary, when we consider artful thinking routines such as See Think Wonder (STW; Harvard Project Zero, 2007). Students who participate in these inquiry-based AI activities have opportunities to access their prior knowledge and convey their particular orientation or understanding. In this way, cognitive engagement may drive affective and linguistic engagement.

## Engagement as the Umbrella

The following framework addresses issues of how and why AI influences language, cognition, and affect by positing its role as a mechanism of engagement. Further, linguistic, cognitive, and affective engagement may likely influence and reinforce each other, depending on a student's individual strengths and needs.

The following theory of action uses engagement as an umbrella and then postulates contributions from linguistic, cognitive, and affective domains of learning to better understand the influence of AI contexts on individual student learning. For example, linguistic, cognitive, and/or affective dimensions of engagement might influence one another, as well as objective learning outcomes depending on the particular student. In essence, this chapter asks the question of how a dimensional view of engagement supports students with a variety of developmental and academic needs in inclusive classroom environments. Figure 4.1 below shows one-way arrows from the AI context to affective, cognitive, and linguistic dimensions of engagement. Note the bidirectional arrows between affective and cognitive engagement, cognitive and linguistic engagement, and linguistic and affective engagement. This hypothetical model indicates multiple pathways to engagement, all of which are mediated by the AI context.

### Engagement Hypothesis

In the engagement hypothesis of bidirectional pathways to engagement (cognitive, linguistic, and affective), there may be a direct path from AI to engagement, as conceptualized by different dimensions. In this predictive path, we might assume that AI influences either or all dimensions of affective, cognitive, and/or linguistic engagement. Another assumption of this model is that the dimensions of affective, linguistic, and cognitive engagement are mutually influential through AI. In other words, affective, cognitive, and linguistic engagement can occur simultaneously through AI; or one dimension might influence another (e.g., joint attention and interest-based activities may lead to affective and cognitive engagement, driving linguistic engagement). Noteworthy in this model are unidirectional arrows between AI and each of the dimensions of affective, cognitive, and linguistic engagement. This is an important feature of the model since it supports the interpretation that AI may have a differential influence on individual learners, depending on their strengths and needs. It is therefore plausible to consider students' primary and secondary pathways to engagement through AI. For example, students with language-based LD may experience linguistic engagement through AI activities because their oral and written discourse skills are supported through context (Ukrainetz, 2006). A secondary effect would be support for affective and cognitive engagement. Conversely, students with sensory-based processing challenges may primarily respond to activity-centered, joint-attention, and interest-based features of AI in support of affective engagement; dimensions of linguistic and cognitive engagement are influenced as a result. Also, students with EBD may

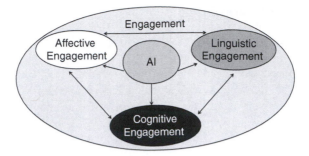

**FIGURE 4.1** A Dimensional View of Engagement: Linguistic, Cognitive, and Affective Relations.

experience primarily emotional, social, and behavioral (i.e., affective) engagement through AI that influences their linguistic and cognitive engagement. Thus, the major lens for this book and the demonstrations of practice that follow in Part II reflect a multidimensional view of engagement through AI across a range of individual learners.

## References

Abedin, G. (2010). *Exploring the potential of art-based education for adolescents with learning disabilities: A case study of engagement in learning through the arts*. Retrieved from ProQuest Dissertations & Theses (3409864).

Anderson, A. (2012). The influence of process drama on elementary students' written language. *Urban Education, 39*(4), 1–24.

Anderson, A., & Berry, K. (in press). The influence of creative drama on teachers' language use and students' on-task behavior. *Preventing School Failure*.

Anderson, A., Loughlin, S. M., & Berry, K. (2013a, April). *Differential language use in elementary arts integrated and conventional language arts activities*. Paper presented at the Council for Exceptional Children 2013 Convention and Expo, San Antonio, TX.

Anderson, A., Loughlin, S. M., & Berry, K. (2013b, April). *The influence of dramatic arts integration on teacher and student language in language arts contexts*. Paper presented at the 2013 AERA Annual Meeting, San Francisco, CA.

Berry, K., & Anderson, A. (2013, April). *Teachers' speech acts in elementary arts integrated and conventional language arts contexts*. Poster presented at the Council for Exceptional Children 2013 Convention and Expo, San Antonio, TX.

Berry, K., & Anderson, A. (2014, April). *Behavioral engagement of students with language-based learning disabilities in elementary arts integrated and conventional language arts contexts*. Presentation at the 2014 CEC Convention, Philadelphia, PA.

Bloom, B. S. (1956). *Taxonomy of educational objectives: The classification of educational goals*. New York: Longman.

Bruner, J. S. (1966). *Toward a theory of instruction*. Cambridge, MA: Belknap Press of Harvard University Press.

CAST. (2011). *Universal Design for Learning Guidelines version 2.0*. Wakefield, MA: CAST. Retrieved from http://www.udlcenter.org/aboutudl/udlguidelines

Comber, B. (2001). Classroom explorations in critical literacy. In H. Fehring & P. Green (Eds.), *Critical literacy: A collection of articles from the Australian Literacy Educators' Association* (pp. 90–111). Newark, DE: International Reading Association.

Deshler, D. (1998). Grounding interventions for students with learning disabilities in "powerful ideas." *Learning Disabilities Research and Practice*, 13(1), 29–34.

Dewey, J. (1934). *Art as experience.* New York: Minton, Balch & Company.

Durham, J. (2010). *The effects of an arts-based and integrated curricular approach on the cognitive processes and personal learning characteristics of students with learning disabilities.* Retrieved from ProQuest Dissertations & Theses (193944440).

Eccles, J. S., Wigfield, A., & Schiefele, U. (1998). Motivation to succeed. In N. Eisenberg (Ed.), *Handbook of child psychology* (Vol. 4, 5th ed.). New York: Wiley.

Fredricks, J. A., Blumenfeld, P. C., & Paris, A. H. (2004). School engagement: Potential of the concept, state of the evidence. *Review of Educational Research*, 74(1), 59–109.

Furlong, M. J., Whipple, A. D., St. Jean, G., Simental, J., Soliz, A., & Punthuna, S. (2003). Multiple contexts of school engagement: Moving toward a unifying framework for educational research and practice. *California School Psychologist*, 8, 99–114.

Gambrell, L. B., & Morrow, L. M. (1996). Creating motivating contexts for literacy learning. In L. Baker, P. Afflerbach, & D. Reinking (Eds.), *Developing engaged readers in school and home communities* (pp. 115–136). Mahwah, NJ: Erlbaum.

Greenspan, S. I., & Wieder, S. (1997). Developmental patterns and outcomes in infants and children with disorders in relating and communicating: A chart review of 200 cases of children with autistic spectrum diagnoses. *Journal of Developmental and Learning Disorders*, 1, 87–142.

Greenspan, S. I., & Wieder, S. (1999). A functional developmental approach to autism spectrum disorders. *Research and Practice for Persons with Severe Disabilities*, 24(3), 147–161.

Greenspan, S. I., Wieder, S., & Simons, R. (1998). *The child with special needs: Encouraging intellectual and emotional growth.* Reading, MA: Addison-Wesley Longman.

Harvard Project Zero. (2007). *Visible thinking: See Think Wonder routine.* Retrieved from http://www.visiblethinkingpz.org/VisibleThinking_html_files/03_ThinkingRoutines/03c_Core_routines/SeeThinkWonder/SeeThinkWonder_Routine.html

Jimerson, S. R., Campos, E., & Greif, J. L. (2003). Toward an understanding of definitions and measures of school engagement and related terms. *California School Psychologist*, 8, 7–27.

Joffe, V., & Nippold, M. A. (2012). Progress in understanding adolescent language disorders. *Language, Speech, and Hearing Services in Schools*, 43(4), 438–444.

Kasari, C., & Patterson, S. (2012). Interventions addressing social impairment in autism. *Current Psychiatry Reports*, 14(6), 713–725.

Katz, J. (2013). The three block model of Universal Design for Learning (UDL): Engaging students in inclusive education. *Canadian Journal of Education*, 36(1), 153–194.

Klem, A. M., & Connell, J. P. (2004). Relationships matter: Linking teacher support to student engagement and achievement. *Journal of School Health*, 74(7), 262–273.

Laban, R. (1956). *Principles of dance and movement notation.* London: Macdonald & Evans.

Loughlin, S. M., Anderson, A., & Berry, K. (2013, April). *Reading between the lines: Classroom discourse and academic rigor in traditional and drama-integrated language arts.* Presentation at the 2013 AERA Annual Meeting, San Francisco, CA.

Mastropieri, M. A., Scruggs, T. E., & Fulk, B. J. M. (1990). Teaching abstract vocabulary with the keyword method: Effects on recall and comprehension. *Journal of Learning Disabilities*, 23(2), 92–96.

Merriam-Webster, Inc. (2013). *Webster's American English dictionary.* Springfield, MA: Federal Street Press.

Montgomery, J. K. (2013). Teaching words to adolescents with language disabilities. *Perspectives on Language Learning and Education*, 20, 67–74.

Morrow, L. M., Gambrell, L. B., & Duke, N. K. (Eds.). (2011). *Best practices in literacy instruction* (4th ed.). New York: Guilford Press.

Mulcahy, C. (2011). The tangled web we weave: Critical literacy and critical thinking. In J. L. DeVitis (Ed.), *Critical civic literacy: A reader* (pp. 1–10). New York: Peter Lang.

Nordoff, P., & Robbins, C. (1971). *Music therapy in special education*. New York: J. Day Co.

Novosel, L., Deshler, D., Pollitt, D., Mark, C., & Mitchell, B. (2011). At-risk learners (characteristics). In N. Seel (Ed.), *Encyclopedia of the science of learning* (pp. 1–5). New York: Springer.

Oldfather, P., & Wigfield, A. (1996). Children's motivations for literary learning. In L. Baker, P. Afflerbach, & D. Reinking (Eds.), *Developing engaged readers in school and home communities* (pp. 89–113). Mahwah, NJ: Erlbaum.

Park, S., Holloway, S. D., Arendtsz, A., Bempechat, J., & Li, J. (2012). What makes students engaged in learning? A time-use study of within- and between-individual predictors of emotional engagement in low-performing high schools. *Journal of Youth and Adolescence*, 41(3), 390–401.

Piaget, J. (1967). *Six psychological studies*. New York: Random House.

Reschly, A. L., & Christenson, S. L. (2012). Jingle, jangle, and conceptual haziness: Evolution and future directions of the engagement construct. In S. L. Christenson, A. L. Reschly & C. Wylie (Eds.), *Handbook of research on student engagement* (pp. 3–19). New York: Springer.

Skinner, E. A., Kindermann, T. A., & Furrer, C. J. (2009). A motivational perspective on engagement and disaffection: Conceptualization and assessment of children's behavioral and emotional participation in academic activities in the classroom. *Educational and Psychological Measurement*, 69(3), 493–525.

Smith, S. L. (2000). *The power of the arts: Teaching academic skills to the non-traditional learner through the arts*. Baltimore: Paul H. Brookes.

Stevens, L. P., & Bean, T. W. (2007). *Critical literacy: Context, research, and practice in the K-12 classroom*. Thousand Oaks, CA: Sage.

Tomlinson, C. A. (2001). *How to differentiate instruction in mixed-ability classrooms* (2nd ed.). Alexandria, VA: Association for Supervision and Curriculum Development.

Torgesen, J. K. (1989). Cognitive and behavioral characteristics of children with disabilities: Concluding comments. *Journal of Learning Disabilities*, 22(3), 166–168.

Ukrainetz, T. A. (1998). Stickwriting stories: A quick and easy narrative notation strategy. *Language, Speech, and Hearing Services in the Schools*, 29, 197–207.

Ukrainetz, T. A. (2001). Narrative assessment: Coherence, cohesion, and captivation. *Perspectives on Language Learning and Education*, 8(2), 11–15.

Ukrainetz, T. A. (2006). *Contextualized language intervention*. Eau Claire, WI: Thinking Publications.

Vasquez, V. (2014). *Negotiating critical literacies with young children* (10th ed.). New York: Routledge.

Wang, M. C. (1997). *Serving students with special needs through inclusive education approaches*. Philadelphia, PA: National Research Center on Education in the Inner Cities. (ED419076)

Wigfield, A., & Eccles, J. S. (2000). Expectancy-value theory of achievement motivation. *Contemporary Educational Psychology*, 25(1), 68–81.

Winner, E., & Hetland, L. (Eds.). (2001). *Beyond the soundbite: What the research actually shows about arts education and academic outcomes*. Los Angeles: J. Paul Getty Trust

Ye, L., Varelas, M., & Guajardo, R. (2011). Subject-matter experts in urban schools: Journeys of enacted identities in science and mathematics classrooms. *Urban Education*, 46(4), 845–879.

Zyngier, D. (2008). (Re)conceptualising student engagement: Doing education not doing time. *Teaching and Teacher Education: An International Journal of Research and Studies*, 24(7), 1765–1776.

**PART II**

# Arts Integration Demonstrations of Practice in Inclusive Classrooms

## Introduction

Part II illuminates the theory of action on student engagement presented in Part I, and puts on offer demonstrations of possibility from three special educators who use arts integration (AI) approaches with their students in an inclusive urban school setting. These chapters address questions of what the AI demonstrations of practice have in common in terms of the following: (1) theory guiding each of the chapters; (2) action research and special education methodology, which has been widely recognized in the AI literature (Burnaford, Aprill, & Weiss, 2001; Rabkin & Hedberg, 2011; Winner & Hetland, 2008), and (3) outcomes related to linguistic, cognitive, and affective dimensions of engagement.

In Chapter 5's demonstration of practice, Kristin Nagy's film-making project with eighth-grade students is presented and examined for its contributions to AI methodology, as well as literacy, affective, and cognitive engagement outcomes through students' oral and written expression. Next, in Chapter 6 Christina Bosch's approach using creative drama to support fifth-grade students' written expression of social studies content is presented and investigated for its methodology in supporting three students to reach individual cognitive, social/emotional-behavioral, as well as language-learning goals. In Chapter 7, Robyn Davis provides a detailed account of sixth- and seventh-grade students' use of creative movement and dance therapy in learning mathematics content and in meeting social-emotional and behavioral objectives. It is noteworthy that the teachers describe the relationship between students' engagement, participation, and academic progress through AI activities. Also, evidence of students' cognitive, affective, and linguistic gains are considered as outcome measures in support of the multidimensional engagement framework presented in Part I.

All of the demonstrations focus on students in late elementary to middle school (fifth to eighth graders). Engagement, literacy learning, and participation are outcomes in each of the studies, as these issues existed for students and their teachers across the school and are central to the framework explaining how and why AI facilitates cognitive, linguistic, and affective engagement among the students. As well, the range of exceptionalities is similar in each of the classrooms.

The students involved in the following AI demonstrations of practice had histories of being 'locked out' of conventional literacy learning venues for a variety of linguistic, cognitive, and affective reasons. Arguably, all students might benefit from AI; however, these chapters focus on later elementary- and middle-school-age students identified as 'at-risk' based on disability and environmental factors. At the site where the demonstrations of practice occurred, 100% of the students qualified for free/reduced lunch based on their family's economic status, and 60–70% of the school population had identified language- and sensory-based processing disorders ranging from high-incidence, such as learning disabilities (LD) and attention deficit hyperactivity disorder (ADHD), to lower-incidence disabilities, such as emotional-behavioral disorder (EBD) and autism spectrum disorder (ASD).

This inclusive school setting served students in kindergarten through eighth grade, with classrooms of 14–18 children with and without disabilities learning together with one special education teacher and one general education teacher. Regardless of whether students had Individualized Education Programs (IEPs) or identified disabilities (LD, ASD, or EBD), the majority of the school population was performing significantly below grade level on conventional reading, writing, and mathematics literacy measures.

In addition to the shared elements of the Part II chapters (e.g., participants, setting, problem, and solutions), each chapter provides an introduction to the teacher contributor, each of whom is a highly qualified special educator with at least two Master's-level degrees in special education and an allied service profession (e.g., elementary education, counseling psychology, or arts integration/education). Their AI work has spanned over three years together with me on the conceptual and procedural aspects of these demonstrations of practice. Our shared goals have included: (1) grounding AI interventions (i.e., 'action') in evidence-based special education practice; and (2) disseminating these practices to teachers, administrators, families, and researchers, in order to contribute to the intersecting fields of arts integration and special education.

With these two goals in mind, the three teacher-authors participated in comprehensive Master's-level professional development programs in AI and special education, and developed skills and knowledge to achieve these goals. Formally, each of the teachers earned a Master's-level certificate in curriculum and instruction, focused on AI and special education. In the following chapters, each teacher describes the approaches she used to arrive at her action research, as well as information on what readers can expect. Additionally, a detailed picture of the quality of the teachers' scholarship and thinking around their contributions will be provided in the "Voices from Higher Education and Research" section at the end of each chapter. As each of the teacher-authors describes her AI intervention with her students, keep in mind the following questions about how the engagement framework (see Chapter 4) applies to these practices.

## Guiding Questions

### Contextualization of Language Learning

- How does the teacher contextualize the academic content (e.g., language arts/literature, mathematics, history)?
- How does contextualization through AI support students' understanding?
- How does contextualization through the art form (e.g., film, drama, or dance/movement) influence students' oral or written language?
- How does social interaction support students' language learning (e.g., oral language, reading comprehension, written language)?

## Cognitive and Affective Engagement

- How do students demonstrate their affective engagement?
- How do students show that they are cognitively engaged?
- What is the relationship between students' cognitive, affective, and linguistic engagement?
- Is one dimension of engagement the driver for the others (e.g., affective engagement drives cognitive and linguistic engagement)?

# References

Burnaford, G., Aprill, A., & Weiss, C. (2001). *Renaissance in the classroom: Arts integration and meaningful learning.* Mahwah, NJ: Lawrence Erlbaum.

Rabkin, N., & Hedberg, E. C. (2011). *Arts education in America: What the declines mean for arts participation. Based on the 2008 Survey of Public Participation in the Arts.* Research Report # 52. Washington, DC: National Endowment for the Arts.

Winner, E., & Hetland, L. (2008). Art for our sake: School arts classes matter more than ever – but not for the reasons you think. *Arts Education Policy Review,* 109(5), 29–32.

# 5

# FILM ARTS INTEGRATION AND LITERATURE STUDY

## Influences on Engagement

*Kristin Nagy and Alida Anderson*

## Introduction

Kristin Nagy is a Master's-degree-level special educator of students with language, sensory, and emotional-behavioral disabilities. In 2010, Kristin was a teacher at ARTS Public Charter School (PCS) and embarked on a professional development program at a local university to design and implement arts-integrated learning environments for students with and without disabilities in her inclusive classroom setting. The mission of ARTS PCS was "to provide students with multiple learning styles with a high-quality, arts-infused education." This resonated with Kristin since her own background training and interest was in painting and sculpting.

Kristin's students had language-learning disabilities (LD) relating to reading decoding and comprehension, as well as written language. The majority of her students performed more than two years below their grade level in conventional literacy skills (e.g., reading fluency, comprehension, written language [spelling, mechanics, fluency, semantic diversity]). As a result, most of Kristin's students had problems accessing information through written language (i.e., reading text), and with conveying their thoughts through written language. Kristin developed and implemented a language arts intervention targeting reading comprehension and written expression through film arts integration, focusing on the central question: *How does film arts integration support students with language-based LD to understand written text and use written language?*

Using a combination of survey, conferencing, work sampling, observational, and interview methods with her students and colleagues, Kristin created an arts integrated unit that covered writing about four distinct film art units: sound design, cinematography, editing, and assessment.

## Integrating Film and Literature Study: Kristin Nagy

In the fall of 2010, I started teaching sixth-, seventh-, and eighth-grade writing. My students had LD and required different ways of accessing content. When presented with grade-level literature, students often faced obstacles in accessing the content of that literature. For the first few weeks, I struggled to get my students to write with any type of depth or breadth. They wrote one or two sentences about a topic, ones they thought I wanted to hear, and then they would say they were finished. I started to think about my interest in writing and the topics that made me wonder. At home, I found a copy of the book *Into the wild* (Krakauer, 1997), the story of a young man named Chris McCandless who journeyed across the country to Alaska, where he lived on an abandoned bus alone in the wilderness for several weeks. This story has always fascinated me. The next day in class, I showed my students a photograph of the bus and we discussed what we saw in the photograph and what it made us think and wonder. This is a well-known arts integration (AI) routine called See Think Wonder (STW; Harvard Project Zero, n.d.). The following day, I read a few pages from the book; and the day after that I showed a brief scene from the film version of the book (Linson, Penn, & Pohlad, 2007).

Before long, my students were thinking, writing, and imagining every detail that surrounded the journey of the film's protagonist. Each and every day my students came to class thirsty for more information; students who read several levels below their grade were talking to me about information they found on the Internet in their free time. They could not get enough of Chris McCandless, and were talking and writing about him as if he were another member of our class. "Are we going to talk about Chris today?" they would ask me in the hallways before school. It was amazing how eager students were to learn and how behavior problems in the classroom had become nearly nonexistent.

When the unit ended, so did students' excitement. I thought we were doing interesting activities in class, but the students did not seem engaged. Their writing lacked specificity, focus, and depth. I thought about it for a long time. What caused this *Into the wild* effect? Suddenly, I realized that it was the way I incorporated the film with the literature. It was by accident that I had done this and partly because the film is rated R so I could only show small bits at a time. All it took to keep the students' attention was a five- to six-minute portion of the movie during each class, leaving them with a cliffhanger. So each day when they returned, they could not wait to see what was next. This story had become an all-encompassing investigation. We were watching and listening to the soundtrack of the film, as well as finding and reading information online about the film. Everything that had to do with this story, book, or film – we knew about it, and we were studying it.

### *Why Arts Integration?*

For more than a hundred years, people have been entertained, informed, and inspired by motion pictures. We have laughed, cried, and been transfixed by the stories and characters we meet on the silver screen. But rarely do we recognize and discuss film as a valid art form. When I started my work at ARTS PCS, I had difficulty understanding the difference between arts infusion and AI. I learned quickly that the key difference is the assessment of the arts standards. I used the Kennedy Center's (2011) definition of AI to guide my work: "An approach to teaching in which students construct and demonstrate understanding through an art form. Students engage in a creative process, which connects an art form and another subject area and meets evolving objectives in both."

Through this process, both the arts standards and content standards are assessed. By contrast, arts infusion uses the arts as a means of engagement, but the process involves only assessing the content standards. Because arts infusion focuses around only a superficial understanding of the arts standards at best, it lacks the depth of meaning that AI involves. For students, especially those with LD and emotional-behavioral disabilities (EBD), understanding of both content and arts standards can be a powerful undertaking (Mason, Steedly, & Thormann, 2008). As I reviewed the research surrounding literature and film studies for students with exceptionalities, I discovered little on the topic of incorporating film and literature. One study conducted in the late 1960s detailed various ways of incorporating films into literary units in a language arts classroom (Katz, 1969). More influential to my practice were the Universal Design for Learning (UDL) principles in providing my students with multiple means of representations to support their comprehension and expression (CAST, 2011). Since my students had language-based disabilities and required different ways of accessing content, it was essential for them to be able to approach the curriculum from various angles. Universal Design for Learning Guideline 3 states, "Proper design and presentation of information – the responsibility of any curriculum or instructional methodology – can provide the scaffolds necessary to ensure that all learners have access to knowledge." When my students were presented with grade-level literature, they often faced cognitive processing obstacles in reaching the content of that literature (Johnson, Humphrey, Mellard, Woods, & Swanson, 2010). Pairing films with literary text was a means of multiple representation and a way for students to combat their literacy learning challenges. These paired activities allowed them to think deeply about literary elements and make connections to other texts, to themselves, and to the world, regardless of whether they could decode the words on the pages.

## Problems and Goals

Arts integration provides instruction and assessment of both academic and arts content standards. Since my students' engagement with *Into the wild* (Krakauer, 1997) happened by chance, I wanted to find a way to recreate it using a more deliberate AI model. I had assessed only language arts content standards with *Into the wild* (Krakauer, 1997), so the aim of my demonstration of AI practice was to incorporate instruction and assessment of both film arts and language arts content standards to understand how this approach supported student learning better than instruction in each isolated area. I was admittedly cautious and a bit skeptical about the use of film with my class since I had seen more ineffective than effective use of movies (e.g., as an alternative means of 'teaching' for un- or under-prepared teachers rather than as a springboard for inquiry and discussion). However, films engage students, and as an educator, I did not want to discount the positive influence that they can have on students, especially those with language-based LD such as dyslexia, who seem to 'think in pictures' (Shoffner, De Oliviera, & Angus, 2010; Silverman, 2003).

Beyond holding students' attention and providing access to content, films can bring the details of characters, settings, and plots from classic literature to life visually. The most important aspect of incorporating film in the classroom, and that which I have studied here, is the ability of film to help students with language-based LD demonstrate increased levels of thinking and processing through the combination of visual and verbal expression. Broadly, my central question was: *How can film studies help increase the level of understanding and expression for students with LD in reading/language arts?*

## Designing my AI Intervention Unit

To recreate the *Into the wild* effect, I chose an age-appropriate, engaging, and accessible book and film combination. After discussing options with colleagues, and spending hours at the bookstore, I selected *The outsiders* (Hinton, 1967), a classic among middle school students. The film (Frederickson & Ross, 1983), directed by Francis Ford Coppola, closely mirrors its novel counterpart. I discussed my AI plan with my colleagues, some of whom incorporated themes from the unit into their own classes.

In my eighth-grade writing class, we watched the film, studied the art elements, read aloud from selected parts of the novel, and wrote about the story to incorporate standards from both language arts and drama. The eighth-grade literature teacher used a novel study in his class, in which students read and discussed the entire book. In social studies, the teacher incorporated a mock trial based on the story. Our science classes made stop-motion animation movies relating to science content, incorporating the film elements that students were learning in my language arts classes. Although pieces of our AI unit were present in other subject areas, the focal point of the four-week AI intervention was aimed at writing in relation to film production, and was broken down weekly by focusing on the following elements/skills:

- week one: sound design
- week two: cinematography
- week three: editing
- week four: assessments.

In **week one**, students learned about sound effects, musical scores, and sound-tracks. During **week two**, students learned about the three parts of cinematography: movement, composition, and lighting. In **week three**, students studied editing techniques, such as cross-cutting, fade in/out, and montage. Each lesson began with a journal prompt related to the film and literature elements, for instance, "How is film editing like the editing process in writing?" During the first 5 to 10 minutes of each class, students wrote in their journals. In **weeks three and four,** we discussed the journal entries and these became vehicles for my assessment of learning. Following discussions, we read excerpts from the novel and discussed our thoughts and feelings. Then we viewed the corresponding scene from the film and continued our discussion, focusing on more abstract parts of the story. Each lesson ended with a quick-write related to the objectives, in which students wrote about something they learned or were thinking about related to the lesson.

Some lessons deviated from this plan when I realized that two versions of the film existed. One version was the original release of 1983 (Frederickson & Ross, 1983). The second version, a director's cut called *The outsiders: The complete novel* (Aubry, Coppola, Frederickson, & Ross, 2005), came out in 2005 and included key scenes from the book that were excluded from the original film. I discovered that different music was used in each version, and showed parallel scenes from each film in which only the soundtracks differed. Students compared the effect of the soundtracks in each version. I also used the parallel versions of the film as a way to compare editing techniques. Students watched parts of each film, and discussed the effect of a scene's being included or not. This means of comparison sparked great debates and discussions among students.

In order to achieve our goal of improved thinking and processing skills, as we discussed the story, I prompted students to delve further into the underlying themes, moods, and tones of the novel that were present in the film. We began with basic questions relating to the characters, setting, and plot: who, what, and where. Next, we discussed how and why those story elements were enhanced through the filmmaker's use of sound, cinematography, and editing. This process allowed students to explore the literary elements through a visual and auditory lens. In doing this, they had multiple representations of concepts and ideas, and were thus better able to understand the deeper ideas conveyed within the story (e.g., the unique dynamic of the Curtis brothers, Johnny's loneliness through-out the story, each character's feelings toward the social constructs of the time and place).

Throughout the AI process, we covered various language arts standards related to both reading literary text and writing. Our class focused on producing and revising multi-paragraph essays, as well as the *6 traits of writing* (organization, ideas, voice, sentence fluency, word choice, and conventions: Education Northwest, 2013). These traits assess the quality of the writing outlined in the Common Core State Standards (CCSS) for language arts and have been shown to be useful in monitoring students' growth. The traits focus on writing features applicable to a range of modes, purposes, and types of writing, including the argumentative, informative, and narrative modes that are the focus of the CCSS (Education Northwest, 2013).

## My Action Research Method

I used a combination of survey, conference, work samples, observations, and interview methods over the course of the AI intervention with my students and colleagues. I worked to establish students' baseline language and engagement levels from surveys, interviews, and work samples. I triangulated this information with baseline data gathered during our faculty team meetings through interviews and conferences, as well as through observations of my students at times other than my class periods.

### Surveys

I surveyed my students on their feelings about using film as a learning tool. I asked the students 15 multiple-choice questions related to reading, writing, and watching films, in which students responded by answering "always," "often," "sometimes," or "never." Additionally, I asked them to write a short response that answered the question, "What activities have you enjoyed most in writing or literature class this year?"

### Conferences

Class discussions were also a large part of this AI practice because I wanted to show how film could support students with thinking and verbal processing skills. I videotaped class discussions to examine how students responded to comprehension questions and analyzed story elements. Videotaping allowed me to re-examine their responses and evaluate how they arrived at their answers.

### Work Samples

During the unit, I collected multiple work samples and used daily journals with students to understand and monitor their progress on expressing thoughts and feelings. I did not grade these journals, but rather used them as checkpoints to make sure students were on track. I assessed students on their understanding of film art elements and language arts content standards. For the film arts standards, we examined three elements of film: sound, cinematography, and editing. Students took multiple-choice quizzes on vocabulary associated with each of these elements. Additionally, they wrote brief constructed responses related to each of the three topics. Their written responses served two purposes. First, they demonstrated understanding of the film component, and second they demonstrated their ability to make connections between film techniques and literary elements.

Students' work samples included final five-paragraph essays on topics related to the film. Although this objective is well below the writing expectations for a typically developing middle school student, my students performed between two and four years below grade level on conventional literacy measures (reading [decoding, fluency, and comprehension] and writing [fluency, spelling, mechanics, grammar/syntax]). Students chose topics that varied greatly in subject and complexity. Some chose to write about the film elements we had studied and how those elements related to the mood and tone of the story. Others chose topics that focused directly on the literary elements of characters, setting, or plot. Students' essays were then evaluated using a standard writing rubric that they had been using since the start of the school year which assessed students' expression of ideas, organization, voice, style, and use of writing conventions.

The other final work sample was the creation and production of a short film using the targeted film elements that we studied. Students wrote important scenes from the film and acted out each scene. We used a silent film format to focus on the visual techniques of editing and cinematography. Students chose different scenes to focus on and then we edited the scenes together to create a complete summary of the film. Students were assessed on their understanding of film techniques and ability to summarize the story, both of which were aligned with the language arts standards.

## Observations

Throughout the AI unit, I collected data on student engagement and behavior. Our school-wide behavior plan required us to record merits and demerits for students throughout each class period. During the unit, I continued to record these as usual. In addition, I recorded participation points based on student engagement during each class throughout the AI unit.

## Interviews

In addition to work sampling, observation, and conference data collection methods, I interviewed my middle school team colleagues to see how students were using the skills from our film unit within other content area classes. Throughout the AI unit, teachers were eager to discuss developments in their own classrooms related to our unit. Students created art projects in various classes related to the film unit.

After this data collection, I assembled a team of educators from across disciplines and conducted a collaborative assessment conference (CAC). The team looked at work samples from before and after the AI unit to assess the depth of understanding that students expressed in their writing samples. Examining work samples from before and after the AI unit, we established a baseline for where the students were going into the unit. The team looked at work samples from one month before we began the AI and also at the students' final essays for the unit.

## Findings

### Surveys

The results of pre/post student surveys showed that prior to beginning our AI unit, the majority of my students reported that they rarely or never understood what they read. Thirteen students completed the survey. Of those students, eight reported that they understood what they read sometimes or never. In addition, 10 students reported that they always or often understood story elements when text is read aloud to them. Likewise, 10 students reported that they always or often understood story elements when they watch films or video clips. Students' responses included:

> "*Into the wild* [Krakauer, 1997]. I liked watching that movie."
> "This year what I liked was watching *Into the wild* [Krakauer, 1997]. I liked the essay contest. I like being in here sometimes!"
> "I liked *Into the wild* [Krakauer, 1997]. It was cool."
> "What I liked about writing and literature class was talking about the *Tell-tale heart* [Poe, 1903]. And I liked doing writing projects."
> "The lessons I enjoyed in this class is when we did the art."
> "I liked learning different character traits."
> "When we did drawings of the characters. *Into the wild* [Krakauer, 1997] *project!* When we watched cartoons about conjunctions. Writing Projects! When we impersonate people. I wish we would have studied more books! Doing the 'Do Now.' Doing the spelling tests."
> "The lessons about *Into the wild* [Krakauer, 1997] and the *Tell-tale heart* [Poe, 1903]. I liked that the lesson about *Into the wild* [Krakauer, 1997] was very curricular. I liked how we looked at parts of the movie. The *Tell-tale heart* [Poe, 1903] was phenomenal. I loved how we read the story and then we watched the short movie to give me the movement of the whole story. It made me imagine and see the story."

### Conferences with Students

The most inspiring aspect of the process was listening to the students discuss the literary elements of the story. Students who struggled all year with understanding basic concepts presented verbally were talking in-depth about a character's motivation, the impact of setting, and central themes. They were excited to share their insights with their classmates and beyond the classroom as well. Students looked up information related to the book online at home, watched video clips on the Internet, and discussed film elements with their friends and families. Their engagement in the AI unit was evident at every turn. During the unit on *The outsiders*, as well as the *Into the wild* unit we studied earlier in the year, behavior problems were minimal. Students came to class ready to learn and were excited to collaborate with their classmates. There was a sort of Renaissance feeling toward learning that was created during this unit and it seemed to be shared by students and teachers alike. Moreover, extending the concepts beyond our writing class into literature, science, social studies, and art classes created a dynamic learning community for students in which they had even greater opportunities to access the content and create meaning. Other teachers also noticed students' improved behavior across their content area classes.

## Understanding and Engagement

During class discussions, it was evident that students were gaining a deep level of understanding related to the story. Students made connections between themselves and the characters on screen. For instance, students carefully analyzed the relationship between the three brothers in the story and described how each was affected by the rising and falling action of the plot.

One of the most enlightening activities, however, was our comparison of the two versions of the movie. Each version had a very different soundtrack, and students were able to explain their preferences, which they acknowledged did not 'fit' with the mood of the film. One student explained:

> The music in the original version was slow and quiet. The music from the second version was fast and exciting. It sounded like an adventure. But the people were running away because of what happened. They weren't excited about it. I think the music from the first version was better for what was going on.

Students continued to bring up topics related to *The outsiders* (Hinton, 1967) throughout the remainder of the school year, just as they had continued to talk about Chris McCandless of *Into the wild* (Krakauer, 1997) and his great journey. Their oral and written expression as well as their performance in other classes reflected their deep level of understanding and ability to analyze and evaluate the texts. This level of comprehension would not have been possible for many of the students without the AI lessons. Students needed to use the films as catalysts for knowledge. Had they been exposed only to the book in its text version, students with LD would have spent more time decoding the text and less time engaged in thinking and comprehension. Further, some students would have been so overwhelmed by the density of the text itself that they would not have attempted to read the book at all.

Students expressed that the film helped them feel more comfortable with the text. In the initial survey of students' feelings on reading, writing, and films, 45% reported that they sometimes or never understood what they read. Kevin, an eighth grader, reported:

> [The film] helped me better understand the book because the movie gave us an easy glimpse of how the book was going to turn out. Sound helped me in the movie because the sad music or sounds gave you like a sad moment. Or, if there was this hyped-up type music you knew something was about to happen. If I did not watch the movie and just read the book I would not have had the same understanding of the book. The movie helps me get a clear idea of the characters and setting and what's going on.

Kiera, another eighth-grade student, explained:

> It helped me understand because first, it told what they were going through. The movie shows more conflict and what's going on between the two groups and what's happening so far. It would have been hard to understand the book without watching the movie because I would probably not have understood what was going on between the two groups or why they are having conflicts against each other.

## Work Samples

### Influences on Reading and Writing

The students' writing improved across content, form, and mechanics. Students were better able to construct sentences, organize their writing, and incorporate their own voices. Even students' sentence mechanics improved in their use of capitalization and punctuation to demarcate their ideas and expressions. What amazed me most about this *Into the wild* effect was the difference in students' seeming ability to think (i.e., their cognition), as well as their ability to verbalize or 'show what they know.' The multiple contexts in which information was presented seemed to fill in the gaps that existed for my students with LD. When students had difficulty reading, they often exerted so much energy and concentration to decode, that they lost the chance to understand and analyze what was happening. Arts integration is a way to combat this problem. For my class, pairing the book with the movie meant less time decoding and more time accessing information to be able to engage in higher-level thinking processes, such as analysis, synthesis, conceptualization, symbolization, as compared to lower-level (recall, recognition) thinking skills (Bloom, 1956).

During the course of the unit, students had various writing tasks to complete. The first film element that we studied was sound. We talked about soundtracks and how the rise and fall of the music related to the mood or tone in the film. Students were asked to listen to and compare three clips from movie soundtracks and choose one that would best fit into a movie about their school year. Students wrote extremely thoughtful and reflective answers. One seventh-grade student wrote:

> I chose song number 2 because it gets faster and faster, also like a crescendo. The title of my movie would be called *The growing life of Jane at ARTS*. It relates to my school year because something good happens, then something sad happens but something gets me back up. Also, I think I've grown this year. My grades are getting better and I made the Honor Roll. At the end, I'm going to be an organized, professional, young lady.

These feelings were evident in the students' final essay work, as well. In their final essays, students made meaningful connections and pensive statements relating to each of the literary elements we studied in class. Kevin wrote:

> There were many obstacles I faced in my young life. One obstacle that I had was that people disliked me for who I am, and I tried to conform myself. I would try to emblazon myself as well so that everyone would know that I'm just like my peers. I had struggles in school and at home. There would be a group of students making fun of me because I wasn't smart like them. Ponyboy and the Greasers were disliked by the Socs in a similar way. The Socs would beat up the Greasers one by one. Also, Soda had to drop out of school to help his brothers after the death of their mother and father. For me, people didn't believe that I was going to be successful. And for the Greasers, the Socs thought that the Greasers were mean and unhelpful. Well, that was wrong, as well.

## Observation

I expected to find the most challenges relating to teaching the film elements, since I had no formal background in film studies; however, I observed that students caught on quickly to the film techniques. In no time at all they were using terms such as cross-cutting, backlighting, and pan shot. They understood the reasoning behind the filmmaker's choice of certain camera angles, musical scores, and editing techniques. By the end of the unit, students explained how backlighting creates shadows; why a filmmaker might light a shot in a particular way; what feeling it would create; and how it would help the viewer better understand a character.

It was not long before students were asking to make their own movie, but we waited until the very end of our unit. After their final essays were completed, we spent one full day on the production of our own version of *The outsiders* (Frederickson & Ross, 1983). Together, the class summarized the story and made a list of the most important plot points. Then, we broke it down into about 10 scenes. Each class was responsible for recreating two or three scenes from the film without using sounds. We filmed the scenes in black and white on my smartphone using a vintage movie application and added an old-timey piano sound and the sound of an old-fashioned filmstrip. Using editing techniques, we created a five-minute short film that summarized the story.

To track student behavior and engagement each day throughout the year I gave students daily participation points. Each student started with 7 out of a possible 10 points and could earn or lose points based on their involvement in the class and interactions with peers. Students earned points for asking and answering meaningful questions, demonstrating positive behavior, helping peers, contributing to the class discussion, etc. They lost points for disrupting the class or other off-task behavior, such as interacting inappropriately with peers, and failure to listen or follow directions. Because of the high percentage of students with special needs in the class, each student's behavior points focused on the specific academic and/or behavioral skills they were working on. For example, a student without an Individualized Education Program (IEP) who was reading on grade level would earn points for thoughtful questions or answers and contributions to class discussions, but not for following class directions because following directions was a skill s/he already possessed. In contrast, a student who had behavioral goals on his IEP earned participation points for following classroom rules and procedures. The goal was for students to challenge themselves to be active participants in their learning. Participation points were tracked on the board and students could see when they earned or lost points during activities.

Throughout the school year, students were very focused on these participation points; sometimes their focus was on trying to earn them, and other times certain students were very focused on trying to lose them. However, during both film units, all students showed very little interest in these points and their attention was focused exclusively on the learning activities. During the film units, students gained points quickly and rarely lost any points at all. Each day, nearly all students ended the class with 10 points. This was seldom the case during other language arts units or content area classes. The average participation scores one and two weeks before the film integration unit were 80%, but during the weeks of the film unit the average scores were 95%.

## Interviews with Teachers

I conducted two types of interviews with colleagues focusing on the participating students in my AI unit. First, I did standard pre/post interviews across subject areas with my colleagues who taught students involved in my AI unit. Second, I interviewed an outside group of eight educators who had no connection to these students, through collaborative conferencing.

## Pre/post Interviews

Teachers across subject areas reported positive effects from our film unit in their own classrooms. Matt Samuelson, the middle school literature teacher, stated:

> For me, the biggest thing was the comprehension piece. When we were answering specific questions about the book during our literature class, students could refer back to the movie to activate prior knowledge about the setting, characters, details, et cetera, which in turn helped them have a higher-order understanding of the intricate details of the actual text.

Even in science class, students demonstrated deeper understanding of the concepts being studied. Science teacher Ron Green observed:

> While we were studying tornados, the students paid attention to how dramatic a film could be and how realistic sound effects could change the feeling. Once we had a video that showed a tornado but the commentators were telling jokes during the video, so for the students, all the dramatic elements were gone because of the comments. But then we had another video in which there were no conversations but a dramatic soundtrack, and that video was viewed with more emotion from the kids. They were affected emotionally because of that.

In their social studies classes, students created a court case involving the events from the story. Students acted out each part of a real court case: defendants, prosecutors, witnesses, judge, jury, and even a court reporter and a bailiff. They used facts and evidence from the book and film. Laura Brown, the middle school social studies teacher, reflected:

> I thought that the students were really invested in the court case. I think that when it came to the judgment in the case the students were so tied to the story that they weren't able to separate their emotion of the story to actually just being in the moment in the room. Ashley's case was a lot stronger than Kavon's but because they were so tied to the story the students weren't able to separate from that.

## Collaborative Assessment Conference

With the help of a colleague, I conducted a Collaborative Assessment Conference (CAC; Siedel, 2010). We closely examined student work using the CAC protocol, which involved three main activities:

1. Group members were asked to respond objectively, without interpreting or evaluating the work, and point out what they notice about the work.

2. Following the observations, the group was asked, "What questions does this raise for you?" During this part of the protocol, participants brought up questions related to the work, the student, the assignment, and the process of creating the work.
3. The group members were invited to speculate about the work. The facilitator asked, "What do you think the student is working on? What problems or issues is she trying to understand?"

I followed this protocol and other research designed to assess the influence of AI on student learning (Giudici et al., 2001; Weinbaum et al., 2004). Participants of the CAC noticed a variety of aspects of the students' work. Initially, the participants reflected on the students' use of writing conventions, organization, and structures, but as the facilitator encouraged them to look beyond basic writing conventions, participants noticed a variety of things related to the synthesis and analysis of the themes from the story. Particularly, members of the group responded to students' use of self-to-text connections. They also pointed out students' ability to use evidence to support their arguments and to make emotional connections, similar to findings on the use of improvisational activities with students in urban settings (Smith & McKnight, 2009).

One participant noticed that a particular student, Amy, included "an example of [the student making text-to-self connections] on line 45, 'Family is an important part of life. They're the entertainment of your day.' Then the student explains how her siblings make her laugh."

The second part of the CAC asked participants to discuss any questions the work raised for them. The responses in this second phase focused mainly on the assignment and what the students were asked to do. Participants seemed particularly interested in issues of instruction and classroom routines. A few questions, however, focused on students' home lives, which were common themes of students' essays. Two of the participants said they would be interested in gaining more context about the students and where they were coming from in terms of home/family. One participant wondered about Amy's writing: "I'm curious ... I guess this is apart from the content of the writing, but I'm curious about the student's family/home life, the background of the student from the assignment." Arguably, these wonderings are evidence of Amy's attempts to make meaningful connections in her essay as well as her engagement with the literature.

Part three of the protocol asked participants to consider what students were working on and trying to understand. In this phase, participants' responses varied between the structure of the essay, how the students planned and organized their work, as well as how they created and identified with the characters. Again, during this phase of analysis, there was a lot of speculation surrounding the process of creating the piece. Some participants asked whether students had written an outline, or whether writing a five-paragraph essay was a class objective. Other members of the group commented on students' connection with the text, such as, "I would speculate that the student's being intentional about connections and also the added piece of providing specific evidence for those connections ... and working on providing the personal connection, but also a connection to the text." Similar comments regarding students' work indicated that students were trying to identify with the characters in the story, thus creating meaning on a personal level through analysis of the content.

The perspective of this group of outside educators was important because it could acknowledge any potential source of bias, and in this way, it is more bias-free than most assessments. Also the CAC focused solely on the outcome of students' work rather than their behavior. This focus helps us to better understand the impact of the film-based AI intervention through its close and isolated examination of these concrete outcomes. The results of the CAC indicated that the AI film and literature unit influenced students' engagement remarkably.

## Voices from Research and Higher Education

This final part of the chapter presents the implications from Kristin's demonstration of practice through the lens of higher education research and practice in AI and its allied disciplines of education, developmental psychology, special education, and linguistics. First, a summary of the demonstration of practice is presented, followed by the application of the AI practice to the engagement framework presented in Chapter 4. The final section considers research and practice implications through the lenses of critical literacy, authentic learning, and UDL.

### *Demonstration of Practice Summary*

Kristin Nagy's AI unit was designed to meet the needs of students with language-based LD, most of whom were several years below their grade level in both reading and writing. Kristin understood that her students could not comprehend the meaning behind texts because they could not visualize or grasp the decontextualized information presented via text. To address this obstacle, she developed an AI intervention which paired film arts with literature. Kristin hoped that film arts would provide a means to contextualize the narratives, in order to facilitate comprehension, and engagement, while developing cognitive and linguistic skills associated with reading and writing.

To effectively integrate film and literature and writing, Kristin asked her students to compare the novel to the film and analyze the filmmaker's interpretation of characters, theme, mood, and tone. This encouraged deeper reading of the text and higher-order cognition, evaluating how story elements were enhanced by the filmmaker's use of sound, cinematography, and editing. This process allowed students to look at the literary elements through different (visual and auditory) lenses. In doing this, they were better able to understand and express the deeper ideas within the story.

To evaluate the success of her project, Kristin used a combination of observations, surveys, samples of student work, conferences, and statements from observers (including both colleagues and outside educators). The findings indicated students' increased affective, cognitive, and linguistic engagement during the film AI unit. Student behavior and class participation improved, their analysis of the film and text showed more sophisticated cognition, and students used more specific, complex, and decontextualized language during both class discussions and in written responses.

## Theoretical Framework Questions Explained

This section explores how Kristin contextualized the language arts content (literature); how contextualization through AI supported students' understanding of written language; and the role of social interaction in supporting students' reading comprehension and written language. We also explore how students showed their affective and cognitive engagement over the course of the AI unit. This section considers the relationship between students' cognitive, affective, and linguistic engagement and asks whether one dimension of engagement drives the others (e.g., affective engagement drives cognitive and linguistic).

## Contextualization of language learning

Contextualized language is concrete and familiar and is used in everyday, informal situations to reference objects, people, and actions in the immediate environment (Westby, 1994). When academic content is contextualized, it facilitates students' understanding, and becomes more meaningful and applicable to their daily lives. Yet most curriculum materials are decontextualized, employing unfamiliar, formal language, and explaining abstract constructs (Westby, 2006). By integrating film arts with literature, Kristin was able to introduce and illustrate highly specific and precise vocabulary related to film studies, which augmented students' ability to include decontextualized language in their written discourse. As students analyzed the two films based on *The outsiders* (Hinton, 1967) and then created their own films, the decontextualized language of film design became concrete and immediate.

We see evidence of the students' increasingly decontextualized language use, not only in their writing samples and oral language samples through interview, but also in their use of technical and specialized terminology to communicate and understand the aspects of film making. For example, a peer discussion on the importance of camera angles solidified the students' understanding of themes and use of higher-level thinking, concepts, and language. As noted in Chapter 2,

"As children engage in … social interaction, they use increasingly complex and specific language features such as adverbs, conjunctions (causal, temporal, and sequential), noun phrases, and mental/linguistic verbs." The decontextualized language outcomes of literate oral and written language as well as field-specific vocabulary is an area that has very recently become a target for intervention by speech-language researchers and practitioners (see Joffe & Nippold, 2012; Montgomery, 2013) working with adolescents who have language- and sensory-based disorders.

The film itself also served as a contextualized version of the decontextualized novel; it gave students familiarity and access to the more complex literary content by providing a visual reference of the characters and story line. Students were able to identify with characters more easily, follow narrative developments, and therefore write with greater confidence. Literature was no longer a complex and frustrating medium, but rather a compelling and engaging art form, through which students could express themselves and make connections to their personal lives. The experience that students gained in verbalizing their thoughts and ideas through discussion with their peers and teachers had a facilitating effect on their understanding and use of language. In this way, the social dimension of the intervention could also be considered contextualized (Mariage, 2001).

## Influences on cognitive and affective engagement

Kristin's AI intervention also facilitated greater affective and cognitive engagement by scaffolding students' reading, discussion, and interpretation of the text. Kristin's students had difficulty decoding words due to their LD. Therefore, when attempting to read grade-level texts, the students were expending their cognitive resources on individual words instead of higher-level thinking. The visual and auditory presentation of information allowed students to gain background knowledge that provided for deeper and more critical thinking about literary and cinematic elements. The visual representations offered by the film were scaffolds to the students as they created their own internal, visual images while reading, rereading, and then acting out elements of the story.

Kristin knew that the students were cognitively engaged for three reasons: students were making personal connections to the story; they were discussing and critiquing the filmmaker's decisions; and every student was able to complete the unit objectives. Students' deeper level of cognitive engagement was possible because the medium of film was familiar and, therefore, intrinsically motivating, and the film made the literature content accessible unlike any time before. The accessibility of the content, a change that heightened students' sense of self-efficacy, allowed them to access their critical thinking, problem solving, and higher-level questioning skills. These cognitive tasks could only be developed through an engaging unit such as the film/literature pairing.

Kristin's AI intervention supports the idea that affective engagement leads to increased cognitive engagement. When students were excited about the things they were learning, they were more willing to express themselves through writing and discussion. The more they expressed their ideas, the better they ultimately became at expressing themselves. As language is acquired through verbal processing, knowledge is formed. This in turn, leads to a cyclical relationship between both cognitive-linguistic and affective engagement, illustrated by work done by Sideridis, Morgan, Botsas, Padeliadu, & Fuchs (2006), which showed that cognitive deficits may lead children to struggle with acquiring key academic skills, which in turn leads to decreased motivation, more task-avoidant behavior, and, eventually, more generalized sets of deficits. However, high motivation can ameliorate considerable deficiencies caused by language and cognitive deficits (Dornyei, 1998). Kristin's AI unit was designed to heighten students' affective engagement as well as provide scaffolding for cognitive-linguistic engagement. Students' interest in the film techniques motivated and equipped them for greater cognitive and linguistic engagement.

## Quality of Scholarship and Thinking around Research and Practice Contribution

This section considers the quality of the scholarship and thinking around the contributions of Kristin's demonstration of practice to AI research and practice. In particular, we consider the connections to critical literacy, authentic learning, and UDL.

### Connections to critical literacy

The question arises of how arts approaches, such as film, might enable exceptional students to become critical readers. Kristin's work was inspired by pioneers in using the arts in special education (e.g., Sally Smith and Beverly Gerber), who advocate that all individuals are capable of critical inquiry because of our shared membership in the human community. This is one of the most essential elements of the arts – that is, the facilitation of critical inquiry, thought, and expression. By encouraging students to evaluate the themes, moods, and tones within the novel and then compare them to the filmmaker's interpretation in the film, Kristin's AI unit encouraged critical analysis. Her students went beyond the "I like it" or "I don't like it" attitude, a concept emphasized by Vivian Vasquez's (2003) multicultural approach to children's literature, also known as critical literacy. Critical literacy is the process of identifying new, multiple, and diverse perspectives on the text and its effects. The students practiced critical literacy through the process of critiquing existing film interpretations and then creating their own. This creative act required students to develop their own perspective on the text from their experience with understanding a variety of different perspectives.

## Authenticity and learning standards

Critics may believe that an inverse relationship exists between incorporating authentic learning experiences and meeting standards-oriented criteria in academic classes. Kristin's AI intervention offers evidence that it may be possible for students to engage in authentic learning and simultaneously achieve district-wide curriculum objectives. This unit addressed several of the Common Core State Standards (CCSS) for literacy. Kristin's students refined and improved their writing skills generally; they also were able to use textual evidence to back up their claims (RL.8.1), use precise language and domain-specific vocabulary in their written expression (W.8.2d), and determine the theme of a text and analyze its development over the course of the text, including its relationship to the characters, setting, and plot (RL.8.2). All three are required skills in the CCSS for sixth- to eighth-grade language arts (CCSSI, 2012a, 2012b).

Students demonstrated authentic learning throughout the unit as they made self-to-text connections in their writing, reflected on character motivations and relationships, and used specific evidence to support their arguments. During class discussions, students participated more and could talk about the film elements using specific vocabulary. This likely increased their sense of self-efficacy and encouraged their engagement with the material. Near the unit's end, students used the film techniques they had learned to recreate scenes from the book in their own short movies. All of these activities indicated students' deeper interaction with the material and authentic learning.

## Universal Design for Learning

Kristin's use of film arts integration with literature exemplified Universal Design for Learning (UDL) principles such as the incorporation of multiple teaching and assessment strategies in order to increase student access and engagement (Hall, Strangman, & Meyer, 2003). When Kristin used film as an alternate means of presenting content information, she unlocked the stories for these students, giving them a key to literature that they had never had before. Student engagement is often increased when using a multi-modal approach because it affords numerous opportunities for students to access information (CAST, 2011). Kristin also employed multiple means of expression both with modality and context. She utilized several modalities, including visual, auditory, kinesthetic, speech, listening, reading, and written work. In addition, she varied the contextual forms by allowing the use of the Internet in research for written work, role-playing for expressive language, and reading for content in the literature. It is important to engage various senses in learning to increase opportunities for understanding and expression, especially for students who have deficits in one or more areas of their sensory processing system that affect what Gardner (1983) refers to as areas of intelligence. Students were empowered because the film/literature pairing addressed their diverse needs by presenting and assessing knowledge in multiple ways.

## *Barriers and Facilitators*

One of the barriers Kristin experienced in implementing the AI unit was the school's dedication to student success as measured by standardized tests. School administrators hesitated to approve a unit of study that might endanger the students' mastery of academic content (CCSS) through district-approved and highly scripted curricula. However, research and practice supporting the use of arts to promote students' more meaningful engagement with content encouraged Kristin's supervisors to permit her AI intervention. Also, the availability of extensive technological resources at Kristin's school facilitated this film/literature AI unit. Kristin needed ample technology to successfully implement her lessons: a means to show the films, side-by-side capabilities for comparing films, equipment to record the students' scenes, and desktop computers with editing software for students' creation of their final films. Without this array of technology, Kristin's AI unit would have been much more challenging to implement.

In spite of the challenges, Kristin ultimately found that her project resulted in significant changes in her students' affective, cognitive, and linguistic engagement. Students' improved engagement was demonstrated through reports of increased understanding of written material as well as through observation of her students' interest and excitement about learning in general. Kristin found that her students' writing abilities increased markedly, as they became involved in the story content, the literary style, and various representations of the novel, allowing them to generate more fluid and detailed pieces of writing.

## References

Anderson, L.W., & Krathwohl, D.R. (Eds.). (2000). *A taxonomy for learning, teaching, and assessing: A revision of Bloom's Taxonomy of educational objectives*. New York: Allyn & Bacon

Aubry, K., Coppola, F. F., Frederickson, G., Ross, F. (Producers), & Coppola, F. F. (Director). (2005). *The outsiders: The complete novel* [Motion picture]. Hollywood, CA: Warner Home Video.

Bloom, B. S. (1956). *Taxonomy of educational objectives: The classification of educational goals*. New York: Longman.

CAST. (2011). *Universal Design for Learning Guidelines version 2.0*. Wakefield, MA: CAST. Retrieved from http://www.udlcenter.org/aboutudl/udlguidelines/principle1

Common Core State Standards Initiative. (2012a). *English language arts standards*. Retrieved from http://www.corestandards.org/ELA-Literacy

Common Core State Standards Initiative. (2012b). *English language arts standards: Writing: Grade 8*. Retrieved from http://www.corestandards.org/ELA-Literacy/W/8

Dornyei, Z. (1998). Motivation in second and foreign language learning. *Language Teaching*, 31(3), 117–135.

Education Northwest. (2013). *Crosswalk between 6+1 traits and CCSS English language arts standards for writing and language*. Retrieved from http://educationnorthwest.org/traits/ccss/crosswalk-between-traits-ccss

Frederickson, G., Ross F. (Producers), & Coppola, F. F. (Director). (1983). *The outsiders* [Motion picture]. Hollywood, CA: Zoetrope Studios.

Gardner, H. (1983). *Frames of mind: The theory of multiple intelligences.* New York: Basic Books.

Giudici, C., Rinaldi, C., Krechevsky, M., Barchi, P., Gardner, H., Filippini, T., Seidel, S., & Reggio Children. (2001). *Making learning visible: Children as individual and group learners.* Reggio Emilia, Italy: Reggio Children Publishing.

Hall, T., Strangman, N., & Meyer, A. (2003). *Differentiated instruction and implications for UDL implementation.* Wakefield, MA: National Center on Accessing the General Curriculum. Retrieved January 15, 2014 from http://aim.cast.org/learn/historyarchive/backgroundpapers/differentiated_instruction_udl#.VBnk5BZibKd

Harvard Project Zero. (n.d.). *Artful thinking.* Retrieved March 27, 2014 from http://www.pzartfulthinking.org/see_think_wonder.php

Hinton, S. E. (1967). *The outsiders.* New York: Viking Press.

Joffe, V., & Nippold, M. A. (2012). Progress in understanding adolescent language disorders. *Language, Speech, and Hearing Services in Schools,* 43(4), 438–444.

Johnson, E. S., Humphrey, M., Mellard, D. F., Woods, K., & Swanson, L. H. (2010). Cognitive processing deficits and students with specific learning disabilities: A selective meta-analysis of the literature. *Learning Disabilities Quarterly,* 33(1), 3–18.

Katz, J. S. (1969). An integrated approach to the teaching of film and literature. *English Quarterly,* 2(1), 25–29.

Kennedy Center. (2011). Definition of arts integration. Retrieved from http://www.kennedy-center.org/education/ceta/arts_integration_definition.pdf

Krakauer, J. (1997). *Into the wild.* New York: Anchor Books.

Linson, A., Penn, S., Pohlad, W. (Producers), & Penn, S. (Director). (2007). *Into the wild* [Motion picture]. Hollywood, CA: Paramount Vantage.

Mariage, T. V. (2001). Features of an interactive writing discourse: Conversational involvement, conventional knowledge, and internalization in morning message. *Journal of Learning Disabilities,* 34(2), 172–196.

Mason, C. Y., Steedly, K. M., & Thormann, M. S. (2008). Impact of arts integration on voice, choice, and access. *Teacher Education and Special Education,* 31(1), 36–46.

Montgomery, J. K. (2013). Teaching words to adolescents with language disabilities. *SIG 1 Perspectives on Language Learning and Education,* 20, 67–74.

Poe, E. A. (1903). *The works of Edgar Allan Poe.* The Raven edition. Vol. 2. New York: P. F. Collier and Son.

Seidel, S. (2010). Reflective inquiry in the round. In N. Lyons (Ed.), *Handbook of reflection and reflective inquiry* (pp. 299–313). New York: Springer.

Shoffner, M., De Oliviera, L. C., & Angus, R. (2010). Multiliteracies in the secondary English classroom: Becoming literate in the 21st century. *English Teaching: Practice and Critique,* 9(3), 75–89.

Sideridis, G. D., Morgan, P. L., Botsas, G., Padeliadu, S., & Fuchs, D. (2006). Predicting LD on the basis of motivation, metacognition, and psychopathology: An ROC analysis. *Journal of Learning Disabilities,* 39(3), 215–229.

Silverman, L. K. (2003). Gifted children with learning disabilities. In N. Colangelo & G. A. Davis (Eds.), *The handbook of gifted education* (3rd ed.) (pp. 533–543). Boston: Allyn & Bacon.

Smith, K., & McKnight, K. S. (2009). Remembering to laugh and explore: Improvisational activities for literacy in urban classrooms. *International Journal of Education and the Arts,* 10(12), n.p.

Vasquez, V., Muise, M., Nakai, D., Shear, J., Heffernan, L., & Adamson, S. (2003). *Getting beyond "I like the book": Creating spaces for critical literacy in K-6 classrooms.* Newark, DE: International Reading Association.

Weinbaum, A., Allen, D., Blythe, T., Simon, K., Seidel, S., & Rubin, C. (2004). *Teaching as inquiry: Asking hard questions to improve practice and student achievement.* New York: Teachers College Press.

Westby, C. E. (1994). The effects of culture on genre, structure, and style of oral and written texts. In G. Wallach & K. Butler (Eds.), *Language learning disabilities in school-age children and adolescents* (pp. 180–218). New York: Macmillan.

Westby, C. E. (2006). There's more to passing than knowing the answers: Learning to do school. In T. A. Ukrainetz (Ed.), *Contextualized language intervention* (pp. 319–387). Eau Claire, WI: Thinking Publications.

# 6

# PROCESS DRAMA ARTS INTEGRATION AND SOCIAL STUDIES

## Influences on Engagement

*Christina Bosch and Alida Anderson*

## Introduction

Christina Bosch is a Master's-degree-level special educator of students with learning disabilities (LD) and emotional-behavioral disabilities (EBD). Christina was a teacher at ARTS Public Charter School (PCS) and embarked on a professional development program at a local university to design and implement arts-integrated learning environments for students with and without disabilities in her inclusive classroom setting. Christina's fifth-grade students had language-learning difficulties relating to reading decoding and comprehension, as well as written language. Similar to Kristin's sixth-, seventh-, and eighth-grade students, Christina's students performed more than two years below their grade level in conventional literacy skills (e.g., reading decoding, fluency, comprehension, written language [spelling, mechanics, fluency, and vocabulary]). As a result, most of Christina's students had problems accessing information through reading text, and with conveying their thoughts through written language. Christina developed and implemented a language arts intervention targeting reading comprehension and written expression in social studies through dramatic arts integration (AI), focusing on the central question: *How does process drama integration enable students with language-based LD and EBD to understand and express social studies concepts?* She hypothesized that process drama would support her students to engage more fully in class activities, and thereby gain experience with the academic language and vocabulary necessary to express social studies concepts.

Using a combination of survey, conferencing, work sampling, observation, and interview methods with her students and colleagues, Christina created an AI unit that covered improvisational acting and tableau as the basis for writing historical fiction letters from the perspective of African American soldiers during the American Civil War.

## Integrating Drama and Social Studies: Christina Bosch

Most of my fifth-grade students struggled to be engaged during content area (e.g., social studies, language arts, science, and mathematics) classes. One particular student, Kevin, struggled daily with engagement and expression in all academic areas. On most days, Kevin quietly destroyed his work and wedged himself into a corner, despite the efforts of me and a team of educators to reach him. In hindsight, I was excited to embark on an AI intervention unit because I hoped it would provide a point of entry for Kevin socially, emotionally, and cognitively.

On the first day of the AI unit, while my other students were busy analyzing photographs taken by Matthew Brady, the Civil War photographer, Kevin lay face down flipping through a book he could not read. The other students were practicing an artful thinking routine called See Think Wonder (STW; Harvard Project Zero, n.d.) that supported their deductive reasoning skills. Students were analyzing the photographs, and then linking the photographs to improvised frozen physical stances by practicing *thought-tracking* (Neelands, 1998) for the first time. In thought-tracking, students used their physical gestures and facial expressions to embody their photographs' characters. Everyone was giving their best effort, except for Kevin. Kevin did not participate in the STW routine of responding to observational questions (e.g., *what do I see … what do I think … what do I wonder?*), so he was unprepared for the concluding activity. Although Kevin had become interested in the lesson by that time, he was not ready to participate in the drama activities. He paid attention to the other students, quietly and intently watching their dramatic interpretations from the first portion of the social studies class. When students sat down to write their exit ticket (a quick comprehension-checking question at the end of the class), Kevin started to complete the worksheet on his desk – untouched for hours – independently.

Kevin was one of 14 fifth-grade students in my social studies class. The class was evenly split between genders, as well as between those receiving special and general education. Peace and Briana were two additional students who were 'chronically disengaged' from academic activities. All three struggled to participate in academic activities. These students were among the seven students in my social studies class who received special education support from me in the areas of reading, written language, and social-emotional/behavioral skills. However, Kevin, Briana, and Peace were the most difficult to reach because of their disengagement in academic activities.

I provided both general and special education in my inclusive classroom to meet the legal requirements surrounding inclusive instruction for students with and without disabilities. I intended for my classroom to be imbued with self-expression and acts of creation, but incorporating art and creativity into academic lessons was a source of struggle. I felt an intense pressure to bring all my students up to grade level because their futures seemed dependent upon whether they stayed in school. All of my students struggled to sustain their attention during social studies classes. I had learned, however, that contextualization supported their engagement and this was what sparked my interest in AI. I wanted to know how to foster and promote my students' intellectual growth through contextual supports such as drama. In the process, I hoped to create an intrinsically motivating classroom environment with natural, authentic learning experiences for the human mind and soul.

## Why Arts Integration?

Arts integration is the instruction of academic content in tandem with the instruction of art forms. As Cornett (2011) writes, it is when art and artistic processes are used meaningfully in academic lessons and act as a vehicle for achieving a deeper understanding and the ability to express such understanding. It seemed to me that my students were not making connections with the material. They failed to express their understanding by citing details or recalling facts, so I needed an approach that would help them engage with the material on a deeper level, in a more personal and experiential way. I believed that my students' increased engagement would lead to their improved ability to express understandings in more conventional ways, an ability that is necessary for continued academic success.

I was inspired by specific cases in which AI was connected to students' improved expression. For example, a teacher from an arts-focused elementary school explained that drawing is essential to the writing process because creating art compositions *before* they write significantly increases the quality of students' writing (Cornett, 2011). Using this structure, students first engaged with the material in order to create a visual representation, and their engagement enabled higher-quality written expression. I wanted to know if similar benefits might come from using drama activities prior to writing, particularly in terms of linguistic specificity (how specific and precise students' writing was) and productivity (how much they wrote).

My students' impediments to learning in the classroom seemed to be many: they came to school hungry, tired, depressed, abused, poorly socialized, and below grade level. Some of my students had linguistic and cognitive deficits, and/or difficulties managing their attention. Frequently these obstacles drained my students of self-esteem, social skills, persistence, and focus during classes. But something magical happened when my students created and imagined; they became more interested and focused. My students became driven to understand subjects and to complete tasks. In short, they became engaged in learning. They also showed improved communication with one another and developed the ability to express themselves in multiple modes.

Paula Groves' (2002) analysis of the effects of AI and standardized test preparation on student achievement showed that students worked better in groups, and that disengaged students were more active and excited about learning. She also found that parent participation and communication improved, along with student attendance. Although similar results have been documented in the existing body of literature on AI (see Chapters 1 and 3 for reviews), it is more difficult to find evidence of what happens on the most micro-level of all: within each student. It seemed to me that when my students used AI approaches, they made interdisciplinary connections, confronted paradoxes, used metaphors and allegories, and generally employed more advanced, abstract thought. In these ways, my students were exercising their intellect, and most significantly, this occurred through AI in populations of students whose intellectual potential is often overlooked. My observations were supported by Jesl Cruz's (2009) description of the use of AI in a public, urban, special education classroom:

> In the midst of an academic world where student achievement is based on numbers, it is heartbreaking to face the reality that, as educators, we may be turned in to the head slave of slaves. We are left with a choice: maintain a plantation or choose to trust ourselves and our students to become the artists and thinkers we and they actually are.
>
> *(p. 154)*

Studies have shown that students with LD demonstrate gains in academic achievement in social studies when instruction incorporates multisensory activities (Ferreti, MacArther, & Okolo, 2007). After analyzing the use of narrative frameworks in text to describe historical events, these authors concluded that:

> Students with LD were less able to use the narrative framework that they were provided to organize the historical content. … Students with LD, who generally began instruction with less content knowledge than their typically achieving peers, may have needed more instructional support to use the narrative framework to organize and guide their understanding of this historical period.
>
> *(p. 151)*

A review of the literature base reinforced for me how influential AI could be in bringing material to life for my students through experiential learning. If we read only content area texts in class, regardless of how important or interesting I deemed them, my struggling students would show waning engagement because the content was simply inaccessible. I hoped that my demonstration of AI practice would reveal that struggling readers and writers could benefit from arts-based instructional methods when trying to access and demonstrate their knowledge of social studies content.

## Why Process Drama?

My students needed to access the content of our Civil War unit in order to access their highest potentials of thought and to generate improvements in their written expression. Also, my students needed direct instruction in learning important facts as well as in cognitive processes, such as comprehension of product (who, what, where) and process (how, why) questions. I had benchmark evidence that my students' reading skills were gradually improving. Although I supported all of their content reading with specialized instructional strategies, the 'reading to learn' avenue yielded painfully few 'light bulb' moments for my students; perhaps because of the well-researched evidence that "textbooks require unrealistic levels of background knowledge for comprehension" and that "the reading-level of textbooks is often up to two grade-levels above the level of the intended audience" (Rosler, 2008, p. 265). To understand history as an academic subject and as an influence on our lives today, my students needed to understand and explain, from their own perspectives, how and why certain historical events and figures were important. My students' lack of background knowledge and emotional connection with social studies content prevented their engagement in cognitive and linguistic activities. I thought that in order to explain the significance of the material in our study of the Civil War, my students needed to empathize with and embody the problems of that era. The most concrete embodiment in the arts is found in drama. Lemke (1990) explains that a "word, diagram, or gesture does not have meaning. A meaning has to be made for it, by someone, according to some set of conventions for making sense of words, diagrams, or gestures" (p. 186). I saw a parallel between this idea and the possibility that drama offered the opportunity for my students to 'make meaning' for themselves within our social studies material.

Drama possesses several other qualities that reinforced my initial interest in it as an intervention approach with my students: improvisation, the use of personal experience to shape dramatic expression, and a prioritization of the student as an essential presenter of the content. Our dramatic exercises often became 'process drama,' or the improvised actions of students and teachers in imagined, unscripted scenarios, "framed by curricular topics, teacher objectives, and students' personal experiences" (O'Neill, 1985; Rogers & O'Neill, 1993, as cited in Schneider & Jackson, 2000, p. 38). The most-cited definitions of process drama can be traced back to O'Neill's work (1985), in which dramatic improvisation was first recognized as pedagogy. The use of process drama changes the classroom focus from the content to the students, without sacrificing the former. Using process drama, I presented my students with the relevant academic content and then facilitated their use of this knowledge along with their personal experiences to engage with the subject matter of the Civil War.

Allowing for this shift in leadership from teacher to students is supported by well-researched educational methodologies, such as Culturally Relevant Teaching (Ladson-Billings, 1995), Universal Design for Learning (UDL; CAST, 2011), and Discovery Learning in the tradition of Jerome Bruner (1966) and John Dewey (1934). For example, process drama frequently utilizes role-inverting activities such as *mantle of the expert* (Heathcoat & Herbert, 1985), in which students rather than the teacher are the primary transmitters of knowledge. Each student adopts a character or experience as his or her own, and conveys their expertise drawn from personal experience and academic learning to maintain a convincing character-in-role. The improvisational aspects of process drama techniques encourage every student to make meaning out of events through discovery and interaction.

Process drama aligns with instructional design that is intended to reach the whole child, such as UDL (CAST, 2011). The UDL guidelines provide teachers with ways to structure their lesson plans and activities so that each student has an opportunity to learn and demonstrate their understanding through an area of strength. Process drama corresponds with UDL principles by providing students with multiple means of representation, expression, and engagement. The UDL-inspired process drama techniques are also aligned with Gardner's (1983) Multiple Intelligences theory, in which Gardner identifies seven forms of intelligence through which individuals may learn (i.e., kinesthetic, visual-spatial, musical, interpersonal, intrapersonal, logical-mathematical, and linguistic). Process drama provides access to several of the intelligences that conventionally are not included in standard academic pedagogy. For instance, in drama activities, interpersonal skills are tapped through dialogue and scenes; visual-spatial skills are involved in creating sets, props, and in the physical portrayal of the dramatic scene; students draw on bodily-kinesthetic intelligence when choosing how to use body language and positioning on stage; and intrapersonal intelligence is essential for embodying a character. If each student can be encouraged to participate, then no student is excluded from the learning activity because of individual variance in cultural background, content-level knowledge or learning ability, or interest. Sally Smith's (2001) Academic Club model also inspired my integration of process drama into my social studies classes because Smith created active learning environments in which students engaged in experiential and multisensory experiences of living and learning within the context of their content knowledge.

## Problems and Goals

In the spring of our school year, having worked for several months with my fifth graders, I found that they struggled to reconcile the complexities and analyze the details of the Civil War. My students had a tenuous grasp of American history, geography, and ethnography, and in a broader sense, they struggled to understand units of time. For example, one of my main goals in our social studies classes was to clarify that Martin Luther King, Jr. was a Civil Rights leader of the 1960s rather than a slave, which was the understanding that all of my students shared on this important leader. It seemed that the resources available to my students for their constructions of self-identity were scarce. Particularly for my students with LD, I could not discern whether they had limited knowledge of familial, cultural, and national history, or whether they experienced obstacles to understanding and expression of their knowledge. My students struggled all year long to make connections, integrate facts, generate dynamic opinions, and synthesize ideas. These struggles were illustrated by my students' writing assignments using information from a previous unit on the Colonial era. Students chose events to write about and used a familiar color-coded, graphically organized expository writing system, but this was a taxing assignment for the class as a whole. Many students had significant difficulties with the various processes inherent in the task: comprehending and analyzing a prompt or question; recognizing, recalling and/or applying relevant factual knowledge; explaining, comparing, categorizing, and/or organizing historical causes and events; and evaluating claims with supporting evidence. Of course, this succession of thinking skills associated with reading and writing literacy outcomes culminated in the goal of expressing all of the information within a complete essay format.

In addition to the need for contextualizing historical events to promote literacy learning among my students, I believed that history provides one of the most important sets of conventions by which we culturally construct an understanding of our place in the world (Levstik & Barton, 1996). It seemed that developing the ability to contextualize historical events would directly support my students' abilities to construct independent and individual identities as they entered adolescence. I hoped that drama AI would support my students to gain a deeper understanding of the American Civil War. I hoped that this would be a capstone unit of study in their fifth-grade year, a formative intellectual moment in their education, and the foundation for a more historical understanding of their own identities.

Academic content standards and objectives, identified by our district's school system (District of Columbia Public Schools, 2011) and National Standards for Theater Arts (John F. Kennedy Center for the Performing Arts, 2014), provided an outline for my AI intervention unit. These standards and objectives are presented in Table 6.1.

My AI intervention was intended to benefit all of my students; however, as mentioned previously, I identified three students as my primary participants because of their severe challenges due to LD and EBD. Each of these students had an Individualized Education Program (IEP) with reading, written expression, and social-emotional/behavioral goals. Kevin, Peace, and Briana consistently scored 'Below Basic' on school and state achievement literacy measures and struggled during curriculum-based assessments of reading and writing. Their conventional literacy skills placed them between kindergarten and first-grade level, between two and four years below their peers. Not surprisingly, these three students typically needed prompting and sustained encouragement from an adult to complete any assignment that involved text. These students could not recall or express their background knowledge on a topic, whether this was knowledge or experience gained inside or outside of school. My three students' in-class behaviors could be either disruptive or passively disengaged. In addition to IEP goals for social-emotional skills and behavior, each of these students had a history of more serious behavioral concerns that qualified them for additional, weekly counseling outside of the classroom. Based on my students' IEP goals, I identified activities that would support their individual objectives. These goals are shown in Table 6.2.

**TABLE 6.1** Social Studies, Language, and Theater Content Area Standards and Objectives

| Content Area | Standards and Objectives Addressed during Intervention Period |
|---|---|
| Social Studies Standards | 1. To summarize the causes and consequences of the Civil War<br>2. To describe the experience of the war on the battlefield and home front |
| Theater Standards | 1. Acting: To develop basic acting skill to portray characters who interact in improvised and scripted scenes<br>2. Designing: To develop environments for improvised and scripted scenes<br>3. Researching: To use cultural and historical information to support improvised and scripted scenes |
| Written Expression Objectives | 1. To express time-related concepts of cause–effect, sequence, or comparison in a written paragraph<br>2. To relate historical events and characters to information about the setting in a written paragraph |
| Arts-/Social Studies-Connected Objectives | 1. To increase engagement with the in-class task at hand, particularly in students who are chronically disengaged<br>2. To increase higher-order comprehension of a historical event, particularly for students who struggle to comprehend and express understanding during text-based lessons |

**TABLE 6.2** Students' Social-Emotional Goals Addressed during AI Intervention Unit

| Student | Social-Emotional Goals Addressed during Intervention Unit |
|---|---|
| Kevin | 1. To demonstrate positive coping skills when experiencing frustration or anger in 4 out of 5 situations<br>2. To express feelings and mood when asked with 80% accuracy |
| Peace | 1. To initiate positive interaction with peers by using direct eye contact and audible voice tone in 4 out of 5 situations<br>2. To increase range of verbal and non-verbal expression of emotions when engaging in real or simulated situations with 80% accuracy |
| Brianna | 1. To work steadily on a task for a 30-minute period without need for verbal prompts in 4 out of 5 situations<br>2. To identify constructive ways to resolve conflicts in real and simulated situations with 80% accuracy |

## Designing My AI Intervention Unit

I designed my AI intervention unit using the foundational materials from our social studies curriculum, which included textbooks, practice work books, and audio CDs. I also collected relevant supplementary material, such as Matthew Brady's photographic portraits and letters written during the Civil War to use in the process drama activities and to scaffold my students' comprehension. My sequence of activities was adapted from Linda Krakaur's (2005) intervention study using process drama with students to achieve literacy gains. I designed a two-week AI unit for my social studies class, which integrated process drama as an intervention with a total of five separate lessons occurring over the course of two days each. Each of the five drama-integration lessons is listed here in a lesson plan with relevant content standards and objectives (see Tables 6.3–6.7). A description of each lesson's activities follows.

### *Lesson 1 Description*

After a warm-up activity or 'hook,' students chose a photographic portrait. They were asked to consider what their photo depicted, who might be in it, and when and where it would have been taken. Then they turned to a partner and shared their thoughts. As a whole-class activity, students had the opportunity to share their partner's thoughts with the class. Next, students completed the STW routine through independent writing in a graphic organizer. In this routine, they: (1) listed concrete objects that they saw in a set amount of time; (2) listed conjectures about what they thought about from what they saw; and (3) listed questions or things they wondered about, in a more conceptual or abstract way, from the photo. After we had finished the STW routine, students shared their questions and thoughts with the class.

Students established broad conceptions and questions about the time period through the use of the photographs. For example, students asked whether cameras existed during the time period and whether anyone filmed the battles. The

**TABLE 6.3** Lesson 1: Social Studies Content Standards and Drama Objectives

| *Lesson 1* | *Social Studies Content Standards* | *Drama Objective* |
|---|---|---|
| (Day 1) | Students will:<br>1. Develop a concept of time related to historical social studies content<br>2. Research cultural and historical information to support improvised and scripted scenes<br>3. Increase higher-order comprehension of a significant historical event | Students will be able to make observations and ask questions about the people, places, and technology of the Civil War by using Matthew Brady's famous photographs as a focal point for class discussion |

**TABLE 6.4** Lesson 2: Social Studies Content Standards and Drama Objectives

| Lesson 2 | Social Studies Content Standards | Drama Objective |
| --- | --- | --- |
| (Days 2 & 3) | Students will:<br>1. Describe the experience of the war on the battlefield and home front<br>2. Develop basic skills to portray characters who interact in improvised and scripted scenes<br>3. Increase engagement with the in-class task in hand | Students will be able to incorporate different physical expressions of an imaginary Civil War era character into a frozen stance and demonstrate an initial understanding of *thought- tracking* as the basis for a *tableau* |

photographs also fostered students' novel questions about what the time period was like for ordinary people at home and at war. Many of the students expressed insightful 'wonders' during the STW routine about the individuals pictured in the photographs and did some initial perspective-taking during our follow-up discussion.

## Lesson 2 Description

The following day, I introduced the social studies period by playing a game called *Environment* (Krakaur, 2005). In this process drama technique, students learned how to use their bodies to express different aspects of the dramatic environment. For instance, students learned to position their bodies in one of three heights, high, middle, or low, based on whether their 'environment' was affected by a flood, earthquake, or tornado. Students practiced maintaining focus, experimenting with body language, and developing self-control through sustained silence during the activity.

At this point, I introduced the technique of *tableau*, which refers to a scene that appears frozen, or stopped, in time (Neelands, 1998). Tableau scaffolds students towards full dramatic improvisation because it puts an emphasis on physical positioning and bodily expression rather than oral expression. I gave each of my students a photograph that they had studied during their previous class. After choosing one of the characters in the photograph and thinking about the setting, each student froze into high, middle, and low positions that their character might be found in, if their photograph had come to life. We practiced *thought-tracking* by having each student come to life when I touched them on the shoulder and then freeze again when I left. Students had the option to say something, make a sound, or simply move and carry through an action. Thought-tracking was also an effective scaffolding method when teaching drama techniques because it gave the students the option to express an idea orally or through physical movement within a very limited amount of time. It also reinforced summarizing because students

**TABLE 6.5** Lesson 3: Social Studies Content Standards and Drama Objectives

| Lesson 3 | Social Studies Content Standards | Drama Objective |
|---|---|---|
| (Days 4 & 5) | Students will: <br> 1. Describe the experience of the war on the battlefield and home front <br> 2. Design environments for improvised and scripted scenes <br> 3. Research cultural and historical information to support improvised and scripted scenes <br> 4. Increase engagement with the in-class task at hand | Students will be able to collaboratively create a 'set' by discussing, drawing, and then arranging likely objects from either a rural home or a battlefield during the Civil War (*paper location*) |

needed to convey their character's main feeling, thought, or idea through oral and/or physical expression. This activity also fostered students' sustained attention because they maintained their tableaux positions throughout the entire thought-tracking exercise. Last, each student wrote their ideas about the setting and character, and titled their photograph.

I repeated this lesson to help my students become familiar with the techniques, terminology, and expectations involved in their dramatic interpretation of a cue – in this case, a photograph. In our second tableau, students could choose a new photograph or continue to develop their ideas from their original photograph.

## Lesson 3 Description

During the third lesson of the drama integration unit, students did a *paper location* (Krakaur, 2005) activity in two groups: a home front group and a battlefield group. On the second day of this lesson, the groups switched locations so that each student enacted scenes from the perspective of a civilian as well as a soldier. The activity required students to draw an object that might be found in their corresponding character's setting. Then they worked together to construct a scene by placing the objects around a specified area or 'stage.' Following this activity, students created a tableau using thought-tracking to show the audience what objects were in their scene, without using physical props. After practicing in groups, the student groups presented their work to one another.

One important social-communication dynamic during this activity was that the students took turns justifying the placement of each object to the other group. As the facilitator, I posed questions to build the context as well as to support each student's ideas about their scene. The other students contributed to this process as well. For example, if students identified a particular object in the scene as a stove, I asked what they might be cooking on the stove. This discussion would prompt

**TABLE 6.6** Lesson 4: Social Studies Content Standards and Drama Objectives

| Lesson 4 | Social Studies Content Standards | Drama Objective |
|---|---|---|
| (Days 6, 7, 8) | Students will:<br>1. Describe the experience of the war on the battlefield and home front<br>2. Develop basic acting skill to portray characters who interact in improvised and scripted scenes<br>3. Increase engagement with the in-class task at hand<br>4. Increase higher-order comprehension of a significant historical event | Students will be able to create a tableau with thought-tracking and different physical elements (e.g., posture height, pantomime) in response to a given scenario and explain their choices |

students' recollection of the major crops that were staples of the Southern economy. When students identified one of their objects in the scene as a light, I asked what generated light at that time in history. The students correctly concluded through group discussion that most likely it was candlelight.

## Lesson 4 Description

This lesson began our second week of the AI intervention and lasted three days. On the first day, the students received one of two 'telegrams' that I wrote using historical, primary source material from the Civil War. Some of my students were the 'battlefield soldiers' and received orders to march on the Confederate capital of Richmond. The other group, the home front soldiers, received a letter from a fellow soldier on the battle lines, also based on real letters I found online. They used the class period to plan a tableau, which would dramatize the characters and their responses to the telegram or letter. The second day consisted of student practice and individual conferences with me to assess comprehension and expression of social studies objectives. On the third day, the students gave performances of their tableaux, followed by group STW routines to brainstorm titles for each tableau. The follow-up discussion period provided opportunities for students to express and confirm understandings of cause/effect and sequence and to use content-area vocabulary.

## Lesson 5 Description

To conclude the second week, my students recreated their tableaux and wrote a *letter in role* from the perspective of the person they had portrayed in their tableau. I played the battle and national anthems of the Union and Confederate sides

**TABLE 6.7** Lesson 5: Social Studies Content Standards and Drama Objectives

| Lesson 5 | Social Studies Content Standards | Drama Objective |
|---|---|---|
| (Days 9 & 10) | Students will:<br>1. Describe the experience of the war on the battlefield and home front<br>2. Portray characters and historical figures<br>3. Use cultural and historical information to support improvised and scripted scenes | Students will be able to present a revised version of their tableau with thought-tracking and then write a letter in role from the point of view of their character in the tableau |

while my students worked to describe what they had seen and were feeling in the very moment of their tableau. This took us into the final class period on the tenth day. Students then had the option to share their letters with their peers, which several did. To close, we discussed our learning from this set of drama activities, focusing on the experiences of people at home and on the battlefield.

## My Action Research Method

I generated my research question, hypothesis, and objectives, and selected the content area standards for focus after several months of working with my students on thinking skills related to historical events. I administered two weeks of process drama AI lessons, also known as my intervention, in order to increase my students' engagement with social studies content. I believed that my students' engagement and experience in the social studies content through process drama activities would result in their greater linguistic specificity and productivity in their written expression. Data on my students' engagement and written expression were gathered through observation, video recording, student conferencing, teacher survey, and writing samples. I used these data-collection tools to assess affective and cognitive engagement. Also, I measured my students' written language outcomes across contextualized writing activities (drama-based, referred to as W3) and decontextualized language arts activities involving letter-writing to a pen pal (genre-based, referred to as W1 and W2).

### Baseline Writing Samples

I gathered work samples written before the AI intervention unit and discussed these with colleagues at my school in order to establish a baseline level of my students' content area comprehension and expression prior to the AI unit. We discussed my students' needs in learning content-specific vocabulary and key ideas, higher-order thinking skills (using Bloom's Taxonomy; Anderson & Krathwohl, 2000), and adherence to the assignment or question (e.g., topic focus or topic maintenance). We also considered individual students' (Kevin, Peace, and Briana) needs and their academic history to evaluate the most appropriate learning objectives in drama, social studies, and social-emotional/behavioral skills.

Baseline writing samples gathered before the start of the AI unit included a descriptive paragraph explaining the cause–effect relationship between two events selected from a list of possibilities that we had studied as part of our larger exploration of the American Civil War. All of my students had access to graphic organizers and other accommodations for this assignment. Also, I examined students' ability to take the perspective of African Americans during the mid-nineteenth century in their written responses following a STW routine focused on Samuel L. Dunson, Jr.'s contemporary painting, *The cultivators*, which we studied as part of a unit on African American standards of living just prior to the Civil War. The third work sample was a paragraph about William Carney, the first African American to earn the Congressional Medal of Honor, in which only two out of 14 students mentioned a key detail related to the paragraph prompt. The results of these baseline measures showed that all of my students, including Kevin, Peace, and Briana, had limited or no ability to express understanding of social studies content through written language.

### Intervention Writing Samples

Over the course of my AI intervention unit, I collected and compared students' writing samples to examine the influence of the drama integrated activities on their cognitive and linguistic engagement. I collected writing samples that utilized the conventions associated with letter writing (e.g., date, direction, closing, etc.) at three points before, during, and after the two-week AI intervention period.

The first sample (W1) involved decontextualized writing, or writing that typified what most students do in school. In this case, students spent two weeks participating in a highly scaffolded reading of a Chinese fable from their language arts textbooks. Near the end of the unit, students worked with a teacher at one of three rotating stations to write a letter from the point of view of the main character to her mother. It is important to note that this primarily decontextualized sample included both decontextualized (the story/fable) and contextualized (in-role perspective as the character) elements because of the students' literacy levels. Without the perspective-taking element of contextualization, the students could not express the content of the fable (e.g., in the form of a book report or narration). The second writing sample (W2) was also primarily decontextualized, because the students wrote a letter to a pen pal describing their experience at a museum during a class field trip, making references to events and items outside of the immediate environment. I met with each student individually during the writing process to provide specific support for his or her writing. The third writing sample (W3) was the most contextualized and was generated at the end of the AI intervention unit as an assessment of content knowledge comprehension, written expression, and perspective-taking. This sample was considered to be primarily contextualized because it focused on the content of the dramatic activities and allowed for students to draw upon their previous experiences in-role as the characters, as well as their experiences with the other elements of the dramatic context (setting, characters, problem/conflict, and resolution).

## Rating of Cognitive Levels

To measure students' cognitive engagement, I distributed their writing samples to my teaching colleagues in primary and secondary education. These educators had from two to over 20 years of teaching experience, and included general education as well as special education teachers and therapists. All were familiar with Bloom's Taxonomy of Learning Domains (Bloom, 1956), a model for planning and assessing learning based on a hierarchy of six increasingly complex orders of thinking (Anderson & Krathwohl, 2000). These levels range from lower-order skills in recognition, recall, and comprehension, to higher-order skills in evaluating, analysis, synthesis, and interpretation. Three raters were assigned to each of my target students. Each rater was given an informational packet explaining Bloom's Taxonomy with descriptions of the six main cognitive levels that make up the taxonomy and instructions asking the rater to determine the level of the taxonomy that best described each utterance in each sample, with a practice item for self-checking. Students' writing samples were transcribed into sentences and for each sentence, raters determined which of the six levels of cognitive processing each statement best exemplified.

## Behavioral Observations

Most of my students were on behavior plans to manage chronic disruptive behavior throughout the school day, including Kevin, Peace, and Briana. Each student's plan usually involved a daily sheet to chronicle behavior, which I used to record significantly disruptive incidents through incident reports or individual behavior tracking notes. This data allowed me to report on students' IEP goals in the area of social-emotional and behavioral skills, serving simultaneously as a source of data on participation and engagement during the AI unit.

## Video Recordings

I video recorded my students' performances – from their initial attempts to their final, polished, dramatic enactments. The recordings allowed me to review what students said and how they were behaving when other students were speaking or leading the group. Also, my review of the videotaped AI lessons allowed me to reflect on individual students' participation within the group dynamic.

## Conferences

I held conferences with each of my students individually as well as in small working groups throughout the intervention period. To prepare for these conferences, I drafted questions to scaffold students' comprehension of content through their reflections on the drama activities. My initial questions targeted students' objectives in comprehension and expression in order to support their learning achievement of content standards. Also, I carefully progressed from product (who, what, when) to process questions (why, how) in order to assess students' comprehension and expression of higher-order thinking throughout the intervention unit.

## Findings

The AI intervention unit findings focus on the progress made by my three most struggling students. Although I conducted the intervention and collected data with all 14 of my students, I am presenting findings relative to the affective (social-emotional/behavioral), linguistic, and cognitive engagement of Kevin, Peace, and Briana for the expressed purpose of demonstrating the nature of the relationship between the drama AI activities and observed outcomes.

## Affective Engagement

To measure affective engagement, Kevin, Peace, and Briana's social, emotional, and behavioral goals were compared to the demands and requisites of each intervention lesson to describe any relationship between their behaviors during the lessons and the content. As a second measure of affective engagement, videos of the students participating in the intervention were analyzed for on-task behavioral engagement (time on task, eye contact, gesture, prosody, on-task comments/questions). Behaviors were coded and the percentage of on-task behavior was calculated for each student in each context over the course of the intervention period. Table 6.8 summarizes the percentage of on-task behavior observed across the AI lessons for each student.

In addition to providing general evidence of students' affective engagement, my analysis of their behavior through video recording enabled me to focus on them individually and to observe my students in ways not possible when facilitating group activities. Specific activities within the intervention provided opportunities for Kevin, Peace, and Briana to work toward their individual social-emotional and behavioral IEP goals. Group activities involving decision-making enabled these students to work on their individual social and behavioral goals. Group improvisational activities such as paper location and negotiating the roles and actions of

**TABLE 6.8** Contextualized Intervention: Affective Engagement

|          | Lesson 1 % | Lesson 2 % | Lesson 3 % | Lesson 4 % | Lesson 5 % |
|----------|------------|------------|------------|------------|------------|
| Kevin    | 55         | 65         | 66         | 75         | 79         |
| Peace    | 45         | 75         | 85         | 89         | 91         |
| Briana   | 60         | 82         | 88         | 92         | 95         |

characters in tableau required the students to cooperate, compromise, and debate ideas with their peers. Kevin and Briana, who had IEP goals relating to emotional control and conflict resolution (see Table 6.9), both demonstrated the ability to control their frustration and resolve disagreements during the AI group activities. Peace needed prompting to interact with her peers and to use an audible voice during conversation and classroom discourse. Over the course of the intervention period, she was a key contributor of ideas within her group. Beyond that, Peace engaged in dialogue with her classmates on decision-making necessitated by the activities (e.g., who should speak when, how to arrange a scene, etc.). Also, Peace had an IEP goal to increase her range of verbal and non-verbal expression of emotions when engaging in real or simulated situations. Our various activities (e.g., tableau and perspective-taking) allowed Peace to practice verbal and embodied expression of emotions in a safe environment, which encouraged her creative expression of emotion.

My behavior records showed that during the AI social studies lessons, none of my students incurred referrals or incident reports for behavior issues. Each student's daily behavior log showed that they averaged close to a score of 2 (the highest possible score on a scale from 0 to 2) in social studies classes during our two-week AI unit. During this same two-week period, in contrast, the three students' social-emotional and behavioral rating scores in their other classes were much more variable. The students' affective engagement with the AI activities was demonstrated through their active participation and the lack of behavioral incidents. Table 6.9 summarizes the observed behaviors of Kevin, Peace, and Briana in relation to their IEP goals in the areas of emotional, social and behavioral development, and how the AI unit directly addressed supporting progress toward each student's goals.

## Linguistic Engagement

To measure linguistic engagement, each of the students' writing samples was analyzed for productivity through total number of words used in each writing sample. Linguistic specificity was taken into account by coding for students' vocabulary or semantic diversity, and their use of literate language (e.g., frequency of conjunctions, adverbs, mental/linguistic verbs, simple and complex elaborated noun

**TABLE 6.9** Summary of Students' IEP Goals, Related AI Activities, and Progress

| Student | IEP Baseline | IEP Goal | Related AI Unit Activity | IEP Goal Reached? |
|---|---|---|---|---|
| Kevin | Difficulty using positive coping skills and de-escalation procedures in the classroom setting | Kevin will demonstrate positive coping skills when experiencing frustration or anger | Group improvisational activities (paper location, tableau) required cooperation, negotiation, and debate | **Yes:** In 8/10 lessons, Kevin showed positive coping skills. In 2/10 lessons, Kevin followed de-escalation procedures outlined in his behavior plan |
| | Kevin has difficulty expressing his emotions through appropriate outlets | Kevin will express feelings and mood when asked | In group work, participants shared ideas constructively and respectfully. Perspective-taking was required during activities of conveying the emotions of a character | **Yes:** Kevin followed de-escalation procedure and molded play-dough for a few minutes in a quiet space. Afterwards, he verbalized his emotions and asked to rejoin his group |
| Peace | Peace needs prompting to interact with peers by using a louder voice so that others can hear her speak. This withdrawn, quiet behavior often reflects feelings of low self-esteem | Peace will initiate positive interaction with peers by using direct eye contact and audible voice tone | The activities in the unit required dialoguing. Students practiced appropriate pragmatics and expression of ideas during decision-making; e.g., who should speak when, how to arrange a scene, etc. | **Yes:** Per videotape analysis, Peace audibly contributed ideas to her group, using eye contact, and initiating conversation |
| | Peace often demonstrates a flat affect and lethargy with minimal awareness of her surrounding environment | Peace will increase verbal and non-verbal expression of emotions when engaging in real or simulated situations | Tableau, role-play, and STW routines required identification and imagination of the emotions of characters and historical figures. Students used body language, poses, words, and/or sounds | **Yes:** Peace demonstrated a range of verbal and nonverbal expressions of emotion on perspective-taking activities |

| Briana | | | |
|---|---|---|---|
| Briana is easily distracted and requires external prompts to maintain focus on task | Briana will work steadily on a task for a 30-minute period without need for verbal prompts | Multiple modes of engagement offered throughout each AI lesson (observing peers, choice of activity, choice of leadership or follower role) | **Yes:** Briana maintained engagement, without prompts, for 30 minutes |
| Briana continues to have difficulty resolving conflict in a peaceful manner with peers when experiencing an emotionally charged situation | Briana will identify constructive ways to resolve conflicts in real and simulated situations | Conflicting opinions during group work in relation to decision-making about drama elements (tableau, scenes, etc.) | **Yes:** Briana assumed a leadership role to resolve peer conflicts and decreased the number of conflicts with peers |

**TABLE 6.10**  Linguistic Productivity through Total Number of Words Used

| Writing Context | Kevin no. of words | Peace no. of words | Briana no. of words |
|---|---|---|---|
| W1: decontextualized genre | 52 | 22 | 65 |
| W2: decontextualized letter | 69 | 59 | 89 |
| W3: contextualized in-role | 120 | 89 | 151 |

**TABLE 6.11**  Linguistic Specificity through Semantic Diversity

| Writing Context | Kevin % | Peace % | Briana % |
|---|---|---|---|
| W1: decontextualized genre | 50 | 40 | 65 |
| W2: decontextualized letter | 55 | 20 | 66 |
| W3: contextualized in-role | 70 | 65 | 70 |

phrases within each sentence) in each of their writing samples. Table 6.10 shows the number of words produced by each student across contextualized drama (W3) and decontextualized genre (W1) writing samples.

In terms of how much students wrote, all students showed significant increases from the conventional genre-based samples (W1 and W2) to the dramatic writing activity (W3). The number of words each student used in writing samples was more than double in the dramatic in-role letter written after the Civil War process drama intervention. Table 6.11 shows students' semantic diversity (number of different words/number of total words; Greenhalgh & Strong, 2001) across contextualized drama (W3) and decontextualized genre (W1) writing samples.

Across writing samples, students increased in their semantic diversity, or the number of different words as a proportion of the total number of words in their writing samples. The contextualized in-role writing activity yielded semantic diversity between 65 and 70% across students, as compared to decontextualized samples, in which students' vocabulary diversity was between 20 and 66%. When looking at the vocabulary used by students in the drama writing sample (W3), they were using the targeted knowledge-specific vocabulary that we had covered throughout our two-week intervention period, showing some degree of fluency and automaticity. Table 6.12 shows the rate of literate language features (LLFs) produced by each student across contextualized drama (W3) and decontextualized genre (W1) writing samples, as a more precise measure of linguistic specificity (Anderson, 2011).

Students' use of LLFs across drama and non-drama writing samples provided another measure of their linguistic specificity. The use of LLFs has been shown to mark linguistic specificity, beginning in early school age across children with

**TABLE 6.12** Linguistic Specificity through Literate Language Use

| Kevin | Context | ADV[a] | CONJ[b] | MLV[c] | SENP[d] | CENP[e] | LLF[f] |
|-------|---------|-----|------|-----|------|------|-----|
| | **W1**[g] | 0.23 | 0.77 | 0.38 | 0.31 | 0.54 | 2.23 |
| | **W2**[h] | 0.00 | 0.64 | 0.09 | 0.18 | 0.82 | 0.58 |
| | **W3**[i] | 0.00 | **0.81** | 0.29 | **0.69** | **0.85** | 2.06 |
| **Peace** | **Context** | **ADV** | **CONJ** | **MLV** | **SENP** | **CENP** | **LLF** |
| | **W1** | 0.12 | 0.53 | 0.47 | 0.71 | 0.35 | 2.18 |
| | **W2** | 0.00 | 0.48 | 0.16 | 0.48 | 0.32 | 1.44 |
| | **W3** | **0.13** | **0.57** | **0.48** | 0.33 | **0.60** | 2.00 |
| **Briana** | **Context** | **ADV** | **CONJ** | **MLV** | **SENP** | **CENP** | **LLF** |
| | **W1** | 0.00 | 0.82 | 0.36 | 0.45 | 0.45 | 2.09 |
| | **W2** | 0.00 | 0.42 | 0.08 | 0.58 | 0.58 | 1.67 |
| | **W3** | 0.00 | 0.74 | **0.38** | 0.48 | 0.58 | **2.50** |

Notes

Percentages are given in bold where they show the W3 exercise yielding the highest percentage of LLF usage from across the three tasks.

a  ADV: adverbs
b  CONJ: conjunctions
c  MLV: mental and linguistic verbs
d  SENP: simple elaborated noun phrases
e  CENP: complex elaborated noun phrases
f  LLF: literate language features in total
g  W1: decontextualized genre writing
h  W2: decontextualized letter writing
i  W3: contextualized in-role writing

and without language impairments (Anderson, 2011; Curenton & Justice, 2004). Literate language use is important as it is a marker of decontextualized language competence and has been identified as important for specificity and precision of communication (Anderson, 2011; Snow, 1991). As Table 6.12 indicates, individual students used more conjunctions (CONJ) to express relationships of cause, sequence, and/or time. The higher rate of adverb use (ADV), and simple and complex elaborated noun phrases (SENP and CENP, respectively) indicated that more elaboration and description was occurring in dramatic writing samples (W3) as compared to conventional writing activities (W1 and W2). Also, the increased use of mental and linguistic verbs (MLV) indicated that students understood and expressed feelings and motivations of characters in the Civil War.

## Cognitive Engagement

Evidence of students' cognitive engagement was gleaned from coding of each of the sentences in their writing samples on the six levels of Bloom's Taxonomy (Anderson & Krathwohl, 2000), ranging from the most basic level of processing

**TABLE 6.13** Students' Cognitive Engagement (Score out of 6) across Writing Samples

| Writing Context | Kevin | Peace | Briana |
|---|---|---|---|
| **W1: decontextualized genre** | 2.2 | 2 | 2.1 |
| **W2: decontextualized letter** | 2.5 | 3.2 | 2.7 |
| **W3: contextualized in-role** | 3.9 | 4 | 3.8 |

(remembering/knowledge) to the most advanced (creating/synthesis). An average rating for a whole sample was determined by creating a composite score for each sample consisting of the mean and standard deviation (SD). In all cases, the contextualized samples (W3) had higher averages than the decontextualized samples (W1 and W2), indicating higher cognitive levels of engagement in students' written language. To ensure inter-rater reliability, I assigned more stringent criteria for sentences within students' samples to fall within one SD of the mean among raters (see Table 6.13). The mean score for students' written language samples is reported in Table 6.13, with 1 indicating the lowest level of cognitive processing (recognition, recall) and 6 indicating the highest level of cognitive processing (analysis, synthesis, integration of ideas).

The results of this analysis indicate that students' writing samples in the dramatic in-role activity contained higher-level reasoning and evidence of cognitive processing, as compared to predominantly lower-order thinking skills expressed in W1 and W2.

## Summary and Conclusions

My students in general, and Kevin, Peace, and Briana in particular, lacked emotional connections to social studies content prior to the AI intervention. My plan was to strengthen my students' emotional connections to Civil War material through a sequence of process drama activities that enabled them to live and co-create the content. Setting the scene, writing the script, and portraying Civil War characters gave my students opportunities to create meaning from academic content. Because my students became the primary sources or the 'meaning makers,' our social studies content became more accessible, and it related directly to their expression of meaning. From this meaning-making, I observed that students' communicative intentions were clearer, both in socially mediated classroom discourse and as in their written expression on academic tasks. Creativity through drama integration gave my students with language limitations the opportunity to learn and use their new knowledge to challenge those limitations. In short, the results of my AI intervention unit indicated that my students' emotional engagement influenced their linguistic and cognitive engagement with the material.

## Voices from Research and Higher Education

This final part of the chapter presents the implications from Christina's demonstration of practice through the lens of higher education research and practice in AI and its allied disciplines of education, developmental psychology, special education, and linguistics. First, a summary of the demonstration of practice is presented, followed by the application of the AI practice to the engagement framework presented in Chapter 4. The final section considers research and practice implications through the lenses of critical literacy, authentic learning, and UDL.

### *Demonstration of Practice Summary*

This demonstration of practice took place over the course of two weeks, as the students learned about aspects of Civil War history through various forms of process drama. To measure the effectiveness of AI in her classroom, Christina compared writing samples of students throughout the unit and analyzed them for cognitive, linguistic, and affective engagement. The AI intervention unit consisted of five main activities that presented social studies content in an engaging way through student-centered drama supported by written responses. Scaffolded from small- to large-group involvement, students participated in dramatic activities such as tableau or thought-tracking to establish conceptions about the time period, developed empathy for self-created characters living in the time period, and completed written assignments assessing their comprehension of the unit.

Writing samples before and after the unit were analyzed for linguistic, cognitive, and affective engagement. Linguistic engagement was measured by counting the number of words in, or productivity of, each writing sample. Professionals judged the cognition of particular utterances in the writing samples on a scale of 1 to 6, 1 being simple recall and recognition and 6 being analysis, synthesis, and integration of ideas. To measure affective engagement, Christina filmed the students participating in the activities and observed particular behaviors such as time on task, eye contact, gesture, and on-task comments/questions. Three students were targeted for monitoring of the observed influence of the AI intervention on their affective, linguistic, and cognitive engagement during the study. The three students' semantic diversity and literate language use, written language productivity, and cognitive and affective engagement all consistently improved when students' written language was contextualized through process drama.

### *Theoretical Framework Questions Explained*

This section explores how Christina contextualized the social studies content; how contextualization through AI supported students' understanding and written language; and the role of social interaction in supporting students' comprehension and written expression. We also explore how students showed their affective and cognitive engagement over the course of the drama AI unit. This section considers the relationship between students' cognitive, affective, and linguistic engagement for students and asks whether one dimension of engagement drives the others (e.g., affective engagement drives cognitive and linguistic).

## Contextualization of language learning

Christina created an AI unit intended to bridge the gap between students' use of casual, contextualized language and the more formal, decontextualized language of the social studies curriculum. Through process drama activities, she contextualized the Civil War content by tying it to the students' immediate environment. Students progressed from simple observation and discussion based on photographs of the time period, to theorizing about and making connections between the photographs and the larger historical context, to constructing and physically representing their ideas in dramatic tableaux. Each step augmented students' affective, cognitive, and linguistic engagement with the material through emotion, oral expression, interpretation, and physical demonstration, all of which enabled students to form more comprehensive understandings of the events of the Civil War.

Students' linguistic engagement was enhanced by bridging the gap between contextualized and decontextualized language. Process drama activities provided the context for students to use decontextualized, content-specific vocabulary in group settings, in order to create tableaux. After two weeks of 'living' the Civil War through the process drama activities, students' oral and written language referenced the people, actions, and objects of the 1860s. Connecting process drama to academic content comprehension was particularly effective by way of written assignments, which are typically regarded as highly literate. Students' initial writing assignments about their photographs and tableaux served as scaffolds for their final in-role letters, as did their experiences during process drama exercises. The activity of the final week, writing letters in role (W3), incorporated the two forms of language. Literacy activities required the formality of decontextualized, content-specific language use, along with contextualized dialogue and familiarity with the social studies material that had been gained through AI. Christina's findings indicated that contextualization increased comprehension and engagement, which facilitated students' use of specific vocabulary, which in turn increased the quality of students' content-based writing.

## Influences on cognitive and affective engagement

The arts (drama especially) require close collaboration; this became one of the most apparent aspects of the students' affective engagement in the AI intervention unit. Other than written assignments, little individual work occurred throughout the process drama unit. Class discussion and group collaboration activities required students to orally question, organize, reinforce, and construct criticism of ideas with their peers to effectively complete their tableaux.

Also, process drama provided the opportunity for students to physically communicate their engagement when they "practiced maintaining focus, experimented with body language, and developed self-control through sustained silence" during the tableau activities. Particularly significant for the three targeted students was reduced disruptive behavior and increased prosocial behavior during the intervention. Another sign of students' affective engagement was their increased ability to visualize, design, and create environments in which their scenes were staged by placing objects around the room. Finally, the freedom and creativity inherent in the process drama activities allowed students to thoroughly explore, experiment with, and finally demonstrate concepts, vocabulary, causal relationships, and personal connections to the material without the pressure of producing a written product. Students had ample exposure to the material and their own reactions before being asked to express those ideas either orally or in writing.

## Relationships between cognitive, linguistic, and affective engagement

It is possible that affective engagement led to cognitive and linguistic engagement in this AI intervention. In other words, students needed to want to learn, and then try to learn (i.e., cognate), which lead to either the products or byproducts of linguistic engagement (wider vocabulary, complex and specific expression, etc.). Christina acknowledged her students' lack of background knowledge, and specifically pointed to an absence of emotional engagement as the cause of students' inability to cognate on academic content. It was not until Christina was able to 'hook' students through dramatic contextualization that they showed positive outcomes. Process drama was chosen for its ability to provide enticing affective engagement. Once students experienced this form of engagement, their cognitive and linguistic engagement seemed to follow, as evidenced in Christina's findings.

The linguistic productivity and specificity of students' final letters written in-role required higher-level thinking skills. Christina's opportunity to contextualize the language in the AI setting may have been a scaffold for students to use semantically diverse language and literate language features in their written expression. Also, students' cognitive processing around the events and characters of the Civil War supported them to be linguistically engaged, both in group discussions and activities as well as in individual written language tasks.

Other activities served the purpose of channeling students' affective engagement toward cognitive and linguistic engagement. Some of the intervention activities were designed primarily to engage students' interest and emotion; this type of engagement with the process drama activities may not have led to cognitive engagement if students had not been asked to reflect upon it afterwards in linguistic (oral and written) thought-tracking activities. Students' interest and emotion seemed to have been piqued during their initial analysis of the Civil War photographs; it was maximized and directed toward cognitive and linguistic engagement by directing them to share ideas with a classmate and then to write a brief reaction to the photograph. It has been shown that arts integration increases engagement because of the level of active learning that occurs during arts-based activities, as shown by Abedin (2010) and Spence-Browne (2007). One part of this engagement is affective, accessing the emotional and behavioral attributes students possess such as perseverance and overall general effort. Christina contended that her fifth graders' content comprehension increased because they were able to emotionally engage with it. Students with disabilities often struggle to produce language that is specific and precise in academic settings; they may also display emotional and/or behavioral issues that impact upon their affective engagement. Students who have not succeeded academically in the past would have much lower self-efficacy than their general education counterparts and, therefore, a declining motivation to learn. By developing a plan of instruction that was both social and interactive, Christina visually, kinesthetically, physically, and emotionally contextualized their learning, and supported her students with language-based LD and EBD to participate and progress in an inclusive educational setting.

## Quality of Scholarship and Thinking around Research and Practice Contribution

This section considers the quality of the scholarship and thinking around the contributions of Christina's demonstration to AI research and practice. In particular, we consider the connections to critical literacy, authentic learning, and UDL.

### Connections to critical literacy

Christina's AI demonstration reflects current and important research and practice in education, specifically in the area of critical literacy. Freire (1970) describes critical literacy as a pedagogy that co-constructs meaning, with readers as active agents "producing and acting upon their own ideas – not consuming those of others" (p. 108). It invites readers to move beyond passively accepting the text's message to question, examine, or dispute the power relations that exist between readers and authors (Comber, 2001; Vasquez, 2010). Critical literacy focuses on issues of power and promotes reflection, transformation, and action (Freire, 1970). Arts integration specifically relates to the practice of critical literacy because of the active engagement of students in the reading of content. One example of critical literacy from Christina's AI practice was when she provided students a telegram that was based on actual letters and correspondence during the Civil War era. Even though the telegram provided useful background information on its own, students were then instructed to create tableaux illustrating how their character would react to the telegram, and then justify their tableau to the class. Such engagement removed the barrier between the reader and author, especially when the students were instructed next to write their own letter through the lens of their character. Such an approach demonstrates critical literacy because students were empowered to be their own creators of knowledge, rather than passively taking in the content from a textbook or another source.

## Authenticity and learning standards

Christina's intervention demonstrates the practices of authentic learning and learning of content standards simultaneously. Authentic learning involves real-world applications of the desired skills (Moore, 2012). Authentic learning extends the question of whether a student understands the content to what their real-life takeaways will be. In Christina's AI unit, her class showed empathy with the time-period-specific struggles of individuals on the battlefield or on the home front during the Civil War. Students' real-world understandings could then be extrapolated to their understandings of the social studies content standards on a deeper level than would have otherwise been possible. Students demonstrated cause–effect reasoning in relation to the events of the Civil War, both when they were asked to write about specific historical events at the beginning of the unit, and when they had to develop their own tableaux based on previous events. Through these cause–effect learning experiences, they reached the school district's social studies standard of "summarize[ing] the causes and consequences of the Civil War." At the same time, students placed themselves into the mindsets of their characters, which helped them individually to understand causes and consequences on a personal level.

The intervention also demonstrated students' authentic learning through their willingness to participate in both tableau activities and discussions that followed. Students showed cognitive and affective engagement with their characters through acting out scenes and tableaux, meeting Standard 2 of the National Standards for Theater, Grades 5–8 (John F. Kennedy Center for the Performing Arts, 2014). Further, students' understanding of an object's relevance and its placement in their tableau showed their mastery of Standard 3 of the National Standards for Theater, "designing … by developing environments for improvised and scripted scenes" (John F. Kennedy Center for the Performing Arts, 2014).

## Universal Design for Learning

Using process drama engaged students through the use of Multiple Intelligences, as described by Gardner (1983). Students with language- and sensory-based processing disorders (e.g., LD, ASD) may not engage with conventional activities that require linguistic intelligence (Greenspan, Wieder, & Simon, 1998). Process drama integrates intelligences such as bodily-kinesthetic, interpersonal, intrapersonal, linguistic, and spatial. Christina's use of multiple intelligences also aligns with UDL through her use of multiple means of representation by presenting content through verbal communication and photographs. Multiple means of engagement were incorporated through active portrayal of characters, reading documents, and designing sets. Students used multiple means of action and expression, such as collaborative post-tableau thought-tracking, reflective writing, and abstract reasoning about causes and effects to convey thoughts and ideas about the Civil War social studies content.

## Barriers and Facilitators

Barriers to the intervention might have included the overreliance on visual or kinesthetic approaches, especially for students who were more accustomed to verbal-linguistic learning approaches. It is also possible that the process drama activities may have distracted some students from learning the social studies content if they were unable to integrate the drama and social studies content. Christina might have over-contextualized the social studies content in a way that prevented students from working independently using decontextualized language. Further, we do not know the extent to which students' experiences in contextualized written language might generalize to more standard and typical writing assessments. However, the creativity inherent in this AI intervention coupled with evidence of students' learning of content knowledge indicates students' affective, cognitive, and linguistic engagement throughout the intervention.

Also noteworthy in relation to the strength of this demonstration was that through collaboration, students developed communication skills that could support their learning and development of concepts later on in their education. Christina tapped into an art form that the students clearly connected with, and because of this the content became more accessible. Christina noted other challenges in maintaining focus during highly stimulating and relatively unstructured activities, as well as the challenge of collecting data on students' behavioral engagement, which limited her sample size. Nevertheless, Christina's AI demonstration of practice in her social studies classroom demonstrated various poignant elements of special and general education, such as the importance of contextualization, the importance of all forms of engagement, authentic learning, and UDL. Each of these components reflects the goals that every student should have ample opportunity to (1) meaningfully engage in and (2) authentically demonstrate understanding of their content learning. As demonstrated by Christina's intervention, AI is a key factor in contextualizing the academic content so that these goals can be possible.

## References

Abedin, G. (2010). *Exploring the potential benefits of arts-based education for adolescents with learning disabilities: A case study of engagement in learning through the arts* (Unpublished doctoral dissertation). University of Maryland, College Park.

Anderson, A. (2011). Linguistic specificity through literate language use in preschool-age children with specific language impairment and typical language. *Child Language Teaching and Therapy*, 27(1), 109–123.

Anderson, L. W., & Krathwohl, D. R. (Eds.). (2000). *A taxonomy for learning, teaching, and assessing: A revision of Bloom's Taxonomy of educational objectives.* New York: Allyn & Bacon.

Bloom, B. S. (1956). *Taxonomy of educational objectives: The classification of educational goals.* New York: Longman.

Bruner, J. S. (1966). *Toward a theory of instruction.* Cambridge, MA: Belknap Press of Harvard University Press.

CAST. (2011). *Universal Design for Learning Guidelines version 2.0.* Wakefield, MA: CAST. Retrieved from http://www.udlcenter.org/aboutudl/udlguidelines/principle1

Comber, B. (2001). Negotiating critical literacies. *School Talk*, 6(3), 1–2.

Cornett, C. (2011). *Creating meaning through literature and the arts: Arts integration for classroom teachers.* Boston: Pearson.

Cruz, J. X. R. (2009). Stepping into America: An educator's journey to the intersection of special education and the arts. *Teaching Artist Journal*, 7(3), 145–154.

Curenton, S. M., & Justice, L. (2004). African American and Caucasian preschoolers' use of decontextualized language: Use of literate language features in oral narratives. *Language, Speech, and Hearing Services in the Schools*, 35, 240–253.

Dewey, J. (1934). *Art as experience.* New York: Minton, Balch & Company.

District of Columbia Public Schools. (2011). *Social studies: U.S. history and geography: Growth and conflict: Grade 5.* Retrieved from http://dc.gov/DCPS/Files/downloads/In-the-Classroom/5th%20SS%20standards.pdf

Dunson, S. L., Jr. (2000). *The cultivators.* Oil on canvas. The Kinsey Collection.

Ferreti, R. P., MacArther, C. A., & Okolo, C. M. (2007). Students' misconceptions about U.S. westward migration. *Journal of Learning Disabilities*, 40(2), 145–153.

Freire, P. (1970). *Pedagogy of the oppressed.* New York: Herder and Herder.

Gardner, H. (1983). *Frames of mind: The theory of multiple intelligences.* New York: Basic Books.

Greenhalgh, K. S., & Strong, C. J. (2001). Literate language features in spoken narratives of children with typical language and children with language impairments. *Language, Speech, and Hearing Services in Schools*, 32, 114–125.

Greenspan, S. I., Wieder, S., & Simons, R. (1998). *The child with special needs: Encouraging intellectual and emotional growth.* Reading, MA: Addison-Wesley Longman.

Groves, P. (2002). "Doesn't it feel morbid here?" High-stakes testing and the widening of the equity gap. *Journal of Educational Foundations*, 16(2), 15–31.

Harvard Project Zero. (n.d.). *Artful thinking.* Retrieved March 27, 2014 from http://www.pzartfulthinking.org/see_think_wonder.php

Heathcote, D., & Herbert, P. (1985). A drama of learning: Mantle of the expert. *Theory into Practice*, 24(3), 173–180.

John F. Kennedy Center for the Performing Arts. (2014). *ArtsEdge: Arts standards by art form: Theater standards and achievement standards.* Retrieved from http://artsedge.kennedy-center.org/educators/standards/national/arts-standards/collections/by-art-form/theater-standards.aspx

Krakaur, L. (2005). *Using process drama to engage minority students to read for meaning* (Master's dissertation). Trinity College, Dublin, Ireland.

Ladson-Billings, G. J. (1995). Toward a theory of culturally relevant pedagogy. *American Education Research Journal*, 35(3), 465–491.

Lemke, J. L. (1990). *Talking science: Language, learning, and values*. Westport, CT: Ablex Publishing Corporation.

Levstik, L. S., & Barton, K. C. (1996). "They still use some of their past": Historical salience in elementary children's chronological thinking. *Journal of Curriculum Studies*, 28(5), 531–576.

Moore, K. (2012). *Effective instructional strategies: From theory to practice*. Los Angeles: Sage.

Neelands, J. (1998). *Beginning drama 11–14*. London: David Fulton Publications.

O'Neill, C. (1985). Imagined worlds in theatre and drama. *Theory into Practice*, 24(3), 158–165.

Rogers, T., & O'Neill, C. (1993). Creating multiple worlds: Drama, language, and literary response. In G. E. Newell & R. R. Durst (Eds.), *Exploring texts* (pp. 69–89). Norwood, MA: Christopher-Gordon.

Rosler, B. (2008). Process drama in one fifth-grade social studies class. *Social Studies*, 99(6), 265–272.

Schneider, J. J., & Jackson, S. A. W. (2000). Process drama: A special space and place for writing. *Reading Teacher*, 54(1), 38–51.

Smith, S. (2001). *The power of the arts: Creative strategies for teaching exceptional learners*. Baltimore: Paul H. Brookes.

Snow, C. E. (1991). The theoretical basis for the relationships between language and literacy in development. *Journal of Research in Childhood Education*, 6, 5–10.

Spence-Brown, R. (2007). Learner motivation and engagement in a pedagogic and assessment task: Insights from activity theory. In H. Marriott, T. Moore, & R. Spence-Brown (Eds.), *Learning discourses and the discourses of learning* (pp. 12.1–12.15). Melbourne: Monash University ePress.

Vasquez, V. (2010). *Getting beyond "I like the book": Creating space for critical literacy in K-6 classrooms*. Newark, DE: International Reading Association.

# 7

# DANCE/MOVEMENT ARTS INTEGRATION AND MATHEMATICS

## Influences on Engagement

*Robyne Davis and Alida Anderson*

## Introduction

Robyne Davis is a Master's-degree-level dance/movement therapist and counselor of students with language, sensory, emotional, and behavioral disabilities. In 2010, she was a counselor at ARTS Public Charter School (PCS), and embarked on a professional development program at a local university to design and implement arts-integrated lessons for students with and without disabilities in her therapeutic settings.

Robyne's caseload of students had learning difficulties relating to reading decoding and comprehension, as well as written language. Robyne's students performed significantly (more than two years) below their grade level in conventional literacy skills, such as reading fluency, comprehension, and written language (spelling, mechanics, fluency, and semantic diversity), similar to Kristin's and Christina's students. As a result, most of these students had problems accessing information through written text and with expressing ideas through written language. In the mathematics classroom, these language-based difficulties translated into problems mastering the specialized vocabulary, understanding textbook examples, and comprehending explanations.

In addition to students' language-based learning challenges, most of Robyne's students had diagnoses or displayed characteristics of attention deficit disorder and attention deficit hyperactivity disorder (ADD/ADHD). Students with ADD/ADHD have difficulties with sequencing, organizing information, and following procedures, which have significant consequences in math. Students with these symptoms find it difficult to follow multi-step instructions, whether given by the teacher, presented in the textbook, or demonstrated in the lesson. The mission of ARTS PCS was "to provide students with multiple learning styles with a high-quality, arts-infused education," which resonated with Robyne's background training and experience as a dancer. Robyne developed and implemented a combined mathematics and behavioral intervention targeting self-regulation through Dance/Movement Therapy (DMT). Her guiding research question asked: *How does the use of DMT in the inclusive classroom setting contribute to students' learning of mathematics, social-emotional, and dance/movement skills?*

Using a combination of survey, conferencing, work sampling, observational, and interview methods with students and colleagues, Robyne created a DMT arts-integrated unit that covered movement sequences and vocabulary, as well as mathematics concepts and procedures related to students' Individualized Education Program (IEP) goals.

## Dance/Movement and Mathematics: Robyne Davis

As a dance/movement therapist and licensed professional counselor at ARTS PCS, I had the opportunity to provide counseling services in and out of the classroom to students with special needs in grades K–8. During these sessions, I saw at first hand the healing power of the creative arts as my students began to make positive changes, both academically and emotionally. I decided to focus my arts integration (AI) demonstration of practice with sixth- and seventh-grade students and their teacher in an afternoon mathematics class, due to students' social, emotional, and academic difficulties. My students had one of three types of ADD/ADHD, including: (1) predominantly inattentive type (e.g., inability to sustain task or other activities, to remember to follow through on rules and instructions, and/or to resist distractions while doing so); (2) predominantly hyperactive-impulsive type (e.g., fidgets with hands or feet; squirms in seat; often leaves seat in the classroom; talks excessively; has difficulty waiting for a turn); and (3) combined inattentive-hyperactive type (Barkley, 2003).

When working with my students who showed impulsive, hyperactive, and inattentive behavior, it became clear to me that learning through conventional, verbally based seatwork activities was a challenge. One of the biggest obstacles in the classroom was the students' difficulty focusing on tasks and staying engaged throughout hour-long class periods. In addition to students' hyperactivity and distractibility, they showed low frustration tolerance and poor self-regulation (e.g., following multi-step directions, focusing and identifying necessary skills for task completion) throughout most academic tasks. Understandably, these students experience social-emotional stress, since:

> Kids who can't seem to operate their minds to meet expectations feel terrible about themselves, while their perplexed parents understandably lose sleep over their child who reads with little understanding or has trouble making friends or is out of focus in school.
>
> *(Levine, 2002, p. 14)*

## *Why Arts Integration?*

When I asked my students why they were constantly moving and fidgeting, they seemed to lack self-awareness and responded, "I don't know." They did not seem to understand the powerful connection between body, mind, and spirit. Physical activity has been shown to stimulate mental activity and to engage the connection between mind and body (Barringer, Pohlman, & Robinson, 2010). It was this revelation that sparked my interest in AI with these students. My premise was that using dance in AI would help students to become more aware of how to control their bodies, and subsequently become better able to control their thought processes. I thought that my dance/movement AI approach would help students to find their unique voices within the classroom setting. Arts integration is generally defined as the linking of a content area and an art form for the purposes of reaching a deeper level of engagement, learning, and reflection than without the art form (Anderson, 2012). In an AI classroom, students are working with and through the art form to reach academic, social, and personal goals (Cornett, 2011).

The Individuals with Disabilities Education Act (IDEA, 2004) ensures that students with exceptionalities receive a free and appropriate public education in the least restrictive environment. Depending on an individual student's needs, the inclusive classroom setting may be appropriate depending on how the teacher structures the learning environment. Our school's inclusive classrooms were comprised of students who learned in a variety of ways and were functioning on a variety of levels that challenged teachers to meet the needs of every student within the classroom. I thought that AI would help to level the playing field by providing multiple accessible learning opportunities for students simultaneously, empowering both the students and teachers.

Arts integration aligns with the Universal Design for Learning (UDL; CAST, 2011) guidelines intended to help teachers meet the challenges of instructing diverse learners. The UDL guidelines identify three main principles in designing lesson plans for students with varying learning needs through multiple means of (1) representation, (2) action and expression, and (3) engagement. Universal Design for Learning and AI philosophies are similar (see Anderson, this volume, Chapter 2, for a discussion) in that they rely on a holistic perspective on the student; and they promote the idea that individuals have the capacity to learn when they can access their unique strengths, predispositions, and communication styles. I thought that an AI dance/movement intervention could enable students to use movement to symbolize or represent concepts and ideas. Also, students might use movement exercises as a form of body action and as a way to express their inner feelings. Further, I thought my students would be more likely to stay engaged in our activity as they interacted with peers and became attuned to their own movement responses. Self-awareness and self-regulation skills are crucial for students with ADD/ADHD (Barkley, 1997; Harris, Reid, & Graham, 2004), and have been shown to be fostered through UDL (Katz, 2013). Students are more likely to be affectively engaged when they are self-regulating through their individual means of representations and expressions. In short, I used UDL principles to help my students develop personal coping skills and strategies through multiple means of expression and representation.

## Problems and Goals

My demonstration of practice began with a question: *How will the use of dance in the classroom setting impact the engagement and self-regulation of students with symptoms of ADHD?* After consistently observing my students with ADD/ADHD struggle to maintain their personal space, body control, impulse control, focus, and attention span during a 60-minute class period, I wanted to find an approach that would help them develop self-awareness and control over their mental and physical states.

Attention requires mental energy control, which regulates initiation and maintenance of cognitive energy flow for learning, work, and behavioral control (Barringer et al., 2010). Studies have found a link between executive dysfunction and disorders of behavioral control, attention, and judgment such as ADD/ADHD (Lyon 1996; Naglieri, 2003, as cited in Tomporowski, Davis, Miller, & Naglieri, 2008). Davis and colleagues (2001) found that physical exercise generated an improvement in executive function skills such as planning, monitoring, and regulating behavior. Dance/Movement Therapy (DMT) provides several benefits in addition to physical exercise, as it is designed to heighten awareness of the body, and to help participants become fully conscious of the relationship between their physical and emotional state. In therapy, this leads to increased awareness of the inner conditions that manifest in the body.

In addition to my students' characteristic symptoms of inattention, hyperactivity, and impulsivity, they had problems with body tension, disturbed body image, and fragmented movement patterns (Gronlund, Renck, & Weibull, 2005). For students with ADD/ADHD symptoms, DMT helps them to release tension through increased experiences connecting the body and mind. During a movement sequence, participants may regulate their breathing, move in unison with a defined rhythm, and develop internal organization skills by transitioning from one movement phrase to the next. In one study conducted in an urban public school setting, teachers reported that DMT was associated with a reduction or maintenance of ADD/ADHD symptoms in their students (Redman, 2007).

From a social perspective, the majority of the students in my classroom had social-emotional issues. They appeared unaware of one another's personal space and often intruded without awareness of how their actions might impact others. Students' social conflicts often led to negative name-calling and defensive behavior. Also, students' impulsive behaviors impacted their teacher. For instance, students called out spontaneously while the teacher was talking, preventing the teacher from completing a thought or concept. Based on previous experience, I thought that DMT would help my students to build connections between their body and mind, which would support their increased self-awareness and awareness of others in their community.

In order to address my students' current levels of academic and social-emotional functioning within the DMT intervention, I needed to consider how to integrate their IEP goals in mathematics as follows:

1. To recall basic multiplication facts and related division facts.
2. To complete 2- to 3-step problems using addition, subtraction and multiplication.
3. To add and subtract single-digit numbers using manipulatives.
4. To select and use appropriate operations to solve addition, subtraction, multiplication, and division problems with and without regrouping.

Out of my 14 students, nine had counseling goals on their IEPs, including:

1. To demonstrate the difference between impulsive and self-controlled behavior.
2. To ignore distractions while completing work for a 30-minute period.
3. To identify three signs of frustration and practice self-regulation skills.
4. To work steadily with attention focused on task.
5. To practice positive coping skills to reduce anxiety and stress.
6. To accept responsibility for one's own behaviors.
7. To increase ability to express emotions appropriately.
8. To increase awareness of personal space in relation to others.

With students' IEP objectives in mind, I outlined the mathematics, dance/movement arts, and counseling learning objectives. The objectives and grade-level standards provided a foundation to planning my lessons over the four-week intervention period (see Table 7.1). Based on these goals, I created a three-part movement sequence intended to foster students' increased organization of thought, motor sequencing, gross motor coordination, and emotional self-regulation.

## Designing My AI Intervention Unit

Based on my students' shared goals and objectives across their IEPs, I selected dance/movement as the art form to support students' focus and attention during mathematics classes. The class I selected for the intervention was ideal since nine of the 14 students received special education and the majority exhibited symptoms of ADHD on a daily basis. Our class met during the last period of the day, when students' ADHD symptoms were often at their most severe. Students with ADHD have been reported to demonstrate difficulties with gross and fine motor coordination, motor sequencing, effort allocation, and emotional self-regulation,

**TABLE 7.1** Content Area Standards across Mathematics, Dance/Movement, and Social-Emotional Domains

| Content Area | Standards Addressed during Intervention Period |
| --- | --- |
| Mathematics | 1. To learn basic multiplication skills<br>2. To learn to write dimensional arrays<br>3. To learn to write the area of rectangular shapes |
| Dance/Movement | 1. To apply breath support, initiation of movement, connectivity and transition from one movement to another in performing short phrases<br>2. To identify and demonstrate concentration and focus in dance<br>3. To discuss and explore the concept of personal and general space |
| Social-Emotional | 1. To demonstrate how effort and persistence positively affect learning<br>2. To take responsibility for one's actions<br>3. To understand the need for self-control and practice it |
| Connected Dance/<br>Movement and<br>Mathematics Objectives | 1. To practice self-control by exploring polarities of movement efforts<br>2. To kinesthetically connect math concepts, such as arrays, with personal space<br>3. To increase regulation skills and motivational effort through the use of internal breath work<br>4. To take responsibility for one's actions<br>5. To reduce hyperactivity through body awareness |

Note

Adapted from American School Counselor Association, 2004; Arizona Department of Education, 2006; District of Columbia Public Schools, 2011.

such that their "performance is worse later in the day, when they attempt greater task complexity such that organizational strategies are required and when restraint is demanded" (Barkley, 2003, p. 79).

Additionally, the students were familiar with the concept of movement since the mathematics teachers had already implemented a movement break midway through the period. Most importantly, the teachers were supportive of my use of DMT with the students. Students' social and academic challenges, as well as the teachers' support of my work with this group of students during their math class, created an environment that was well suited to the aim of my AI practice.

The movement combinations I developed to meet the class's unit goals were based on Laban Movement Analysis (LMA; Laban, 1956). Rudolf Laban, a famous choreographer and dancer, created a systematic way of notating expressive movement through *Effort*. Laban developed the concept of Effort as a continuum of "attitudes toward the exertion of energy in flow, space, weight and time. Each move [is] a way of coping [and] has an almost infinite range of possibility from minute to extreme of effectiveness and involvement" (Bartenieff & Lewis, 1980, p. xiii). I hypothesized that when students explored a variety of Effort qualities, they would become more fully engaged on a cognitive, physical, and social-emotional level during the AI lessons. Bartenieff and Lewis (1980) described the use of Effort elements, in support of my hypothesis:

> Choices are continuously being made by all people in motion, consciously or unconsciously, to determine what combinations of Effort elements will best serve the purposes of their intents or modify their behavior. Whatever the action in which the Effort combinations appear ... the whole biological/psychological system is involved.
>
> *(p. 57)*

The first step in the movement combination focused on Weight Effort, one of eight Efforts that are expressed on a continuum (see Table 7.2). Effort elements are described as expressions of the inner state of mind that prepare the mover for a sequence (Laban, 1956, as cited in Bartenieff & Lewis, 1980). Weight Effort defines the mover's intention by creating a strong or light impact. Students were taught to rise and fall within the vertical plane, using Light and Strong Efforts, while asking themselves, "What is my impact?" (Bartenieff & Lewis, 1980, p. 53).

The second step of the movement sequence encouraged students to widen and narrow their movements within the horizontal plane, using sustained and quick Time Efforts. Time Effort is defined as the mover's ability to make decisions about movement by employing a sense of urgency or non-urgency. During this step, students asked, "When do I need to complete the act?" The third step focused on Space Effort, which is defined as the mover's attention and orientation and is described as either direct or indirect. Students were instructed to ask, "How do I approach the space?" (Bartenieff & Lewis, 1980, p. 53).

Throughout the movement combination, students were encouraged to primarily use Free Flow Effort with smaller moments of Bound Flow Effort. Flow Effort is described as how the movement is initiated, and how it is sustained. During Flow Effort, students asked themselves the question, "How do I keep the movement going?" It is important to note that all of the Effort elements fluctuate along a continuum, as seen in Table 7.2.

I introduced our first movement sequence at the beginning of the math class for a two-week period and asked the entire class to participate. Before beginning the first movement sequence, we rearranged the classroom space. When entering the classroom, students picked up a yoga mat, a concrete representation of personal space (theirs and others'). The mat helped students to visualize moving within their kinesphere, a general term used to describe personal space. One's physical kinesphere is defined by the depth, width, and length of the body.

Next, I taught the students dance-related vocabulary to provide verbal support for expressing the nonverbal experience of modulating between Effort movement

**TABLE 7.2** Effort Elements Continuum

| *Effort Elements* | | |
| --- | --- | --- |
| Space | Indirect | Direct |
| Weight | Light | Strong |
| Time | Sustained | Sudden |
| Flow | Free | Bound |

Note
Adapted from Bartenieff & Lewis, 1980, p. 51.

qualities within their bodies. This dance vocabulary was created by Laban (1956) and is part of LMA. After we discussed using Effort qualities, we played music to accompany the dance/movement experience and provide a rhythmic structure. The short three-part movement sequence was designed to promote body awareness and self-regulation. It began with students slowly rolling their heads, then rotating their shoulders, and finally taking a deep breath inhaling (arms rising) and exhaling (arms lowering). This beginning step of the movement sequence was intended to foster students' self-regulation. The movement qualities of Sustained Time and Free Flow were intended to foster self-control in the next two movement components. All three parts of the movement sequence incorporated body awareness techniques to promote students' self-awareness of tension held throughout their bodies.

Dance/Movement Therapy was incorporated in three additional activities to support the math content objectives directly. The next movement activity in the DMT intervention reinforced basic multiplication skills while finding the area of a shape. The math teacher and I co-taught these concepts using physical movement, with an emphasis on students' applying their personal space by using their own bodies as arrays. To find the dimensions of students' kinesphere or personal space, they worked in pairs to measure and record the lengths of their torsos, from head to hip, and the widths of their arm spans, from fingertip to fingertip. The students then multiplied the length times the width to find the area of their kinesphere.

The intervention's second activity focused on writing the dimensions of arrays using a hopscotch grid as an array that I made with floor tape. Students were encouraged to move inside the array, hopping from square to square, while multiplying aloud. Next, students drew arrays on graph paper to practice finding the area (by multiplying the length by width) and writing the array as an equation. Finally, I drew a volleyball court with floor tape to reinforce several aspects of the DMT intervention. Students moved within the volleyball court to show understanding of the mathematical concepts, exemplifying the use of physical activity to enhance cognitive activity. As students moved, they maintained their personal space within individual squares, which supported their self-regulation and body control. Finally, students reinforced their computational skills by counting the total number of squares in the volleyball court, as well as multiplying the length and width of the court.

## My Action Research Method

The initial data sources I used to establish a baseline for my students included their IEPs, weekly related services notes, quarterly progress reports, and classroom observations. My documentation and interaction with the students throughout the year provided a baseline for their behavior and helped me to decide which students on my counseling caseload would benefit most from my DMT AI intervention. The types of data I collected throughout the intervention period included classroom observations, work samples, interviews, surveys, and written reflections.

### Observations

I designed a simple system for measuring student participation and behavioral engagement in the intervention. I used a plus sign to indicate a high level of participation, on-task behavior, and ability to follow directions; a minus sign indicated minimal to no participation, off-task behavior, and difficulty following directions. This system allowed me to track and assess levels of individual and group involvement following each class period throughout the project.

### Work Samples

Assignments and quizzes provided quantitative data regarding students' achievement of mathematics objectives and DMT vocabulary. I collected these samples before, during, and after the DMT–mathematics integrated activities. Also, I gathered reports from the students and teachers to assess students' demonstration of the mathematics, social-emotional, dance/movement arts, and connected learning objectives (see Table 7.1). Each student and the teachers were asked to reflect on the student's performance on the arts-based standards addressed during the intervention and on achievement of social-emotional/behavioral skills such as attention, focus, concentration, hyperactivity, impulsivity, and distractibility.

### Interviews, Surveys, and Written Reflections

I assessed students' progress on dance/movement and social-emotional objectives through individual interviews and written reflections. In order to support students' understanding, use, and integration of kinesthetic learning and dance/movement vocabulary, they practiced using terminology throughout movement sequences and DMT–mathematics integrated lessons. At the end of each lesson, students completed a DMT vocabulary worksheet on: (1) the movement efforts they used that day, (2) the range of personal space used, and (3) the shape-flow made by their bodies. The worksheet also provided space for students to share their thoughts and/or feelings about the movement experience.

## Findings

### Observations

I compiled field notes from my observations focused on student participation levels and on-task behavior (e.g., following directions). Over the course of the month-long DMT intervention, all students showed increased participation and on-task behavior during both DMT and mathematics activities. Results from the first week of the intervention ranged from 0 to 57% participation, with the majority of the students (8/14) not participating actively or consistently. By the second week, participation increased to an average of 64% and by the end of the intervention, 86% of the class (12/14) was demonstrating increased participation in DMT–mathematics activities. It seemed that the students' practice of the modulation of Effort qualities through the DMT intervention improved their ability for self-control through reduced physical tension and increased body awareness. Also, students showed their increased spatial and social awareness through improved understanding of their personal kinesphere, which contributed to increased self-regulation (i.e., longer attention span).

### Understanding and Engagement: Week One

On the first day, I observed students walking over one another's mats without thinking or self-awareness, and fighting over the same mat even though there were enough for each student. Overall, only half of the students focused and followed through with the movement sequence before the math lesson. The following day, the transition from movement to math was much smoother. This orderly transition, as well as a better understanding of expectations, seemed to aid students' participation in the movement activity. Students remained in their seats longer, appeared less fidgety, and some focused for a longer period after the dance/movement sequence was completed. By the end of the first week, teachers and students recognized the shift in attention span and self-regulation. One classroom teacher noticed how quiet the room was when the students were moving their bodies slowly through space. Another teacher commented that students were more focused and showed increased attention span during the academic portion of the class.

### Understanding and Engagement: Week Two

The most significant part of this study took place during the second week. A natural succession of students began to take turns leading the movement sequences, without any suggestion on my part. As leaders of their class, they embodied the dance objectives, which were applying breath support, initiation of movement, and connecting one movement phrase to another. They were able to identify and demonstrate concentration and focus in dance, as well as explore the concept of personal and general space. In the past, these student leaders had received several behavioral referrals and had been extremely disruptive to the rest of the class. However, instead of negatively influencing their peers, they were full participants and positively engaged the entire class in the AI lessons. "The arts transform how learners are perceived by others. Arts integration consistently reveals unrecognized abilities in learners formerly perceived as a problem by teachers and other students" (Burnaford, Aprill, & Weiss, 2001).

## Understanding and Engagement: Weeks Three and Four

During the final weeks of the intervention, the majority of the students continued to assume leadership roles in the movement sequences before, during, and after mathematics lessons. Thirteen of the 14 students volunteered to select music for the movement sequences and their choices changed the quality of Effort required. Also, they were able to use the LMA vocabulary with their peers and teachers. Students enthusiastically participated in the AI lessons and requested additional DMT-integrated activities outside of class. Students reported using DMT techniques to manage feelings of hyperactivity or impulsivity while sitting down in their seats and without drawing attention to themselves. Students reported that they felt most interested in the academic work that involved dance/movement.

## Linguistic Engagement through Work Samples

The academic focus of the study was on mathematics learning; however, my students showed improvement in their understanding and use of oral and written language to convey their thoughts and feelings about the DMT intervention. Students' surveys and self-reflections showed their understanding of attention and effort required to stay alert on both physical and cognitive levels. Students' performance on vocabulary worksheets showed their increased understanding and use of DMT- and mathematics-specific vocabulary associated with activities. Through students' use of dance/movement vocabulary, they were able to describe and elaborate on their experiences and use more specific verbs to describe their feelings. Some of the comments noted on the worksheets included:

"I am happy!!!"
"I like the movement. I feel free."
"My feeling for this exercise was very calming and relaxing."
"I feel calm when I did the dance."
"When I dance I feel like I am alone. I feel like I am advancing. I feel strong."

## Cognitive Engagement through Work Samples

To measure cognitive engagement in the mathematics activities, mathematics curriculum-based assessments were used. On a mathematics pretest of basic multiplication, understanding and use of dimensional arrays, and calculation of the area of rectangular shapes, students' scores ranged from 0 to 25% correct (5/20), with a class average of 13% (3/20). Students' scores increased on post-tests of basic multiplication, dimensional arrays and area calculation, ranging from 65% (13/20) to 100% (20/20) correct, with a class average of 85% (17/20).

### Affective Engagement through Interviews, Surveys, and Written Reflections

Students' survey responses indicated that they understood the meaning of attention and the energy required to sustain their attention on physical, cognitive, and social-emotional levels. The majority (86% or 12/14) of students reported using Free Flow and Sustained Time most frequently. As mentioned earlier, Flow refers to the continuity of the movement. The use of Free Flow aligns with the dance/movement arts objective targeting a smooth transition from one phrase of the sequence to the next, requiring balance and self-control. Time Effort describes the quality of the movement along the continuum from Sustained to Sudden. Sustained Time is linked to decision-making skills, encouraging thinking before acting. As previously mentioned, Flow reflects the quality of continuity of the movement, noting our dance/movement objective to smoothly transition from one phrase to the next, requiring balance and self-control. Time Effort determines the quality of the movement, conveying a message, and is therefore linked to decision-making skills. The internal use of Sustained Time has been reported to encourage thinking before acting, rather than demonstrating impulsive behavior; and Time and Space Efforts are often used to reinforce each other to increase mental alertness (Bartenieff & Lewis, 1980).

Also, my findings indicated that the frequency of students' disruptive and hyperactive behaviors during math class decreased over the course of the intervention period. During each math class, students became more focused and attentive following the initial movement sequence. By the middle of each class they were asking questions, following directions, and were generally enthusiastic when moving through the multiplication arrays together. The DMT AI process supported the students' academic growth and helped to manage behavior through self-awareness and self-regulation, as evidenced through decreased distraction, increased focus, and positive socialization.

### Summary and Conclusion

The use of dance and movement in the mathematics classroom setting is an example of meaningful AI. This arts-based teaching experience was significant for my students because they were engaged cognitively and affectively through physical activity. Researchers have acknowledged that LD and ADHD frequently co-occur, and that students with ADHD experience difficulty decoding in reading and math computation because of working memory problems that interfere with accessing the symbol systems necessary to these skill areas (Maynard, Tyler, & Arnold, 1999). However, when my students with ADHD practiced self-regulation skills through dance/movement, they slowed down their bodies and applied a kinesthetic approach to learning math. They conceptualized multiplication through body and mind connections, similar to the way that dance has been described in relation to math understandings such as sequencing, symmetry/asymmetry, geometric shapes and designs, relationships between metered time and fractions, patterns (rhythm, movement and body shape), and measurement (e.g., movement and space) (Cornett, 2011). The integration of dance/movement with mathematics enabled students to experience academic achievement in ways that had been previously inaccessible.

## Voices from Research and Higher Education

This final part of the chapter presents the implications from Robyne's demonstration of practice through the lens of higher education research and practice in AI and its allied disciplines of education, developmental psychology, special education, and linguistics. First, a summary of the demonstration of practice is presented, followed by the application of the AI practice to the engagement framework presented in Chapter 4. The final section considers research and practice implications through the lenses of critical literacy, authentic learning, and UDL.

### *Demonstration of Practice Summary*

Robyne designed and implemented a unique mathematics and behavioral intervention that explored how DMT influenced students' self-awareness and self-regulation in an inclusive classroom setting. The participants in the study were 14 sixth- and seventh-grade students receiving special education, nine with LD, ADHD, and EBD. The unit objectives targeted students' IEP goals in emotional-behavioral areas and mathematics through the use of DMT. Robyne aimed to improve the students' self-awareness and self-regulation through DMT, which she thought would support students' mastery of mathematics concepts and procedures. She also modeled effort and persistence in learning with her students.

The first element of Robyne's intervention was a three-step movement sequence performed at the beginning of each class, which encouraged students to increase the organization and regulation of their thinking, as well as their motor sequencing and coordination. She also taught several content lessons about multiplication and arrays through activities that incorporated dance concepts and bodily-kinesthetic intelligence (Gardner, 1983). Her data collection methods included survey, conferencing, work sampling, observation, videotaping, and interview with students and colleagues. Robyne found that her students became more focused and attentive during math lessons following movement sequences.

Students' scores on mathematics assessments improved significantly during the intervention. Students' use of dance and mathematics vocabulary increased, with a noticeable decrease in students' disruptive and hyperactive behaviors over the course of the intervention.

### Theoretical Framework Questions Explained

This section explores how Robyne contextualized the mathematics content; how contextualization through AI supported students' understanding and language; and how the role of social interaction supported students' mathematics, social skills, and language learning. We also explore how students showed their affective and cognitive engagement over the course of the DMT AI unit. This section considers the relationship between students' cognitive, affective, and linguistic engagement and asks whether one dimension of engagement drives the others (e.g., affective engagement drives cognitive and linguistic).

### Contextualization of cognition and language learning

Robyne's AI intervention contextualized the dance and mathematics content through students' physical or bodily expressions. Unit activities incorporated the students' use of their bodies in a variety of ways (e.g., concepts of kinesphere, personal space, and finding area through taking measurements of students' dimensions). These physical connections supported students' cognitive engagement with the material as each lesson's content was contextualized within the immediate environment (e.g., objects in the room, fellow classmates, and teachers). Contextualization of the content through dance/movement supported students' language use as well. Many students in the class had difficulty understanding and using social and linguistic symbols; it seemed that dance/movement helped illuminate these concepts by making them concrete. Students honed their expressive social communication skills through the group and partner routines and exercises. Anderson explains in Chapter 2 that as children develop increasingly complex understandings of content through AI, they gain familiarity and experience using more sophisticated language to express their ideas. Robyne noted that her students spontaneously started taking turns leading movement sequences that required their explanation of concepts and dance sequences using specific vocabulary. During these group activities, Robyne's students represented their ideas for their peers and reached academic, personal, and social goals similar to the benefits reported by researchers using creative movement and dance arts approaches with students from at-risk backgrounds (Bradley, 2002; Camilleri, 2007). This was a significant accomplishment for Robyne's students, who struggled to understand academic content and to relate to each other.

Arts integration has the potential to be transformative, particularly for students who struggle in traditional academic contexts. Burnaford, April, and Weiss (2001) suggest that others' perceptions of a student can be changed through the arts by the revelation of previously unrecognized abilities. Several of Robyne's most disruptive students became leaders of the dance/movement sequences and emanated positive peer pressure during the AI intervention. Robyne developed relationships with her students and created a prosocial forum, recognizing the importance of social relationships and the belief that positive interactions between teachers and students can lead to improved self-esteem and a heightened sense of community within the classroom (Battistich, Solomon, Kim, Watson, & Schaps, 1995; Dewey, 1938; Klem & Connell, 2004; Raider-Roth, 2005). The contextualization of mathematics and dance/movement concepts fostered a positive classroom atmosphere and greater familiarity with the material, which in turn increased students' sense of self-efficacy.

## Influences on cognitive and affective engagement

Educational programs for students with EBD and ADHD should emphasize social interaction skills such as self-awareness, self-esteem, and self-control, along with academic content (Belson, 2003). Robyne's project demonstrated student improvement in each of these areas. For example, on the first day of instruction, students were anxious and disengaged; only half of the students completed the initial movement sequence. By the end of the intervention, most students were taking turns leading the initial movement sequences, selecting music, and participating enthusiastically. In this intervention, affective engagement appeared to drive students' cognitive and linguistic engagement. The students were initially engaged in the dance/movement techniques and sustained this engagement, which ultimately led to their increased understanding of math concepts and procedures, and the specific terminology/vocabulary in both math and dance/movement. Students' increased awareness and understanding enabled their improvement in both cognitive processing and self-regulatory behavior (e.g., self-regulation and self-control). After completing the movement sequences, students were more focused and attentive during math lessons. They asked questions, followed directions, and exhibited fewer disruptive and hyperactive behaviors. Students improved in their interactions with teachers and peers, as demonstrated by successful work in pairs. Students' increased affective engagement opened the door to their willingness to engage cognitively and linguistically. Robyne's multisensory mathematics and dance/movement lessons supported students' learning of mathematics content and lesson-specific terminology.

## Quality of Scholarship and Thinking around Research and Practice Contribution

This section considers the quality of the scholarship and thinking around the contributions of Robyne's demonstration of practice to AI research and practice.

In particular, we consider the connections to critical literacy, authentic learning, and UDL.

## Authenticity and learning standards

Authentic learning was promoted by situating the DMT and mathematics concepts within students' prior knowledge to make the information relevant to students' interests and needs. Students learned to use their bodies as tools for learning, and as a means to express feelings and thoughts. Robyne integrated mathematics content standards of basic multiplication, writing of dimensional arrays, and finding the area of rectangular shapes with movement. Students came to appreciate activities such as 'balloon ball' that required mathematics, social-emotional, and movement skills. By the end of the intervention period, students' mastery of mathematics content standards reached 85%. Equally important, students' participation, on-task behavior, and ability to follow directions over the course of the intervention improved significantly.

## Universal Design for Learning

Robyne's practice demonstrated UDL principles by extending the opportunity to learn to all of her students, regardless of their challenges in a traditional classroom. She carefully prepared for the project by reviewing the students' IEP goals; and instead of using a 'one-size-fits-all' approach, she customized her lessons according to students' individual needs. Robyne asked herself, "instead of hyperactivity being viewed as a detriment in the classroom, why not allow students' strengths of energetic movement to become an asset in the creative learning process?" She also continuously reflected on her approach to adjust to her students' needs in relation to the goals of the AI intervention. Through dance/movement and bodily-kinesthetic activities, Robyne provided an alternative to traditional learning contexts that have been reported to exacerbate environmental and learning challenges, as well as to decrease students' affective engagement (Eisner, 1998). Stevenson and Deasy (2005) explain that through arts education, students are included in lessons and classroom activities for which they may otherwise lack the basic skills required for participation. Limitations in math, reading, writing skills, or even physical abilities did not prevent Robyne's students from participating in the AI mathematics activities.

## Barriers and Facilitators

One barrier to the AI intervention was students' increased distractibility at the end of the school day. In Robyne's case, however, this additional challenge adds weight to her findings that students became more engaged with the lessons and that their math performance improved. An additional barrier was the brevity of the intervention period. Robyne and the classroom teachers had hoped to continue the intervention through the end of the school year; however, standardized testing priorities limited instructional time.

Robyne noted that additional structure could have facilitated transitions between dance/movement and math activities. Additionally, music was a facilitator of the intervention and played a role in setting the mood of the environment, but Robyne's research did not focus on the influence of musical genres and dance/movement integration. Future research could explore the contribution of music and art modalities in conjunction with dance/movement AI. The most salient facilitator of the practice seemed to be the students' interest in the intervention activities and their eagerness to participate. They took on leadership roles, reflecting what Cornett (2011) describes as the way "the arts capture attention and develop concentration because they are emotionally compelling" (p. 11). Another key facilitator of Robyne's AI intervention was the collaboration with the general education classroom teachers. All of the professionals shared their classroom and responsibility for the intervention goals integrating mathematics, dance/movement, and social-emotional skills. They carefully co-planned and coordinated their schedules to carry out a wide variety of activities. In summary, this demonstration of practice presents an avenue for addressing diverse learning needs of students at-risk for school failure through the integration of dance/movement arts and mathematics.

## References

American School Counselor Association. (2004). *ASCA national standards for students.* Alexandria, VA: ASCA.

Anderson, A. (2012). The influence of process drama on elementary students' written language. *Urban Education,* 39(4), 1–24.

Arizona Department of Education. (2006). *Arizona dance standards: Introduction and rationale for dance in education.* Retrieved from http://www.azed.gov/standards-practices/files/2011/09/dance.pdf

Barkley, R. A. (1997). Attention-deficit/hyperactivity disorder, self-regulation, and time: Toward a more comprehensive theory. *Journal of Developmental and Behavioral Pediatrics,* 18(4), 271–279.

Barkley, R. A. (2003). Issues in the diagnosis of attention-deficit/hyperactivity disorder in children. *Brain and Development: Official Journal of the Japanese Society of Child Neurology,* 25(2), 77–83.

Barringer, M. D., Pohlman, C., & Robinson, M. (2010). *Schools for all kinds of minds: Boosting student success by embracing learning variation.* San Francisco: Jossey-Bass.

Bartenieff, I., & Lewis, D. (1980). *Body movement: Coping with the environment.* New York: Gordon and Breach Science.

Battistich, V., Solomon, D., Kim, D., Watson, M., & Schaps, E. (1995). Schools as communities, poverty levels of student populations, and students' attitudes, motives, and performance: A multilevel analysis. *American Educational Research Journal,* 32(3), 627–658.

Belson, S. I. (2003). *Technology for exceptional learners: Choosing instructional tools to meet students' needs.* Boston: Houghton-Mifflin.

Bradley, K. K. (2002). Informing and reforming dance education research. In R. J. Deasy (Ed.), *Critical links: Learning in the arts and student academic and social development* (pp. 16–18). Washington, DC: Arts Education Partnership.

Burnaford, G., Aprill, A., & Weiss, C. (2001). *Renaissance in the classroom: Arts integration and meaningful learning.* Mahwah, NJ: Lawrence Erlbaum.

Camilleri, V. (2007). *Healing the inner city child: Creative arts therapies with at-risk youth.* London: Jessica Kingsley.

CAST. (2011). *Universal Design for Learning guidelines version 2.0.* Wakefield, MA: CAST. Retrieved from http://www.udlcenter.org/aboutudl/udlguideline

Cornett, C. (2011). *Creating meaning through literature and the arts: Arts integration for classroom teachers* (4th ed.). Boston: Pearson.

Davis, C. L., Tomporowski, P. D., McDowell, J. E., Austin, B. P., Miller, P. H., Yanasak, N. E., … Naglieri, J. A. (2011). Exercise improves executive function and achievement and alters brain activation in overweight children: A randomized, controlled trial. *Health Psychology,* 30(1), 91–98.

Dewey, J. (1938). *Experience and education.* New York: Macmillan.

District of Columbia Public Schools. (2011). *District of Columbia Public Schools: Learning standards for grades pre-K-8: Grade 6 standards and learning activities.* Retrieved from http://dc.gov/downloads/TEACHING%20&%20LEARNING/Learning%20Standards%202009/DCPS-MATH-GRADE06-STANDARDS-LEARNING-ACTIVITIES.pdf

Eisner, E. (1998). Does experience in the arts boost academic achievement? *Art Education,* 51(1), 7–15.

Fiore, T., Becker, E., & Nero, R. (1993). Educational interventions for students with attention deficit disorder. *Exceptional Children,* 60(2), 163–173.

Gardner, H. (1983). *Frames of mind: The theory of multiple intelligences.* New York: Basic Books.

Gronlund, E., Renck, B., & Weibull, J. (2005). Dance/movement therapy as an alternative treatment for young boys diagnosed as ADHD: A pilot study. *American Journal of Dance Therapy,* 27(2), 8–16.

Harris, K. R., Reid, R. R., & Graham, S. (2004). Self-regulation among students with LD and ADHD. In B. Wong (Ed.), *Learning about learning disabilities* (3rd ed.) (pp. 167–195). San Diego, CA: Elsevier.

Individuals with Disabilities Education Improvement Act of 2004, Public Law 108–446, 20 U.S.C. § 1401 et seq. (2004).

Katz, J. (2013). The three block model of Universal Design for Learning (UDL): Engaging students in inclusive education. *Canadian Journal of Education,* 36(1), 153–194.

Klem, A. M., & Connell, J. P. (2004). Relationships matter: Linking teacher support to student engagement and achievement. *Journal of School Health,* 74(7), 262–273.

Laban, R. (1956). *Principles of dance and movement notation.* London: Macdonald & Evans.

Levine, M. (2002). *A mind at a time: America's top learning expert shows how every child can succeed.* New York: Simon & Schuster.

Lyon, G.R. (1996). The need for conceptual and theoretical clarity in the study of attention, memory, and executive function. In G. R. Lyon & N. Krasnegor (Eds.), *Attention, memory, and executive function* (pp. 3–9). Baltimore: Paul H. Brookes.

Maynard, J., Tyler, J. L., & Arnold, M. (1999). Co-occurrence of attention-deficit disorder and learning disability: An overview of research. *Journal of Instructional Psychology,* 26(3), 183–187.

Naglieri, J. A. (2003). Current advances and intervention for children with learning disabilities. In A. Mastropieri (Ed.), *Advances in learning and behavioral disabilities.* Vol. 16, *Identification and assessment* (pp. 163–190). Amsterdam: Jai Press.

Raider-Roth, M. (2005). *Trusting what you know: The high stakes of classroom relationships.* San Francisco: Jossey-Bass.

Redman, D. (2007). *The effectiveness of dance/movement therapy as a treatment for students in a public alternative school diagnosed with attention deficit hyperactivity disorder: A pilot study* (Master's thesis). Drexel University, Philadelphia, PA.

Sherborne, V. (1990). *Developmental movement for children.* Cambridge: Cambridge University Press.

Stevenson, L., & Deasy, R. J. (2005). *Third space: When learning matters.* Washington, DC: Arts Education Partnership. Retrieved from http://www.artsedsearch.org/summaries/third-space-when-learning-matters#sthash.IhXRdt4s.dpuf

Tomporowski, P. D., Davis, C. L., Miller, P. H., & Naglieri, J. A. (2008). Exercise and children's intelligence, cognition, and academic achievement. *Educational Psychology Review,* 20(2), 111–131.

# PART III

# Reflections and Next Steps for Arts Integration Research and Practice

## Introduction

This concluding section addresses the state of the current research and practice on AI with respect to the proposed theory of action and supporting demonstrations of practice to highlight possible directions for the field. In Chapter 8, Jean Crockett, Katherine Berry, and I provide a review of the current status of arts and special education research, with a focus on arts integration (AI) intervention research with students having a range of disabilities in a variety of educational settings. These findings are considered in relation to the engagement framework presented in Part I, as well as in relation to the AI demonstrations of practice offered in Part II of the book. In particular, the findings generated from the AI demonstrations of practice with a vulnerable student population revealed that for middle-school-age students with a variety of learning and environmental obstacles, access to meaningful content through AI was relevant, motivating, and supported their conceptualization skills, which was interrelated with their development of language skills and academic performance. In Chapter 9, James Catterall provides a conclusion to the book's lessons learned for the research and practice of tomorrow, as well as for the reader's further consideration while reading the demonstrations of practice involving AI practices in a range of educational settings.

# 8

# WHERE ARE WE NOW?

## The Research on Arts Integration and Special Education

*Jean B. Crockett, Katherine A. Berry, and Alida Anderson*

Advocates regard instruction in and through the arts as essential to a high-quality public education that prepares students for success now and in the future. An emerging body of research supports this claim with reference to students' growth in areas such as literacy, mathematics, motivation, engagement, critical thinking, communication, and leadership skills (Arts Education Partnership, 2013). To ensure these benefits, all students, including those with disabilities, need access to arts learning and cultural activities, opportunities to develop appropriate skills, and instruction provided by educators who are well prepared to teach them (John F. Kennedy Center, n.d.). Access to learning in and through the arts provides opportunities for youth with disabilities to aspire to careers in artistic fields and to develop the necessary skills to be successful. Opportunities to learn through the arts also hold potential to enhance students' quality of life, academic learning, and social growth. Successful learning, however, requires arts educators and classroom teachers to include learners with special needs in their instruction.

This chapter explores research findings in arts integration and special education in relation to the theoretical framework outlined in Part I and the demonstrations of practice presented in Part II of this book. The discussion begins with the shared principles at the intersection of arts education and special education in the context of student learning and school improvement. A review of content published in professional journals is provided to illustrate how the intersection of these disciplines has recently been portrayed, and to explore the extent to which inclusive practices, students' artistic growth, teachers' development, and arts integration are reflected in the literature. Empirical studies of arts integration interventions to support engagement and learning for students with various disability-related needs are examined next, followed by a discussion of this research in relation to demonstrations of AI in classroom practice. The chapter concludes with a discussion of the contributions of AI to the interdisciplinary fields of education and developmental psychology, and the role of teachers' professional development in special education and the implementation of AI interventions.

## The Complementary Disciplines of Special Education and Arts Education

In the United States, the dual priorities of including students with disabilities in all aspects of school life (Hehir, 2005) and ensuring all students' access to high-quality arts learning experiences (AEP, 2013) coalesce in the current context of accountability and school improvement. The Elementary and Secondary Education Act (ESEA), most recently reauthorized as the No Child Left Behind Act of 2001 (2002), aims to raise educational achievement by requiring teachers to provide research-based instruction, and by challenging all students to participate in school, district, and state accountability systems. The ambitious goal to improve schools by strengthening learning for all students is supported by the Individuals with Disabilities Education Improvement Act (IDEA, 2004), which ensures appropriate opportunities for special education students to make progress toward meeting challenging standards. "Taken together, IDEA and ESEA provide the basis for inclusion of all students with disabilities in general education, with high expectations for their achievement in high quality education programs," (Malley, in press), including equitable engagement in high-quality education in the arts.

### *Shared Principles*

Special education and arts education can be described as complementary disciplines with shared principles. Figure 8.1 illustrates how these fields work in tandem to advance student learning (Crockett, 2013).

   With regard to special education, four principles of democratic engagement provide a framework to guide policies and practices addressing the education and well-being of people with disabilities in American society including (a) equal opportunity, (b) full participation, (c) independent living, and (d) self-sufficiency (Silverstein, 2000). These principles, derived from over 90 pieces of legislation in the US, were incorporated in the opening section of the IDEA (2004) to chart a course toward productive and meaningful lives for youth with disabilities in their communities. The complement to these values can be found in the principles embedded in the Core Arts Standards designed to guide arts educators in teaching all students ways to create, perform, present, produce, respond, and connect through participation in dance, drama, music, and visual and media arts (National Art Education Association, 2014). The intersection of special education and arts education holds the potential to cultivate full participation, greater independence, and the development of personal and artistic competencies in special needs learners, as well as the motivation to be successful in post-secondary school education,

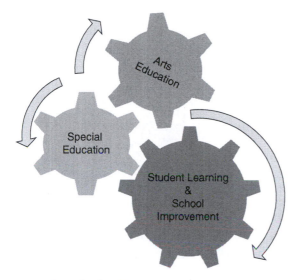

**FIGURE 8.1**   Student Learning and School Improvement as Enhanced by Interactions with the Complementary Disciplines of Special Education and Arts Education.

careers, and community living (Adamek & Darrow, 2012). There is, however, scant evidence beyond descriptive data to support the impact of arts education or arts integration instruction on the educational outcomes of students with disabilities (Mason, Steedly, & Thormann, 2008).

## Addressing the Evidence

There are some positive indicators resulting from qualitative analyses conducted in the 1990s that education in and through the arts can be used successfully in inclusive classrooms to introduce complex content information (Onosko & Joergensen, 1998), and to provide effective media for culminating projects (Qin, Johnson, & Johnson, 1995). Within the past decade, findings from 34 focus groups conducted in 16 states with teachers, parents, artists, students, and other school personnel in inclusive settings and special education centers have also suggested the value of the arts in developing students' voice (i.e., social skill development and communication), choice (i.e., cognitive development and problem solving), and access to artistic skill development (Mason, Thormann, & Steedly, 2004). But many questions remain unanswered. Few researchers, for example, have employed quantitative analysis, as Catterall has done (1998), to assess the effect on academic performance of integrating the arts into the general curriculum. In addition, little is known about how teachers work with students at the intersection of special education and arts education, and Mason and her colleagues (2008) underscored the importance of researching the extent to which teachers are prepared to engage in this instruction, and how school districts, state departments of education, and professional associations are providing them with relevant professional development. To address the need for data informing the intersection of special education and arts education, Crockett (2013) sampled the content of professional journals related to these complementary disciplines to determine how activities at this intersection were studied and portrayed over a 10-year time span.

## Publications at the Intersection of Arts Education and Special Education

Literature related to special education and the arts can be found in local, state, and national reports, books, and chapters, and in professional journals in both special and general education. In this analysis the abstracts of articles published in professional journals were reviewed because these periodicals are intended for educators and reflect current issues. Analyzing the content of professional journals is a useful way to survey the types of articles and the topics of interest within a specific field (Crockett, Becker, & Quinn, 2009; McFarland, Williams, & Miciak, 2013; Mastropieri et al., 2009), and in this case to explore the published scholarship linking the arts with the education of exceptional learners from 2002 to 2012.

### *Searching for Publications*

Abstracts of published articles were identified through an initial rather than exhaustive search of electronic databases including Academic Search Premier and ERIC First Search, using the following keywords in combination: *arts education, disabilities and schools,* and *drama, dance, music, visual and media arts.* Articles were selected for further review if their abstracts indicated content focused on individuals with disabilities in educational settings from pre-school through college. Each abstract was coded and categorized by artistic domain, publication information, type of article, and topical area. To assess the type of article, abstracts were coded as *professional commentaries* (including conceptual pieces, critiques, literature reviews, and program descriptions), or *research studies* (including quantitative and qualitative inquiries, surveys, and program evaluations). Individual abstracts were classified into topical areas based on information about the content of articles contained in the brief summaries.

The limited search terms in this scan of the literature yielded only 100 usable abstracts, with 86% of the content addressing the artistic domains of music (n = 49), visual arts (n = 22), and drama (n = 15). Content addressing dance (n = 8) and media arts (n = 6) comprised only 14% of the articles in this collection. The abstracts summarized articles that were international in scope and contributed by authors from nine countries. Ninety-six percent of the articles represented multiple entries from the United States (n = 68), Great Britain (n = 20), Australia (n = 4), Canada (n = 2), and South Korea (n = 2), and 4% represented single entries from Barbados, Iceland, Israel, and New Zealand.

The 100 articles were published in 55 journals and were distributed equally among arts education journals (n = 42) and special education and psychology journals (n = 42), with fewer articles published in generic education journals (n = 16). Eighteen of the 55 journals (33%) published multiple relevant articles over the decade. The largest number was published in the *Music Educator's Journal* (n = 10), sponsored by the National Association of Music Educators; *General Music Today* (n = 6), a peer-reviewed, practice-oriented, online journal; and a special issue of *Learning Disabilities: A Multidisciplinary Journal* (n = 6), sponsored by the Learning Disabilities Association of America. It should be noted that only one article (Reis, Schader, Milne, & Stevens, 2003) was published during this time frame in *Exceptional Children*, the premier research journal in the field of special education.

## Types of Articles

Sixty-six of the 100 articles were professional commentaries and 34 were research studies. Though commentaries were more prevalent than studies in all domains, the greatest proportion of studies was found in drama (40%), followed by dance (38%), visual arts (36%), music (33%), and media arts (17%). Participants in the studies ranged in age from preschoolers to young adults with a wide range of disabilities, and multiple methodologies were used, including descriptive qualitative approaches (n = 15), single case designs (n = 9), quantitative analyses (n = 7), and mixed method designs (n = 2). One exception to these empirical investigations was a historical study tracing the development of theatricals in the nineteenth century, about people with disabilities and the social impact of these affliction melodramas on fundraising for special schools and institutions (Moeschen, 2006/2007).

## Topical Areas

The content of the abstracts was analyzed and categorized into four topical areas: (a) inclusive practices, (b) students' artistic growth, (c) teachers' development, and (d) arts integration. These categories were not exclusive, and abstracts often addressed more than one topic (e.g., inclusive practices and arts integration), suggesting a modest picture of recent research. For the purposes of this chapter the content in each topical area is briefly described, but greater detail is provided for the research studies addressing AI.

### Inclusive practices

Fifty-eight abstracts addressed inclusive practices with professional commentaries comprising 76% (n = 44) and research studies comprising 24% (n = 14). Coding of the abstracts was based on Silverstein's (2000) framework addressing social aspects of disability and diversity, and access to and participation in arts activities with opportunities for voicing preferences and making personal choices. Abstracts referring to collaboration, accommodations, and Universal Design for Learning in arts education for people with disabilities were also coded in this category, as were abstracts referring to accountability for outcomes aligned with educational policies.

## Students' artistic growth

Twenty-nine abstracts addressed opportunities for students to develop skills in arts-related activities. Of these articles, 69% (n = 20) were professional commentaries, and 31% (n = 9) were research studies. Content included the development of various skills in acting, dancing, mask making, painting, musical performance, and media access to arts experiences for students with cognitive, emotional, sensory, and physical disabilities; several articles addressed employment training through technology and music production.

## Teachers' development

Forty-seven abstracts addressed the preparation and professional development of educators to engage students with disabilities in arts education. Of these articles, 70% (n = 33) were professional commentaries, and 30% (n = 14) were research studies. Content featured practical descriptions of instructional strategies and techniques, and several studies investigated effective ways to support paraprofessionals in inclusive art classrooms.

## Arts integration

Forty-nine abstracts were assigned to the topic of AI because they indicated the arts were used in the teaching/learning process. Of these articles, 63% (n = 31) were professional commentaries, and 37% (n = 18) were research studies. Content included the development of cognition, communication and social skills, disability awareness, literacy and core academic content, self-esteem, self-advocacy, and self-control through engagement with the arts. Abstracts were also included in this area if they addressed art therapies through integration of the arts with therapeutic goals.

Nine abstracts specifically addressed arts therapy for special education students. Five of these abstracts described research studies in which the arts were used to facilitate a group therapy program for school-aged students with social developmental disorders (Epp, 2008); as a prompt to evoke speech sounds (Wan et al., 2011); as a means of reinforcing behavior (Buckley & Newchok, 2006); and in case studies assessing the achievements of a six-year-old child with autism (Bakan et al., 2008), and the emotional well-being of five children with learning difficulties who experienced stress or trauma (Ottarsdottir, 2010).

The remaining 40 abstracts addressed education through the arts for students with disabilities, and only 13 of these abstracts (33%) represented research studies. AI was addressed in these studies through a variety of methodologies. Five studies employed single case designs in the following ways: using a nursery song (Old MacDonald) to prompt preschoolers with autism to identify pictures of animals (Simpson & Keen, 2010); assessing the influence of process drama on the writing productivity and specificity of 16 elementary students with learning and behavioral challenges (Anderson, 2012); evaluating the effect of interactive reading materials using visual cues and music on the active engagement of six students with autism (Carnahan, Musti-Rao, & Bailey, 2009); assessing the effects of a peer group dancing program on the use of appropriate behaviors by socially isolated children (Lee, Kim, Lee, & Lee, 2002); and using video modeling to teach adolescents with intellectual disabilities to play music on mobile devices (Kagohara et al., 2011). Three studies employed quasi-experimental designs, using music to enhance the painting quality and positive behavior of students with significant intellectual disabilities (Riddoch & Waugh, 2003; Waugh & Riddoch, 2007), and using visual cues and music to explore the understanding of emotion by students with significant language impairments (Spackman, Fujiki, Brinton, Nelson, & Allen, 2005). Qualitative case studies were used in three investigations examining approaches typically used with gifted and talented students for strengthening the musical and mathematical skills of young adults with Williams syndrome (Reis et al., 2003); the impact of an apprenticeship in sculpture on the learning engagement of sixth graders with dyslexia and attention deficit disorder (McPhail, Pierson, Goodman, & Noffke, 2004); and the inclusion of children with complex learning needs in drama activities (Whitehurst, 2007). Mixed method designs were used in two studies examining the impact of drama activities on the relationships among students with and without intellectual disabilities (Dodwell, 2002), and the ways in which art educators and special educators determine the qualities of digital media and make decisions about when, why, and how to use digital video with special needs learners (Orr, 2007).

## Future Considerations

The abstracts included in this content analysis represent a small collection of articles, and the use of different search terms and strategies might have yielded different results. This modest collection, however, offers a sampling of recent publications in professional journals and suggests the need for more research. Only 34% of what we know from these publications is based on studies, indicating the need for more empirical data at the intersection of special education and the arts as increasing numbers of students with disabilities are included in general classes for arts and academic instruction (US Department of Education, 2012). Only 14 studies investigated inclusive approaches to instruction, and another 14 studies addressed teacher preparation for working with exceptional learners in the arts. Fewer still, a meager nine studies, focused on cultivating students' artistic development. The 18 studies collectively addressing the integration of the arts in therapeutic and other learning goals included descriptive investigations as well as interventions designed to boost students' achievement. These studies focus attention on the distinctions among arts education, art therapy, and arts integration as vehicles for other forms of learning, work, development, or engagement for students with exceptional learning needs (Ockelford, Welch, & Zimmerman, 2002). Ockelford and his colleagues suggest that teachers need clearer guidance and better resources to understand and utilize the continuum of supports available to special education students across these three approaches to the arts.

Another issue to consider is the importance of intervention research in the education of exceptional learners. Students with disabilities have complex learning needs and research examining the effectiveness of interventions to improve their capabilities, as well as their inclusion in general education environments, forms the foundational knowledge base of special education (Mastropieri et al., 2009). Several intervention studies in this collection (Anderson, 2012; Carnahan, Musti-Rao, & Bailey, 2009; Lee et al., 2002; Spackman et al., 2005) are among the studies considered in greater depth in the following review of AI intervention research.

## Arts Integration Intervention Research

The purpose of this review is to examine the scholarly literature related to arts integration interventions for students with attention deficit disorder (ADHD), autism spectrum disorder (ASD), emotional and behavioral disorders (EBD), learning disabilities (LD), and speech and language impairment (SLI). This section is organized around three broad topic areas: drama interventions, music interventions, and dance and movement interventions. It should be noted that the literature reviewed in this analysis revealed no studies that described visual and/or media arts interventions aligning with the inclusion criteria. Detailed within each topic area is a description of the included students, the intervention context (e.g., inclusive, self-contained, etc.), the types of arts approaches, the findings, and the implications for teacher practice. A summary, limitations, and recommendations for future research follow. This review of the literature was guided by the following questions of interest: (a) what previous research has been conducted related to arts integration interventions (i.e., drama, music, dance and movement, and visual and media arts) for students with ADHD, ASD, EBD, LD, and SLI; and (b) what are the implications of these interventions for future research at the intersection of arts integration and special education?

Several strategies were used to identify relevant theoretical and empirical literature. The following six databases were searched using various search terms: Academic Search Complete, ArtsEdSearch, Education Source, ERIC (EBSCO),

ProQuest Dissertations and Theses Online, and PsychINFO. Key search terms included different combinations of the following: *drama, theater, performance, music, song, dance, movement, physical activity, media arts, film, movie, digital art, photography, visual art, art, painting, drawing, intervention, strategy, disability*, and *students with disabilities*. To narrow the scope of the search, four limitations were employed. First, because this chapter emphasizes the most recent literature at the intersection of arts integration and special education, only literature written or studies conducted between 2002 and 2014 were considered for review. Second, articles must have been published in English-language, peer-reviewed journals. Third, because the purpose of the review was to describe arts integration interventions, studies and articles must have described the specific implementation of interventions in K-12 academic classroom settings. Thus, the review excluded articles describing interventions that were conducted after school, as part of summer programs, in residential facilities, in home environments, and exclusively in arts, music, dance, physical education, or drama classes. Fourth, studies must have included populations of students with ADHD, ASD, EBD, LD, and SLI; however, articles related to students with low-incidence disabilities such as significant intellectual disabilities, serious physical impairment, multiple disabilities, and deaf/blindness were excluded from the review.

## Arts Integration Interventions for Students with Disabilities

### Drama Interventions

The review of drama interventions focused on the use of process drama, a method of teaching and learning that allows learners "to use imagined roles to explore issues, events, and relationships" (O'Neill & Lambert, 1983, p. 11). In contrast to culminating play productions, process drama involves examining ideas that emerge from classroom discussions, considering a situation from multiple perspectives, and taking on the roles of specific characters or actions (Schneider, Crumpler, & Rogers, 2006). The literature reviewed revealed 11 drama intervention studies aligning with the inclusion criteria.

### Student populations

Of the 11 drama intervention studies, five (Cameron, 2007; Corcoran & Davis, 2005; Garrett & O'Conner, 2010; Hubbard, 2009; Whittaker, 2005) involved students with LD, one (Jacobs, 2005) examined students with EBD, one (Kempe & Tissot, 2012) described students with ASD, and three (Anderson, 2012; Anderson & Berry, in press; Guli, Semrud-Clikeman, Lerner, & Britton, 2013) included students from at least two disability categories. All five of the studies involving students with LD consisted of kindergarten through fifth graders while the studies targeting EBD and ASD populations were conducted with middle and high school students. For the studies including students from at least two disability categories, one study (Anderson, 2012) included fourth graders with LD and behavioral challenges, a second (Anderson & Berry, in press) consisted of students with comorbid LD/ADHD, and a third (Guli et al., 2013) involved students with ADHD, ASD, and LD, ages 8 to 14 years.

## Intervention context

The 10 interventions were implemented in a variety of settings, such as inclusive classrooms, self-contained classrooms at special schools, resource classrooms, and a combination of inclusive and self-contained classrooms. Two researchers (Anderson, 2012; Cameron, 2007) conducted studies in inclusive classroom contexts in which students with disabilities learned aside their age peers. Additional researchers (Anderson & Berry, in press; Jacobs, 2005; Kempe & Tissot, 2012) used self-contained classrooms at special schools for students with EBD, ASD, ADHD, and/or LD, while others (Corcoran & Davis, 2005; Hubbard, 2009) utilized resource classrooms where students with disabilities received individualized supports to address their specific learning needs. One drama intervention (Garrett & O'Conner, 2010) was implemented in four different settings: an inclusive kindergarten classroom, a self-contained classroom with third, fourth, and fifth graders with LD, a self-contained classroom with fourth and fifth graders with LD, and a small group of first, second, and third graders with LD. Additional researchers (Guli et al., 2013) recruited students from several schools, but they did not clearly describe the context of their intervention.

## Types of arts approaches

Three main arts approaches emerged from the drama intervention literature: the use of process drama activities and strategies, Reader's Theater, and the development of creative drama-based curricula.

### Process drama activities and strategies

Four studies (Anderson, 2012; Anderson & Berry, in press; Cameron, 2007; Kempe & Tissot, 2012) described using specific drama activities and strategies as part of their interventions. Anderson (2012) embedded elements of tableau (i.e., creating frozen gestures), role play, and in-role writing into her intervention in an effort to improve the written language skills (i.e., linguistic specificity and productivity) of fourth graders with LD and behavioral challenges. During the tableau activities, students used nonverbal gestures and frozen body positions to observe and interpret story events and character motives from *Little Red Riding Hood*. Students also engaged in role play by acting out specific scenes and events from the story. By assuming the roles of specific characters, students then wrote stories from their unique perspectives. Cameron (2007) implemented similar drama strategies, including tableau and role play, to support the story text comprehension of fifth graders with LD. An additional drama intervention (Kempe & Tissot, 2012) was designed to teach social skills to secondary students with ASD. The drama activities consisted of the use of dialogic talk, role play, and puppetry, with the culminating project consisting of an evolving play in which the class wrote a script and developed a short film. A final study (Anderson & Berry, in press) examined students' on-task behavior and teachers' language use across drama (i.e., tableau) and conventional language arts lessons.

## Reader's Theater

Additional drama interventions included the use of Reader's Theater fluency programs designed to connect quality literature, oral reading, and drama (Garrett & O'Conner, 2010). In Reader's Theater, students use their own thoughts and actions to rehearse and perform a play, speech, poem, script, or related text. Several researchers studied this method to improve the comprehension and fluency skills of students with LD. A Reader's Theater program was utilized to support the reading fluency development of 12 students with LD in a combined second- and third-grade self-contained classroom (Corcoran & Davis, 2005). Similarly, Reader's Theater was implemented to evaluate the extent to which participating in three plays increased the reading fluency rates of second and third graders with LD (Hubbard, 2009). An additional researcher (Whittaker, 2005) compared the use of Reader's Theater with readings from a narrative genre to determine which context led to greater reading fluency and attention for 24 third- and fourth-grade students with LD in a language arts resource classroom.

## Creative drama-based curricula

Researchers also developed entire drama-based curricular interventions for students with disabilities. One study (Guli et al., 2013) explored the effects of student participation in a Social Competence Intervention Program (SCIP). As a creative drama-based group intervention, SCIP's goal was to improve the social perception of nonverbal cues, social competence, emotional understanding, and theory of mind of secondary students with ASD. Each of the 13 sessions included student engagement in improvisations through which they assumed the perspectives of characters and practiced appropriate ways to respond to others. A second study (Jacobs, 2005) utilized a Drama Discovery curriculum in conjunction with bibliotherapy, or the use of literary sources to solve problems and develop a deeper understanding of a topic. The Drama Discovery curriculum involved middle school students with EBD, who participated in role play and improvisations of the story characters to which they most related.

*Findings*

The drama intervention literature revealed significant findings for students with disabilities in the areas of linguistic, cognitive, and behavioral development.

## Linguistic development

Researchers found that after exposure to drama interventions, students with LD increased their written language specificity and productivity and were able to connect to literary texts in meaningful ways. Fourth graders with LD who were involved in a process drama intervention using tableau and role play improved their written language skills (Anderson, 2012). Paired sample t-tests were used to compare differences among students' written language specificity and productivity across conventional and drama-based writing activities. Written language specificity was calculated as the number of literate language features (i.e., adverbs, conjunctions, elaborated noun phrases, and mental and linguistic verbs) used, and written language productivity was measured through the number of total words (NTW), number of different words (NDW), and total number of utterances (UTT). Significant increases in students' written language specificity and productivity were observed in the drama activities as compared to the more conventional language arts tasks (Anderson, 2012). Students used twice as many literate language features (e.g., complex elaborated noun phrases, conjunctions, etc.) in the drama context as in the conventional writing assignments, indicating that students' writing was more descriptive and elaborative during the drama intervention.

A case study of 27 fifth graders with LD who participated in role play and tableau intervention activities showed increased reading comprehension scores on the Developmental Reading Assessment from pre- to post-intervention (Cameron, 2007). Direct observations and student interviews also suggested that the drama activities provided greater opportunities for dialogue among students, which allowed them to connect to the literacy text in more meaningful ways than in the conventional language arts lessons.

Students with LD who participated in Reader's Theater interventions improved their letter recognition, fluency, and comprehension ratings as measured by school benchmark assessments (Garrett & O'Conner, 2010). Students with LD also increased their overall oral fluency as measured by the number of words read correctly per minute after participation in Reader's Theater programs (Corcoran & Davis, 2005; Hubbard, 2009; Whittaker, 2005).

## Cognitive development

In addition to improving linguistic skills, drama interventions also supported cognitive competencies of students with disabilities. When students with LD engaged in role play and tableau activities, they reported that they were better able to understand what they read and to access text that may have otherwise been too difficult (Cameron, 2007).

## Behavioral development

Nine of the 10 studies revealed that drama interventions led to improved behavioral outcomes for students with ASD, ADHD, EBD, and LD. Case study findings from observational notes, reflective journals, and staff feedback revealed that secondary students with ASD developed transferable social skills, such as group collaboration and perspective-taking, after participating in drama activities (Kempe & Tissot, 2012). Similarly, students with ADHD, ASD, and LD showed significant improvements in domains of social behavior after exposure to the SCIP intervention (Guli et al., 2013). Findings based on observational data from partial-interval time sampling indicated improved social interactions (e.g., cooperative play, greetings, smiling, turn taking, etc.) for students who participated in the SCIP intervention as compared to the control group. Moreover, qualitative data in the form of parent and student interviews showed improvements in interpersonal relationships, increased empathy, greater self-control, and better understanding of nonverbal cues (Guli et al., 2013).

During drama interventions, students with LD demonstrated increased participation, positive attitudes, greater interest and confidence in reading, and an overall preference for drama over more traditional learning approaches. Anecdotal evidence from the special education teacher and related school personnel emphasized that their fourth graders with LD showed increased willingness to participate in class discussions and positive attitudes towards language activities that integrated drama (Anderson, 2012). Likewise, students with LD who participated in Reader's Theater programs improved their motivation, showed increased participation, and developed a greater interest and confidence in reading, as measured by teacher and researcher reports and observations (Cameron, 2007; Garrett & O'Conner, 2010) and pre- and post-reading surveys (e.g., Elementary Reading Attitudes Surveys; Corcoran & Davis, 2005; Whittaker, 2005). Students with comorbid LD/ADHD increased their on-task behavior during drama as compared to conventional language arts lessons (Anderson & Berry, in press).

For students with EBD, drama interventions led to positive self-efficacy for students regarding their own exceptionalities (Jacobs, 2005). Qualitative assessments of student observations, journals, and interviews, as well as field notes and audio-taped documents, revealed that students were able to develop coping strategies through their relation to the story characters and their participation in process drama activities.

## *Implications*

Several implications for teacher development emerged from the positive linguistic, cognitive, and behavioral findings associated with drama interventions for students with disabilities.

## The importance of context

As teachers develop and refine their practice, they need to consider how the classroom context supports learning. Interventions for students with disabilities should be structured in ways that scaffold student learning through contextualized language-learning activities (e.g., drama) in the immediate environment and that rely on the use of shared knowledge, contextual clues, and high-frequency vocabulary to make meaning (Anderson, 2012; Clyde, 2003; Kelner & Flynn, 2006; Paul, 2002). Embedding contextualized language tasks into teacher practice can support students' understanding of more decontextualized language, such as the language used in literacy texts (Mariage, 2001).

## Meaningful engagement

Teachers also should consider how to meaningfully engage their students with disabilities, both academically and socially. Drama provides an opportunity for these students to succeed and thrive by presenting academic material in a non-threatening way. Moreover, drama creates a space for students to practice and enhance their social skills while also supporting their literacy skill development (Garrett & O'Conner, 2010; Guli et al., 2013; Kempe & Tissot, 2012).

## Reader's Theater

Four studies cited improved outcomes for students with disabilities after participation in Reader's Theater programs. As such, Reader's Theater provides a potentially valuable and creative approach for teaching students with reading fluency challenges (Corcoran & Davis, 2005; Garrett & O'Conner, 2010; Hubbard, 2009).

## Metacognitive skills

Two interventions (Cameron, 2007; Jacobs, 2005) suggested that drama may enhance the metacognitive skills of students with disabilities. By assuming the roles of various characters through improvisations and tableau drama activities, students may develop more complex thinking skills and garner a better understanding of the text (Jacobs, 2005). As such, drama interventions may prove especially helpful for students with ASD, who often have difficulty with reflection and perspective taking.

## *Music Interventions*

The second broad topic area addresses literature related to music interventions. Eleven studies described interventions aligning with the inclusion criteria.

## Student populations

Four music intervention studies (Colwell & Murlless, 2002; Legutko & Trissler, 2012; Register, Darrow, Standley, & Swedberg, 2007; Spackman et al., 2005) included students with LD, one (Brownell, 2002) examined students with ASD, and six (Carnahan, Basham, & Musti-Rao, 2009; Carnahan, Musti-Rao, & Bailey, 2009; De Mers, Tincani, Van Norman, & Higgins, 2009; Ferrell, 2012; Gooding, 2010; Yoshida, 2005) involved students with various disabilities. The studies of students with LD involved children ranging in age from five years old (Spackman et al., 2005) to sixth graders (Legutko & Trissler, 2012). Similarly, the study of ASD students was conducted with first through fourth graders (Brownell, 2002). Of the studies including students with various disabilities, four studies (Carnahan, Basham, & Musti-Rao, 2009; Carnahan, Musti-Rao, & Bailey, 2009; De Mers et al., 2009; Ferrell, 2012) included students varying in age from 5 to 11 years with ASD and behavioral challenges; others included students with ADHD, ASD, and LD, ages 11 to 16 years (Gooding, 2010), and high school students with EBD and LD (Yoshida, 2005).

## Intervention context

The 11 music interventions were implemented in a variety of settings, including self-contained and resource classes in private and public schools. Two studies (De Mers et al., 2009; Gooding, 2010) involving students with ADHD, ASD, and LD were implemented in self-contained classrooms at private schools exclusively for those with disabilities, while others (Carnahan, Basham, & Musti-Rao, 2009; Register et al., 2007; Yoshida, 2005) utilized self-contained classrooms of students with ASD, LD, and/or EBD at public schools. Four additional interventions (Carnahan, Musti-Rao, & Bailey, 2009; Colwell & Murlless, 2002; Ferrell, 2012; Legutko & Trissler, 2012) were implemented in resource classrooms of students with ASD and/or LD. Additional researchers (Brownell, 2002; Spackman et al., 2005) recruited students from several schools, but they did not clearly describe the context of their interventions.

## Types of arts approaches

Three main arts approaches emerged from the music intervention literature. These included the use of music to support students' behavior, the use of music to support students' academic learning, and the use of music to elicit emotions.

### The use of music to support students' behavior

Two researchers (De Mers et al., 2009; Gooding, 2010) examined the effects of music therapy-based interventions for improving students' social skills and decreasing negative behaviors for students with ADHD, ASD, EBD, and LD. The music therapy interventions included a variety of active techniques, including music performance, movement activities, playing instruments, and singing social stories. Other music interventions were specifically designed to support students with ASD. For example, interactive reading materials were paired with music to increase the engagement of students with ASD during small-group picture book reading activities (Carnahan, Musti-Rao, & Bailey, 2009). Social stories also were created for students with ASD to address specific behavioral goals. Original music was composed using the text of a story as lyrics to improve the target behaviors for each student (Brownell, 2002). Interactive books with music provided an additional method for supporting the engagement of students with ASD (Carnahan, Basham, & Musti-Rao, 2009).

## The use of music to support students' academic learning

Several intervention studies were designed to improve students' academic learning in the areas of reading, writing, and math. Music was employed as a strategy for enhancing the reading skills, including word knowledge, decoding, reading comprehension, and accuracy, of second and third graders with LD. The musical approaches were embedded into reading lessons and included activities such as singing, playing instruments, chanting, and movement (Colwell & Murlless, 2002; Register et al., 2007). Background music also was integrated into writing and math lessons to improve the academic performance of students with LD (Ferrell, 2012; Legutko & Trissler, 2012; Yoshida, 2005). In these studies, instrumental and classical music was played on a CD player during independent learning activities and changes in academic performance were assessed over time.

## The use of music to understand emotions

For students with LD, classical music also was paired with picture cards to help students elicit emotion (e.g., happiness, sadness, fear, etc.; Spackman et al., 2005). As the students listened to classical music excerpts, they pointed to the picture card that best represented the emotion the music conveyed.

## Findings

The music intervention literature revealed significant findings for students with disabilities in the areas of linguistic, cognitive, and behavioral development.

## Linguistic development

Researchers found that students with LD who participated in music interventions improved their reading accuracy and comprehension skills. In a study of five students with LD, ages 6 to 8 years, participants were exposed to a conventional reading program during the first week, followed by two music groups: chanting and singing in weeks two and three (Colwell & Murlless, 2002). In the fourth week, students again were presented with the conventional reading program. During each week, students were pre- and post-tested on a new set of target words. Results showed that students improved their reading accuracy across conditions, which suggests that utilizing music as a reading prompt can provide additional value to already existing reading programs. In another study second graders with LD who participated in a reading program that integrated singing, instrument playing, and movement demonstrated significantly improved performance on the Gates–MacGintie Reading subtests of word decoding, word knowledge, and reading comprehension (Register et al., 2007).

## Cognitive development

Music interventions, specifically the use of background music, also have proved beneficial for improving students' writing and mathematics performance. Sixth graders with LD showed increased mean scores on web-based writing probes when classical music was played as compared to scores obtained during non-music conditions (Legutko & Trissler, 2012). In a related study, high school students with EBD and LD demonstrated improved performance on comprehensive mathematics ability tests when background music was paired with algebra instruction (Yoshida, 2005).

## Behavioral development

Seven of the 11 studies indicated that music interventions led to improved behavioral outcomes for students with ASD, ADHD, EBD, and LD. The use of interactive books with background music (e.g., piano, guitar, etc.) led to increased engagement, as measured by the percent of intervals on-task, for students with ASD in kindergarten through fourth grade (Carnahan, Basham, & Musti-Rao, 2009; Carnahan, Musti-Rao, & Bailey, 2009). Additional music programs reduced maladaptive behaviors of first and second graders with ASD and increased the on-task behavior of second graders with LD, and of 11–16-year-old students with ADHD, ASD, and LD (Colwell & Murlless, 2002; Ferrell, 2012; Gooding, 2010). Music therapy programs decreased negative behaviors (e.g., hitting, screaming, etc.) and increased the frequency of positive target behaviors for five-, six-, and seven-year-old students with ADHD and ASD, and for first and second graders with ASD (Brownell, 2002; De Mers et al., 2009).

## *Implications*

Several implications for teacher development emerged from the positive linguistic, cognitive, and behavioral findings associated with music interventions for students with disabilities.

## Academic engagement

Four studies (Carnahan, Basham, & Musti-Rao, 2009; Carnahan, Musti-Rao, & Bailey, 2009; Colwell & Murlless, 2002; Register et al., 2007) cited improved academic engagement for students with ASD and LD who participated in music intervention programs. Teachers should consider the use of music as a remedial, repetitive, and interactive strategy for enhancing reading skills and for promoting student participation in academic lessons.

## Background music

Background music may provide an additional strategy for improving the cognitive development of students with disabilities, particularly in the areas of writing and mathematics. Moreover, background music may serve as an additional support for students with ASD and EBD by calming their inappropriate behaviors (Ferrell, 2012; Legutko & Trissler, 2012; Yoshida, 2005).

## Social skills

Active music therapy interventions that included singing, movement activities, and instruments helped teachers to successfully target and modify specific social behaviors for students with disabilities (Brownell, 2002; De Mers et al., 2009; Gooding, 2010). Thus, music may be an effective way for teachers to support students with disabilities, particularly those with ASD, in overcoming social skills deficits.

## *Dance Interventions*

The third broad topic area for the review highlights literature related to dance and movement interventions. The literature reviewed revealed only two studies that described dance or movement interventions aligning with the inclusion criteria.

## *Student populations*

Of the two dance and movement interventions, one study (Lee et al., 2002) included kindergarteners with ADHD and LD. The second study (Harbin, 2012) described kindergarteners with ASD.

## *Intervention context*

Both studies (Harbin, 2012; Lee et al., 2002) describing dance and movement interventions were conducted in inclusive kindergarten classrooms. In these contexts students with disabilities learned alongside their same-aged peers.

## Types of arts approaches

Two main arts approaches emerged from the dance and movement intervention literature. The first approach utilized a peer group dance program and the second used embedded movement activities.

### Peer group dance program

In one study (Lee et al., 2002), a peer group dance program was developed for kindergarteners with ADHD and LD to improve their verbal communication and socialization skills with their classmates. The program paired dance moves with the arms, legs, and hands to the rhythm of songs (e.g., "Hokey Pokey") in an attempt to increase the appropriate response behavior of socially withdrawn students.

### Embedded movement activities

A similar approach was developed to improve the engagement of kindergarteners with ASD. The intervention consisted of embedding two- to three-minute physical movement activities into classroom circle time routines (Harbin, 2012). The movement activities consisted of having students dance and move their arms and legs while listening to songs such as "Freeze," "I'm Gonna Catch You," and "You Better Run" (Harbin, 2012).

## Findings

The dance and movement intervention literature revealed significant behavioral findings for students with disabilities. In the peer group dance program, the students' free play was video recorded and the percentage of inappropriate and appropriate response behaviors was calculated across baseline, intervention, and maintenance phases. All three kindergarteners showed decreased frequency of inappropriate behaviors (e.g., running around, climbing on the desk, hitting, etc.) and increased frequency of appropriate behaviors (e.g., staying in one's seat, keeping hands and feet to oneself, etc.) upon introduction and continuation of the dance program (Lee et al., 2002).

Similarly, the three kindergarteners with ASD involved in the embedded movement intervention immediately increased their engagement during group circle time and the independent seatwork task following (Harbin, 2012). For all three students, engagement was defined as staying on the carpet, looking at the teacher, and following instructions. The ABAB withdrawal single subject design revealed a functional relation between the embedded movement intervention and the students' behavioral engagement.

*Implications*

One important implication for teacher development emerged from the positive behavioral findings associated with dance and movement interventions for students with disabilities. Both studies (Harbin, 2012; Lee et al., 2002) emphasized the benefits of utilizing dance and movement activities in inclusive classroom settings to improve the socialization and engagement between students with disabilities and their typically developing peers. General and special education inclusion teachers should consider dance and physical activities as a resource for enhancing social interactions, especially for students who have difficulty with their peers in inclusive contexts.

## Summary, Limitations, and Recommendations for Future Research

This review included 24 empirical studies related to arts integration interventions for students with ADHD, ASD, EBD, LD, and SLI. Ten studies described drama interventions, 11 focused on music interventions, two highlighted dance interventions, and no intervention studies to date addressed visual and media arts. A major limitation of the research literature is the limited scope of arts-integrated interventions for supporting students with disabilities. Overwhelmingly, the included studies described drama and music interventions; little is known about the value of dance/movement and visual/media arts interventions for educating students with disabilities. Thus, future researchers should develop and implement dance/movement and visual/media arts interventions to determine their potential linguistic, cognitive, and behavioral benefits for this population of students. Also, of these 24 intervention studies, only five were conducted in inclusive classrooms. Because students with disabilities are often taught in inclusive classrooms where they are expected to master increasingly challenging academic content, future studies should consider how best to support students in these settings. Lastly, the majority of studies examined the influence of arts integration interventions for students with ASD and LD. Far fewer studies considered the potential effects of these interventions for students with ADHD, EBD, and SLI. As such, a need exists for future studies to examine the effects of arts integration interventions for these vulnerable populations.

## Linking Research to Practice and Professional Development

This section uses the engagement framework presented in Part I of this book to examine the intersections among the arts and special education articles and the AI intervention research presented in this chapter, and the demonstrations of AI practice presented in Part II. Taken together, this literature provides a current snapshot of research and practice in integrating the arts and special education, and offers guidance for teachers' professional development.

## Examining the Intersections of AI Research and Practice for Students with Disabilities

The overview of recent articles published on the arts and special education, featured at the beginning of the chapter, outlines topics of interest that have shared rationales with the demonstrations of AI practice featured in Chapters 5, 6, and 7 of this volume. These foci include the use of inclusive practices fostering diversity, access, choice, voice, teamwork, and accountability (e.g., Mason et al., 2008). Additionally, comparison of the demonstrations of practice and the current AI intervention research described above reveals a shared rationale for AI as a value-added intervention model; the AI context was often framed as the additional layer of support over the baseline condition (e.g., reading comprehension through Reader's Theater, with parallel AI activities to support skill acquisition). Moreover, most of the decade's research on the arts and special education, the AI intervention research, and the demonstrations of practice in Part II shared the goal of hypothesis testing and were motivated by the reality that conventional approaches have been insufficient for a large percentage of the school population, especially students with disabilities.

### Participants

Similar to the demonstrations of practice in Part II, the past decade of research has varied in terms of sample size, participant characteristics, and settings. Although the demonstrations of practice have small sample sizes and a heterogeneous population of students at-risk for school failure, the larger body of arts and special education and AI intervention research yields a wider range of sample sizes while reflecting similar heterogeneity with respect to students 'at-risk' due to inaccessibility, lack of participation, and/or progress in conventional academic tasks (also see Robinson, 2013, for review). These challenges are often related to identified disabilities including LD, EBD, ASD, and ADHD. For instance, the majority of participants in the AI intervention research studies included students with ASD and LD; far fewer students identified with ADHD, EBD, and SLI participated; however, these disorders are often comorbid with ASD and LD, making it difficult to determine whether one type of disability group was represented more than others. This is consistent with the demonstrations of practice, which included students with a variety of disabilities, ranging from LD, EBD, ASD, and ADHD, to developmental delays.

Across the literature reviewed in this chapter there was a lack of information about AI research in inclusive classroom settings. In contrast to the majority of the AI intervention research (17 out of 24 studies) conducted in self-contained or resource room settings, the demonstrations of practice address the need for more research aimed at the use of AI in inclusive settings, particularly in establishing best practices and an implementation framework.

## Methodology

In terms of methodology, mixed methods approaches (qualitative, quantitative, survey), including attitude survey, self-report, interview, work sampling, observational measures (time on task, participation rate), and quantitative language measures (reading rate and accuracy, comprehension, oral and written language analysis) predominate the literature base and are consistent with the methods used in the demonstrations of practice, which featured a range of methodologies consistent with the observed outcomes (e.g., cognitive, linguistic, and/or affective). Significantly, in the broader body of arts and special education literature, only 34% of what is known about the relationship between arts and learning for students with disabilities is research-based; these findings point to the need for more data to support the connections between special education and AI.

The broader body of arts and special education literature and the current AI intervention research indicate a need for a continuum of art education and art therapy approaches to meet the range of students' individual needs (see Chapter 2, Figure 2.1, for a model and discussion of the continuum). This is particularly clear in the AI intervention research studies, which focused primarily on affective engagement through social and behavioral skills rather than linguistic or cognitive growth, and the potential for linguistic or cognitive engagement to influence affective engagement (i.e., through social or behavioral skills growth). As such, the demonstrations of practice provide additional evidence of AI approaches for supporting students with LD, EBD, and ADHD across linguistic, cognitive, and affective domains of students' learning engagement.

## Arts integration intervention research and student outcomes

In the review of AI intervention research, nine studies provided evidence for using process and creative drama, with language outcomes observed through dialogue; reading comprehension outcomes also were identified as cognitive outcomes engaging complex reasoning (causal, sequential, relational events) through tableaux. Eight of nine studies examined behavioral outcomes and transferable social skills that could be interpreted as affective engagement (e.g., collaboration, perspective-taking, empathy, self-control, understanding of nonverbal cues, prosocial behavior, confidence, motivation, participation, interest, preference for AI activities). Interestingly, creative drama interventions (Guli et al., 2013; Jacobs, 2005) focused on affective engagement through behavioral outcomes. For students with EBD, positive self-efficacy beliefs were examined through process drama AI intervention (Jacobs, 2005), and students' metacognitive skills were also shown to improve (Cameron, 2007; Jacobs, 2005). It is significant that the demonstrations of practice included linguistic, cognitive, and affective outcomes, providing evidence of the multifaceted and individually based nature of engagement.

The AI intervention research that focused on music interventions (Carnahan, Basham, & Musti-Rao, 2009; Carnahan, Musti-Rao, & Bailey, 2009; De Mers et al., 2009; Gooding, 2010) was conducted in self-contained and resource room settings (no inclusive contexts), featuring therapeutic contexts with process-based and behavioral outcomes. The closest links to these more intensive arts therapeutic approaches can be found in Davis' (Chapter 7) dance/movement AI intervention approach. Davis' use of dance, movement, and music supported students' therapeutic goals (social-emotional and behavioral) in the context of the mathematics classroom. Davis used dance/movement and music to help students understand emotions in the service of promoting improved self-regulation and self-monitoring, similar to Spackman et al. (2005). Also, Davis used music as an environmental accommodation (e.g., background music) to promote cognitive and affective engagement, reporting social-emotional and academic gains, similar to those identified by Colwell and Murlless (2002) and Register et al. (2007) in reading, writing, and mathematics lessons.

The current AI intervention research featured dance interventions (Harbin, 2012; Lee et al., 2002) that shared inclusive settings with the demonstrations of practice, though these studies were conducted with kindergarten and early elementary age children. Group/peer programs integrating dance focused on behavioral outcomes, social interaction, and verbal skills. These studies shared similarities with the demonstrations of practice in the AI context providing for social facilitation among students and with the teacher. The teachers' facilitation in social skills building and peer inclusion was a shared principle across these research studies and the demonstrations of practice. There was no intervention research found on media arts using film and video; however Nagy's (Chapter 5) demonstration of practice shared features of the other AI intervention approaches in music and drama in the ways that Nagy created individualized student objectives and an inclusive learning community that highlighted students' strengths and helped to support their cognitive, linguistic, and affective needs.

The past decade of special education and arts research indicates the need for a continuum of arts education and arts therapies to meet the range of students' individual needs. The demonstrations of practice were developed following this continuum of service provision, such that individual students' goals were addressed through AI demonstrations of practice, ranging from process-based, therapeutic, social-emotional objectives for students with ADHD and EBD (see Chapters 6 and 7), to reading (see Chapter 5), writing (see Chapter 6), and mathematics (see Chapter 7), objectives for students with comorbid LD, ADHD, and/or EBD. Although the broader research on special education and the arts reflects cognitive, academic, and affective outcomes for students with disabilities, the AI research studies primarily focus on students' social skills and behavioral engagement rather than academic growth. The demonstrations of practice included the range of observed outcomes identified in the literature as malleable through the arts, to include cognitive (academic), linguistic, and affective (behavioral, social) outcomes.

## Teacher roles

The special education and arts education literature emphasizes the importance of teacher roles in better understanding how teachers work with students at the intersection of special education and arts education, especially given the extent to which teachers have access to preparation and whether/how school districts, state departments of education, and professional associations support professional development opportunities (Mason et al., 2008). Notably in the demonstrations of practice, teachers simultaneously participated in professional development through a university-sponsored program designed to support their implementation of AI within their inclusive classroom settings. Moreover, and largely unique to many school climates, the commitment to using AI to reach and teach all students in the inclusive classroom setting was shared by the school's administrators.

While the larger body of arts education and AI research highlights the need for more teacher development and preparation for special education and arts education, as well as arts integration, the demonstrations of practice reflect the teacher's critical role as both participant and interventionist. The AI intervention research and the demonstrations of practice revealed the potency of contextualized learning approaches for teacher practice as well as for student engagement via cognitive, linguistic, and affective domains. Unlike the broader arena of arts and special education research, the AI intervention research and the demonstrations of practice reflected teachers' critical roles as facilitators of communication and prosocial activities through AI learning contexts.

The larger body of AI research reviewed in this chapter and the demonstrations of practice in Part II shared the aspect of reframing students' Individualized Education Programs (IEPs) via AI approaches. As seen in the demonstrations of practice, teachers and students experienced the unintended benefits of reaching Common Core State Standards in literacy through the shared objectives across lessons that balanced arts and academic outcomes. Although students' artistic growth was not directly addressed by teachers in their demonstrations of practice in the way that the broader research has identified, the observed affective influences could be considered supports to students' identities as artists through their facilitation of access to, voice in, and choice of activities and materials in the service of learning both arts content and academic content.

### Contributions to the Interdisciplinary Fields of Education and Developmental Psychology

The demonstrations of practice reflect classroom-based inquiries informed by the most current and relevant research on the arts and education, including general and special education, arts education, and AI. This section summarizes the contributions of the demonstrations of practice to the allied disciplinary fields of developmental psychology and linguistics, highlighting the role of AI as a contextualized learning environment to support cognitive, linguistic, and affective engagement.

### AI as a contextualized cognitive, language, and social learning environment

The three demonstrations of practice featured in Part II created contextualized learning environments in which arts–based activities assisted students to engage more fully with academic content. The film, process drama, and dance/movement AI demonstrations each provided experiential and concrete exposure to academic content, as well as intensive social interaction that created opportunity for dialogue. Each of the demonstrations was highly interactive, consisting primarily of group collaboration, class discussion, and cooperative opportunities. During Nagy's film and Bosch's process drama AI interventions, students discussed, analyzed, debated, and created their own interpretations of academic content by working in small groups. Davis's students worked in small groups to apply mathematics concepts in experiential ways, such as measuring one another's arm spans and heights. They also took turns leading the group activity.

In each of these interventions, students had ample opportunities to engage with the content, and to use the more specialized and decontextualized vocabulary that so often is difficult to acquire. Students' increased familiarization with the highly precise and specific academic language of film drama, dance/movement, literature, social studies, and mathematics through discussion and collaboration facilitated their use of this academic language in written expression.

The experiential or contextualized nature of the arts, in addition to the social interaction and collaboration inherent in arts activities, also enabled students to engage in more sophisticated, higher-order thinking. For example, by contextualizing the novel through the visual mode of film, and by encouraging extensive discussion and collaboration among her students, Nagy relieved her students of the cognitive burden of decoding and comprehension, a significant obstacle for many of them. The film's images provided a scaffold for students to more fully understand the novel and to have mental energy left for deeper analysis and evaluation.

## Universal Design for Learning (UDL)

Universal Design for Learning principles, which align with differentiated instruction strategies (see Chapter 2 for a review) in their support of students with and without disabilities, provided a useful tool as the teachers prepared their demonstrations of practice. Each demonstration incorporated primary UDL guidelines as a means of addressing students' diverse needs. Multiple means of representation, or of presenting information, informed all three demonstrations. Nagy utilized film as well as the printed word, and electronic textual sources as sources of content. Bosch used photographs and verbal discussions, and Davis employed several kinesthetic applications of mathematical concepts. Multiple means of engagement were provided through assorted activities including discussion; visual, physical, and spatial depictions; reenactment; analysis; as well as written expression. Finally, the demonstrations provided multiple means of expression for students to demonstrate their understanding of the material. All of the students generated a written assessment, which provided the basis for linguistic-engagement measures, but alternative forms, such as film creation, presentation of tableaux, and use of spatial arrays, were also incorporated.

## Student population: Comorbid needs

The research on arts and special education, as well as research on AI intervention, highlights the comorbid needs of students who seem to benefit most from AI approaches, similar to the student participants in the demonstrations of AI practice. Nagy designed her film AI unit to meet the needs of students with language-based LD, who comprised the majority of her class and who were several years below their grade level in both reading and writing skills. Bosch's classroom population was evenly split between fifth-grade students receiving special and general education, with her most challenging students being identified as those who were "chronically disengaged" in academic content activities and who lacked key social-emotional/behavioral skills. Bosch noted that in addition to environmental/home stressors, her students had linguistic and cognitive difficulties related to self-monitoring, regulation, and sustained attention. Similarly, Davis' students included sixth and seventh graders with social, emotional, and academic difficulties. Most of the students were identified as having ADHD, and showed low frustration tolerance and poor self-regulation (e.g., difficulties following multi-step directions, focusing, and identifying necessary skills for task completion) throughout most academic tasks. The intervention context of AI for addressing the constellation of diverse student needs appears to be a promising model of practice in line with the multi-factorial understanding of student engagement (see Chapter 4 for a review).

## Culturally responsive teaching, learning, and community-building

In the AI demonstrations of practice, Nagy, Bosch, and Davis reported the value of AI to reaching students from their personal and culturally relevant positions. This understanding is echoed in literature valuing the arts as a means to reaching and teaching students with diverse needs, particularly when the teacher is a participant-observer (e.g., Mason & Steedly, 2006). Also, the arts require close collaboration, which was a social-emotional aspect of students' affective engagement throughout the three AI intervention units. Nagy reported that the integration of film with literature reduced students' frustration with reading text, and provided them with an engaging art form through which students could express themselves and make connections to their personal lives. Bosch reported that other than culminating written assignments, little individual work occurred throughout the process drama intervention unit, with class discussion and group collaboration activities requiring students to orally question, organize, reinforce, and construct criticism of ideas with their peers to effectively complete their dramatic representations (e.g., tableaux, etc.). The social and interactive nature of Bosch's intervention helped her students with LD and EBD to participate equally without struggling to produce the specific and precise language used in academic settings, or experiencing lower self-efficacy than their general education peers. Similarly, Davis' students assumed leadership roles in the intervention activities and expressed connections with the music and movement qualities both personally and culturally. The influence of the dance/movement intervention on peer relationships and its emphasis on social relationship building among teachers and students led to improved self-esteem and a heightened sense of community within the classroom, as has been noted by other researchers (Battistich, Solomon, Kim, Watson, & Schaps, 1995; Dewey, 1938; Klem & Connell, 2004; Raider-Roth, 2005).

## Multiple perspectives: A forum for critical literacy

Although literature and social studies disciplines lend themselves more readily to critical literacy, all three demonstrations of practice incorporated elements of ownership, personal investment, and interpretation. Critical literacy asks students to consider information from different perspectives and to reflect on their own relationship to the material. For example, to effectively integrate film and literature and writing, Nagy asked her students to compare the novel to the film, and analyze the filmmaker's interpretation of characters, theme, mood, and tone to facilitate deeper reading of the text and higher-order cognition. Students critically evaluated and analyzed the themes, moods, and tones within the novel and then compared them to the filmmaker's interpretation to demonstrate critical literacy (Vasquez, 2014). As a culminating activity, students designed and filmed their own version of the story. This creative act required them to develop their own perspective on the text from their experiences encountering the multiple perspectives of others. Bosch's practice instantiated multiple perspectives by actively engaging students in the reading of a telegram based on Civil War correspondence, and then creating tableaux to show their character's reaction to the information detailed in the message. Afterward, students explained and justified their tableau to peers and teachers. Students' explanations integrated each of their own perspectives on the material with the events themselves, showing how they became personally invested and embodied in conveying their understanding of the historical events. Davis dance/movement intervention unit more discretely reflected multiple perspectives as a forum for critical literacy in the ways that students related to one another and brought their personal and social understandings into academic and arts activities. In particular, students negotiated social roles, developed leadership skills, and personalized mathematics content in ways that were unique to themselves, and culturally relevant.

## Professional development

The role of professional development in the implementation of AI interventions is underscored by the three demonstrations of practice. All of the teachers had Master's-degree-level training in AI and special education implementation, as well as a school climate that actively supported these approaches. Nonetheless, Nagy and Bosch reported the stress and pressure associated with pending literacy failure as their students approached secondary school age. Both teachers understood how their students' risk increased as they re-experienced literacy failure due to poor reading comprehension and written language, and low levels of learning engagement; as a result they were committed to using AI to simultaneously reach conventional academic literacy goals as well as arts goals. Both Nagy's and Bosch's interventions offer evidence that the combination of carefully crafted and authentic learning experiences through AI can facilitate students' simultaneous achievement of district-wide curriculum objectives (i.e., CCSS for literacy, 2012). Davis designed and implemented her dance/movement intervention to address students' emotional-behavioral and mathematics goals identified in their IEPs. The intervention improved students' overall self-regulation, self-monitoring, and mastery of mathematics content standards (e.g., basic multiplication, writing of dimensional arrays, and finding the area of rectangular shapes).

The professional literature, empirical inquiries, and action research presented in this chapter help to situate where we are now with regard to research at the intersection of arts integration and special education. This synthesis of findings provides further support for arts integration as an inclusive instructional approach for cognitive, affective/motivational, and linguistic engagement through the contextualization of learning. The final chapter addresses the questions of where are we going and where should we go in the research and practice focused on the use of the arts in education with students having a wide range of learning needs.

## References

Adamek, M. A., & Darrow, A. A. (2012). Music participation as a means to facilitate self-determination and transition to community life for students with disabilities. In S. M.

Malley (Ed.), *The intersection of arts education and special education: exemplary programs and approaches* (pp. 101–112). Washington, DC: The John F. Kennedy Center for the Performing Arts.

★Anderson, A. (2012). The influence of process drama on elementary students' written language. *Urban Education*, 47(5), 959–982.

★Anderson, A., & Berry, K. A. (in press). The influence of classroom drama on teachers' language and students' on-task behavior. *Preventing School Failure*.

Arts Education Partnership. (2013). *Preparing students for the next America: The benefits of arts education*. Retrieved from http://www.aep-arts.org/wp-content/uploads/2013/04/Preparing-Students-for-the-Next-America-FINAL.pdf

★Bakan, M. B., Koen, B., Kobylarz, K., Morgan, L., Goff, R., Kahn, S., & Bakan, M. (2008). Following Frank: Response-ability and the co-creation of culture in a medical ethnomusicology program for children on the autism spectrum. *Ethnomusicology*, 52(2), 163–202.

Battistich, V., Solomon, D., Kim, D., Watson, M., & Schaps, E. (1995). Schools as communities, poverty levels of student populations, and students' attitudes, motives, and performance: A multilevel analysis. *American Educational Research Journal*, 32(3), 627–658.

★Brownell, M. D. (2002). Musically adapted social stories to modify behaviors in students with autism: Four case studies. *Journal of Music Therapy*, 39(2), 117–144.

★Buckley, S. D., & Newchok, D. K. (2006). Analysis and treatment of problem behavior evoked by music. *Journal of Applied Behavior Analysis*, 39, 141–144.

★Cameron, K. J. (2007). *"I put myself in the feet of the characters and I understand it more": A look at the influence of drama strategies on the reading comprehension of grade five students.* Retrieved from ProQuest Dissertations & Theses (304753148).

★Carnahan, C., Basham, J., & Musti-Rao, S. (2009). A low technology strategy for increasing engagement of students with autism and significant learning needs. *Exceptionality*, 17(2), 76–87.

★Carnahan, C., Musti-Rao, S., & Bailey, J. (2009). Promoting active engagement in small group learning experiences for students with autism and significant learning needs. *Education and Treatment of Children*, 32(1), 37–61.

Catterall, J. (1998). *Involvement in the arts and success in secondary school.* Washington, DC: Americans for the Arts monograph series, no. 9.

Clyde, J. A. (2003). Stepping inside the story world: The subtext strategy - a tool for connecting and comprehending. *Reading Teacher*, 57, 150–160.

★Colwell, C. M., & Murlless, K. D. (2002). Music activities (singing vs. chanting) as a vehicle for reading accuracy of children with learning disabilities: A pilot study. *Music Therapy Perspectives*, 20(1), 13–19.

Common Core State Standards Initiative. (2012). *English language arts standards.* Retrieved from http://www.corestandards.org/ELA-Literacy

★Corcoran, C. A., & Davis, A. (2005). A study of the effects of Readers' Theater on second and third grade special education students' fluency growth. *Reading Improvement*, 42(2), 105–111.

Crockett, J. B. (2013). *What do we know and how do we know it? What's being published at the intersection of special education and arts education?* Presentation at the 2013 Intersections Conference, a VSA Program of the John F. Kennedy Center for the Performing Arts, Washington, DC.

Crockett, J., Becker, M., & Quinn, D. (2009). Reviewing the knowledge base of special education leadership and administration from 1970–2009. *Journal of Special Education Leadership*, 22(2), 55–67.

*De Mers, C., Tincani, M., Van Norman, R., & Higgins, K. (2009). Effects of music therapy on young children's challenging behaviors: A case study. *Music Therapy Perspectives*, 27(2), 88–96.

Dewey, J. (1938). *Experience and education*. New York: Macmillan.

*Dodwell, C. (2002). Building relationships through drama: The Action Track Project. *Research in Drama Education*, 7(1), 43–61.

*Epp, K. (2008). Outcome-based evaluation of a social skills program using art therapy and group therapy for children on the autism spectrum. *Children and Schools*, 30(1), 27–36.

*Ferrell, M. (2012). *A qualitative study of the effect of background music in the classroom on the maladaptive behaviors of students with multiple disabilities*. Retrieved from ProQuest Dissertations & Theses (1522023).

*Garrett, T. D., & O'Connor, D. (2010). Readers' Theater: "Hold on, let's read it again." *Teaching Exceptional Children*, 43(1), 6–13.

*Gooding, L. F. (2010). *The effect of a music therapy-based social skills training program on social competence in children and adolescents with social skills deficits*. Retrieved from ProQuest Dissertations & Theses (741029264).

*Guli, L. A., Semrud-Clikeman, M., Lerner, M. D., & Britton, N. (2013). Social competence intervention program (SCIP): A pilot study of a creative drama program for youth with social difficulties. *The Arts in Psychotherapy*, 40, 37–44.

*Harbin, S. G. (2012). *The effects of physical activity on engagement in young children with autism*. Retrieved from ProQuest Dissertations & Theses (1035151523).

Hehir, T. (2005). *New directions in special education: Eliminating ableism in education*. Cambridge, MA: Harvard Education Press.

*Hubbard, H. J. (2009). *Readers Theater: A means to improving the reading fluency rates of second and third grade students with learning disabilities*. Retrieved from ProQuest Dissertations & Theses (1463423).

Individuals with Disabilities Education Improvement Act of 2004, Public Law 108–446, 20 U.S.C. § 1401 et seq. (2004).

*Jacobs, M. N. (2005). *Drama discovery: The effect of dramatic arts in combination with bibliotherapy on the self-efficacy of students with emotional and/or behavioral disabilities regarding their understanding of their own exceptionalities*. Retrieved from ProQuest Dissertations & Theses (304994634).

John F. Kennedy Center. (n.d.). *VSA: The international organization on arts and disability*. Retrieved March 30, 2014 from http://www.kennedy-center.org/education/vsa/

*Kagohara, D. M., Sigafoos, J., Achmadi, D., van der Meer, L., O'Reilly, M., & Lancioni, G. E. (2011). Teaching students with developmental disabilities to operate an iPod Touch to listen to music. *Research in Developmental Disabilities*, 32(6), 2987–2992.

Kelner, L. B., & Flynn, R. M. (2006). *A dramatic approach to reading comprehension: Strategies and activities for classroom teachers*. Portsmouth, NH: Heinemann.

*Kempe, A., & Tissot, C. (2012). The use of drama to teach social skills in a special school setting for students with autism. *Support for Learning*, 27(3), 97–102.

Klem, A. M., & Connell, J. P. (2004). Relationships matter: Linking teacher support to student engagement and achievement. *Journal of School Health*, 74(7), 262–273.

*Lee, S., Kim, J., Lee, S., & Lee, H. (2002). Encouraging social skills through dance: An inclusion program in Korea. *Teaching Exceptional Children*, 34(5), 40–44.

*Legutko, R. S., & Trissler, T. T. (2012). The effects of background music on learning disabled elementary school students' performance in writing. *Current Issues in Education*, 15(1), 1–10.

McFarland, L., Williams, J., & Miciak, J. (2013). Ten years of research: A systematic review of three refereed LD journals. *Learning Disabilities Research and Practice*, 28, 60–69.

★McPhail, J., Pierson, J., Goodman, J., & Noffke, J. (2004). Creating partnerships for com-plex learning: The dynamics of an interest-based apprenticeship in the art of sculpture. *Curriculum Inquiry*, 34(4), 463–493.

Malley, S. M. (in press). *Students with disabilities and the core arts standards: Guiding principles for teachers.* Washington, DC: The John F. Kennedy Center for the Performing Arts.

Mariage, T. V. (2001). Features of an interactive writing discourse: Conversational involve-ment, conventional knowledge, and internalization in morning message. *Journal of Learning Disabilities*, 34, 172–206.

Mason, C. Y., & Steedly, K. M. (2006). Rubrics and an arts integration community of prac-tice. *Teaching Exceptional Children*, 39(1), 36–43.

Mason, C. Y., Steedly, K. M., & Thormann, M. S. (2008). Impact of arts integration on voice, choice, and access. *Teacher Education and Special Education*, 31(1), 36–46.

Mason, C. Y., Thormann, M., & Steedly, K. (2004). *How students with disabilities learn in and through the arts: An investigation of educator perceptions.* Preliminary report available at http://www.vsarts.org

Mastropieri, M., Berkeley, S., McDuffie, K. A., Graff, H., Marshak, L., Conners, N. A., … Cuenca-Sanchez, Y. (2009). What is published in the field of special education? An ana-lysis of 11 prominent journals. *Exceptional Children*, 76(1), 95–109.

Moeschen, S. (2006/2007). Suffering silences, woeful afflictions: Physical disability, melo-drama, and the American charity movement. *Comparative Drama*, 40(4), 433–454.

National Art Education Association. (2014). *National coalition for core arts standards.* Retrieved April 4, 2014 from https://www.arteducators.org/research/nccas

No Child Left Behind Act of 2001, Public Law 107–110, 20 U.S.C. §§ 6301–6777 (2002).

Ockelford, A., Welch, G., & Zimmerman, S. (2002). Music education for pupils with severe or profound and multiple difficulties: Current provision and future need. *British Journal of Special Education*, 29(4), 178–182.

O'Neill, C., & Lambert, A. (1983). *Drama structures: A practical handbook for teachers.* Portsmouth, NH: Heinemann.

Onosko, J., & Jorgensen, C. (1998). Unit and lesson planning in the inclusive classroom. In C. Jorgensen (Ed.), *Restructuring high schools for all students: Taking inclusion to the next level* (pp. 71–105). Baltimore: Paul H. Brookes.

★Orr, P. (2007). Digital video intervention with special populations: Looking for inherent qualities. *International Journal of Special Education*, 22(1), 11–17.

★Ottarsdottir, U. (2010). Writing images. *Art Therapy: Journal of the American Art Therapy Association*, 27, 32–39.

Paul, R. (2002). *Language disorders from infancy through adolescence: Assessment and intervention.* St. Louis, MO: Mosby.

Qin, Z., Johnson, D. W., & Johnson, R. T (1995). Cooperative vs. competitive efforts and problem solving. *Review of Educational Research*, 65(2), 129–143.

Raider-Roth, M. (2005). *Trusting what you know: The high stakes of classroom relationships.* San Francisco: Jossey-Bass.

★Register, D., Darrow, A., Standley, J., & Swedberg, O. (2007). The use of music to enhance reading skills of second grade students and students with reading disabilities. *Journal of Music Therapy*, 44(1), 23–37.

★Reis, S. M., Schader, R., Milne, H., Stephens, R. (2003). Music and minds: Using a talent development approach for young adults with Williams syndrome. *Exceptional Children*, 69(3), 293–314.

★Riddoch, J., & Waugh, R. (2003). Teaching students with severe intellectual disabil-ities nonrepresentational art using a new pictorial and musical programme. *Journal of Intellectual and Developmental Disability*, 28(2), 145–162.

Robinson, A. H. (2013). Arts integration and the success of disadvantaged students: A research evaluation. *Arts Education Policy Review*, 114(4), 191–204.

Schneider, J. J., Crumpler, T. P., & Rogers, T. (2006). *Process drama and multiple literacies: Addressing social, cultural, and ethical issues.* Portsmouth, NH: Heinemann.

Silverstein, R. (2000). Emerging disability policy framework: A guidepost for analyzing public policy. *Iowa Law Review*, 85(5), 1691–1796. Retrieved March 20, 2014 from http://disability.law.uiowa.edu/Lhpdc/lawdisabpolicy/index.html

*Simpson, K., & Keen, D. (2010). Teaching young children with autism graphic symbols embedded within an interactive song. *Journal of Developmental and Physical Disabilities*, 20, 165–177.

*Spackman, M. P., Fujiki, M., Brinton, B., Nelson, D., & Allen, J. (2005). The ability of children with language impairment to recognize emotion conveyed by facial expression and music. *Communication Disorders Quarterly*, 26(3), 131–143.

US Department of Education. (2012). *31st annual report to Congress on the implementation of the Individuals with Disabilities Education Act, 2009*, Vol. 1. Washington, DC: Office of Special Education and Rehabilitative Services.

Vasquez, V. (2014). *Negotiating critical literacies with young children* (10th ed.). New York: Routledge.

*Wan, C. Y., Bazen, L., Baars, R., Libenson, A., Zipse, L., Zuk, J., Norton, A., & Schlaug, G. (2011). Auditory-motor mapping training as an intervention to facilitate speech output in non-verbal children with autism: A proof of concept study. *PLoS ONE*, 6(9): e25505.

*Waugh, R., & Riddoch, J. (2007). The effect of classical music on painting quality and classroom behaviour for students with severe intellectual disabilities in special schools. *International Journal of Special Education*, 22(3), 2–13.

*Whitehurst, T. (2007). Liberating silent voices: Perspectives of children with profound and complex learning needs on inclusion. *British Journal of Learning Disabilities*, 35, 55–61.

*Whittaker, J. K. (2005). *Readers' Theatre: Effects on reading performance, attention and perspectives of students with reading disabilities.* Retrieved from ProQuest Dissertations & Theses (3200190).

*Yoshida, E. A. (2005). *The role of music in the mathematical performance of high school students with moderate learning disabilities.* Retrieved from ProQuest Dissertations and Theses (305365798).

# 9

# WHERE ARE WE GOING?

## Trajectories for Research on the Arts and Special Education

*James S. Catterall*

The authors of this book tell a common evolutionary story, one in which a field of research grows – from infancy to contender in exploring *how we come to know* in a social domain, and from its world of simple descriptive scholarship to one of mature scholarly inquiry and analysis. The purposes of this chapter are to comment on this story and to place the narrative in a larger context regarding how research knowledge grows and how it is used, and to suggest directions for the future of research in the arts and special education.

Compared to many fields in education research, arts education and the arts and special education are relative newcomers. They are small, judging by familiar indicators, with relatively few researchers and public commentators, few annual research and professional publications, and a shortfall of the types of scholarship that populate contemporary studies of learning and development. Here is one telling example from research on the arts and learning: the US Department of Education built an enormous database by following 24,000 eighth graders through age 26 beginning in 1988. After 12 years and five panels of data collection, this database, called the National Educational Longitudinal Survey of 1988 (NELS:88), contained more than 1,500 pieces of information about each student (and 36 million pieces of information in all) (National Center for Education Statistics, n.d.). Included were myriad home and school context indicators, course enrollments, student transcripts, extracurricular activities, test scores, college courses and grades, student opinions, motivation and other psychological scales, as well as teacher opinions and parent surveys attached to each subject (National Center for Education Statistics, n.d.). The result was a longitudinal data trove of unprecedented possibilities. More than 1,200 research studies were published based on these data between 1990 and 2005.

Although about 100 of these NELS-based studies addressed mathematics learning and another 100 assessed science learning, only three focused on special education. Thirteen studies looked at students with 13 types of disabilities (National Center for Education Statistics, n.d.), and a whopping single study existed that had anything to do with learning or participation in the arts (Catterall, 2009). This was the case, despite the availability of about 25 indicators over multiple years related directly to the arts – arts courses taken, school offerings, out-of-school instruction, music and dance ensemble participation. As the author of the single NELS-based study on arts participation, which has now sold 5,000 books (Catterall, 2009), I have a couple of thoughts about the environment in which it was produced. First, when it comes to learning across the curriculum, contemporary cognitive psychologists are concerned with language arts, mathematics, science, and not much else – as were their mentors in graduate school. Leading journals showed little interest in a domain that attracted so few scholars. Specialized journals in the arts were overwhelmingly practice-focused and had little standing as, or desire to be, academic publications. Individuals attempting scholarship in the arts were typically not trained in quantitative modeling nor did they have much experience in quantitative research methods beyond counting and averaging.

Research in the arts had little heft a generation ago, at least where empirical attention to student interests, gains, or development was involved. Recognized giants in education philosophy have long discussed the notion and importance of the arts in individual development and society, for example John Dewey, Rudolph Arnheim, Leo Tolstoy, Ludwig Wittgenstein, and Georg Hegel; I will add Elliot Eisner to this list as well. The interest of empirical education researchers, however, has been slower to develop. As of 1990, the annual meeting of the American Educational Research Association (AERA), then with 14,000 members, listed only four or five papers related to the arts out of thousands presented each year – and only one special interest group (SIG) focused on the arts: the Arts and Learning SIG. In the following 25 years or so, AERA's attention to the arts mushroomed, with four SIGs related to the arts and education, and 50 papers presented each year. Several respected academic journals now are focused on learning in and through the arts. Now the premier journals in education and development publish arts-related studies on a regular basis. The popularization of the effects of the arts on learning, including the peculiar if not thoroughly grounded Mozart effect of music on spatial reasoning, seemed to draw not only sizeable public interest but also the curiosity of mainstream cognitive scholars. As new and more interesting stakes were planted, the field grew quickly.

Research on the arts and special education has a similar coming-of-age story, occurring over the same period of time. But the story involves only a small subset of the work going on in the larger field of arts and human development – because research on the arts and children with disabilities comprises only a fraction of the studies focused on the general population. This volume presents a clear picture of where research on the arts and special education stands as of 2014. In Chapter 8, we read that a search for research and professional articles linking the arts with the education of exceptional learners published between 2002 and 2012 produced only 100 usable abstracts. Nearly 50% focused on music, 25% on visual arts, and less than 20% on drama. Studies in movement and dance barely moved the needle. Only 32 studies were research studies, as compared to the majority, which included 68 professional articles. Only one study was related to the arts in education (McDowell, 2010).

The bad news, in a way, is that this oeuvre amounts to about three published research articles per year in the past decade, supplemented by approximately six annual professional publications during the same time period. This status report is wholly consistent with the field's orientation 25 years ago when we mounted a search. When trying in the early 1990s to capture the status of arts-related research trained on special education, our attention was drawn to the Washington, DC organization Very Special Arts. Very Special Arts evolved into VSA, which is now housed at the John F. Kennedy Center for the Performing Arts in Washington, DC. Very Special Arts attended to programming and inquiry related to the arts and children with disabilities and was then a visible repository of 'studies' aimed at the intersection of the arts and populations with special needs. The majority of these studies had a defining quality – they focused on a single child and one-on-one interventions. On the strength of these studies, one could become informed about how music, or drama, or visual art, or movement could generate various responses in this population, how the activities were organized by individual educators, and the sorts of perceived learning that occurred. Most results stemmed from the observations of a teacher, which I do not intend as a criticism – only as an epistemological limitation.

The positive side of the reports offered in this book, and particularly those in Chapter 8, is that high-quality studies have begun to appear in very recent years. The second review of literature, linking arts integration interventions and special education, identified a total of 24 studies published since 2002. Nine of those studies were published between 2011 and 2013. Seventeen studies bear dates between 2009 and 2013. Another impressive indicator is that Chapter 8 lists about 25 research studies in the arts and special education that are effects-focused inquiries, most involving groups of subjects, and many quantitative in methodology. This work evaluates the effects of music (or drama, or process drama, or Readers' Theatre, or dance, or other arts-based interventions) on outcomes for students with disabilities. Moreover, about 20 cited recent studies were published in academic journals, including *Exceptional Children, Exceptionality, Reading Improvement, Journal of Learning Disabilities, Teacher Education and Special Education, Journal of Music Therapy*, and *Communication Disorders Quarterly*. Drama and music studies make up the majority of entries.

While there is a long history of research in special education, research on arts integration and special education is a relatively new field, and one that mirrors (albeit on a much smaller scale) research on the arts and human development more generally. Both areas exhibit trends toward more quantitative, effects-focused research; both are securing beachheads in long-standing, respected, and even top-quality journals. As a natural outcome, both fields are gaining activity and respect in the mainstream academic fields of learning psychology, sociology, and even economics and public policy.

The authors of this book point out that recent studies have contributed basic knowledge about arts and special education, by addressing topics such as:

- using inclusive classrooms to introduce complex content
- providing effective media for culmination projects
- social development
- communication
- cognitive development and problem solving
- artistic skill development.

We note that several of these topics are of wide and deep interest for the education of all children. To wit, if one specializes in cognitive development and problem solving as a general field of interest and inquiry, one may naturally take interest in how the student context impacts the processes and outcomes one researches. These developments in an arts and special education context are likely to join this more general field to share terminology, theoretical models, process and effects indicators, journals, conferences, blogs, and academic societies.

## Where Might the Field Grow?

All of the above may be considered a roundabout way of saying that these authors forecast a promising future for the arts and special education – based on the mounting esteem for research in arts education, the growing sophistication and research interests of scholars in special education, the growing practice of arts integration by teachers, and the generally auspicious convictions of educators, parents, and policy-makers that the arts have a lot to contribute.

Based on recent trends, I would predict that research in the arts and special education will continue on its positive recent path, and exhibit:

- More empirical, effects-focused work. This is because the arts typically are brought to the special education classroom with certain outcomes in mind. Effects-focused research produces understandings of what those outcomes are, for whom, and how they are produced.
- More integration with mainstream academic disciplines concerned with learning and development. Understandings we seek regarding students with disabilities are not much different from what we want to know about all children. As such, learning across populations tends to mutual reinforcement and

shared perspectives. And more general academic journals in learning psychology and social-emotional development will, as they have demonstrated, take increasing interest in how things work for students with special needs.

- This process of integration will lead to more researchers in doctoral programs, as well as in the junior academic ranks, turning their interests to the arts and special education.
- The reinforcing cycle seen in these processes should lead to more and higher-quality research, increasing respect for the sciences of learning in special populations, and advanced conversations across the focal interests of those involved.

## Future Topics for Research

A consideration of topics for future research in the arts and special education can only be speculative, but some informed projections are worth considering. First, the field has exhibited some parallels with research in the arts and human development more generally – an increasing focus on academic and social development, as one observation. The field of arts and human development, as described above, has shown increasing sophistication in conceptual frameworks as well as methods that parallel those enlisted in basic learning research. It seems likely that this research will follow the recent evolution of topics in arts and arts-integration research more generally. I refer mainly to interest in integrated cognitive processes that characterize learning research generally, and learning through the arts more particularly. Here I would be remiss if I failed to mention research on brain function through neuroimaging techniques. Brain imaging studies have been used to probe pathologies of all sorts in children. Using brain imaging to understand more routine cognitive processes is widespread in typical populations. We may see an increased interest in neurological research on arts-related topics in populations with special needs in the future.

Also, we are likely to see expanding interest in creative capacity, performance, and motivation in the arts and special education field. It is difficult to find an education leader, or political leader, or informed parent who does not mention creative development when asked what is important for the nation's youngsters. Creativity research is gaining currency quickly among arts researchers. It is no coincidence that a variety of cognitive and social developments are being seen as not only important in their own right (as they have been for at least three decades), but increasingly important for their roles in creative problem solving and design. I refer here to studies of creativity that attend to:

- self-efficacy (and self-sufficiency)
- collaboration (and attending positively to peers)
- empathy (caring about others).

Our Centers for Research on Creativity (CROC) have built assessments of creative self-efficacy, collaboration, and empathetic orientations into the Next Generation Creativity Survey, commissioned by the Walt Disney Company and piloted with 2,500 students in arts and science programs between 2012 and 2014 (CROC, 2014). This work is generating enthusiasm both among scholars seeking to understand processes of creative development and also program leaders and teachers who want to understand and improve their programs when it comes to cultivating creative problem-solving skills and motivations.

## A Roadmap for Young Scholars?

It may be tempting to dismiss predictions such as these for the usual reasons. We cannot anticipate turns of behavior and randomly intruding factors in social systems. My observations and guesses will spawn reactions from scholars of arts and special education, based on where they feel they themselves are headed and on where they have been. A few may be influenced in their academic choices and activities by informed, but nonetheless speculative, views of what is to come. Perhaps these thoughts will prove helpful to young scholars as they grow to understand their fields, to place their work in larger contexts, and to communicate with established senior colleagues.

That is my greatest hope at the moment.

## References

Catterall, J. S. (2009). *Doing well and doing good by doing art. A 12-year national study of education in the visual and performing arts: Effects on the achievement and values of young adults.* Los Angeles: I-Group Books.

Centers for Research on Creativity (CROC). (2014). *Homepage.* Retrieved May 10, 2014 from http://www.croc-lab.org

McDowell, C. (2010). An adaptation tool kit for teaching music. *Teaching Exceptional Children Plus,* 6(3), Article 3. Retrieved May 14, 2014 from: http://journals.cec.sped.org/tecplus/vol6/iss3/art3

National Center for Education Statistics. (n.d.). *National Educational Longitudinal Survey of 1988 (NELS:88): Overview.* Retrieved May 14, 2014 from http://nces.ed.gov/surveys/nels88/

# INDEX

A reference in **bold** indicates a table and figures are shown in *italics*.